Microsoft® Windows® 98

Simplified Tutorial™

Todd Knowlton

Knowlton & Associates, Inc.

JOIN US ON THE INTERNET

WWW: http://www.thomson.com

EMAIL: findit@kiosk.thomson.com A service of I(T)P®

South-Western Educational Publishing

an International Thomson Publishing company I(T)P®

Cincinnati • Albany, NY • Belmont, CA • Bonn • Boston • Detroit • Johannesburg • London • Madrid
Melbourne • Mexico City • New York • Paris • Singapore • Tokyo • Toronto • Washington

Team Leader: Steve Holland
Managing Editor: Carol Volz
Project Manager: Dave Lafferty
Marketing Manager: Steve Wright
Design Coordinator: Mike Broussard
Electronic Prepress Production: A. W. Kingston Publishing Services

ISBN: 0-538-72045-X Hard Cover Version
ISBN: 0-538-72047-6 Soft Cover Version

1 2 3 4 5 6 CI 03 02 01 00 99

Printed in the United States of America

I(T)P®
International Thomson Publishing

South-Western Educational Publishing is a division of International Thomson Publishing Inc. The ITP logo is a registered trademark used herein under license by South-Western Educational Publishing.

How to Use This Book

Learning Objective

A clearly defined learning objective helps you understand about the new skill.

Units

Unit numbers are clearly indicated on each lesson.

UNIT 3

LESSON 28

Selecting Text

In this lesson, you will learn how to select text in a document.

SKILL PRACTICE

NOTE: Selecting text is also called highlighting.

Before performing an operation on text, you must select the text which you want to effect.

To Select a Word

To *select* one word, you can double-click on the word you wish to select.

1. Start **WordPad**.
2. Choose **Open** from the **File** menu.

   Or

   Click the **Open** button in the toolbar.
3. Open the document named **The Internet** from your work disk.
4. Position the pointer on the word **institutions** in the first paragraph and double-click. The word *institutions* is selected.

To Select an Entire Paragraph

To select a paragraph, you can triple-click anywhere in the paragraph you wish to select.

5. Position the pointer anywhere in the first paragraph and triple-click. The paragraph is selected.

To Select Any Amount of Text

To select any amount of text, click at the beginning of the selection and drag to the end of the text you wish to highlight.

6. Position the pointer at the beginning of the first word of the second paragraph.
7. Drag the pointer to the end of the sentence. The entire sentence is selected.

To Select All Text

8. Choose **Select All** from the **Edit** menu. The entire document is selected.
9. Click anywhere in the document to deselect the text.

TIP: You can also highlight any amount of text by holding down the Shift key and using the arrow keys.

TIP: You can select the entire document by pressing Ctrl+A.

60 **UNIT 3** Introduction to WordPad

Quick Reference Bar

Emphasizes easy-to-use tips and important information to note.

Skill Practice

A step-by-step, hands-on exercise walks you through a specific skill so that you can learn the task by doing it.

Glossary Terms

Introduces and reinforces vocabulary relevant to the lesson.

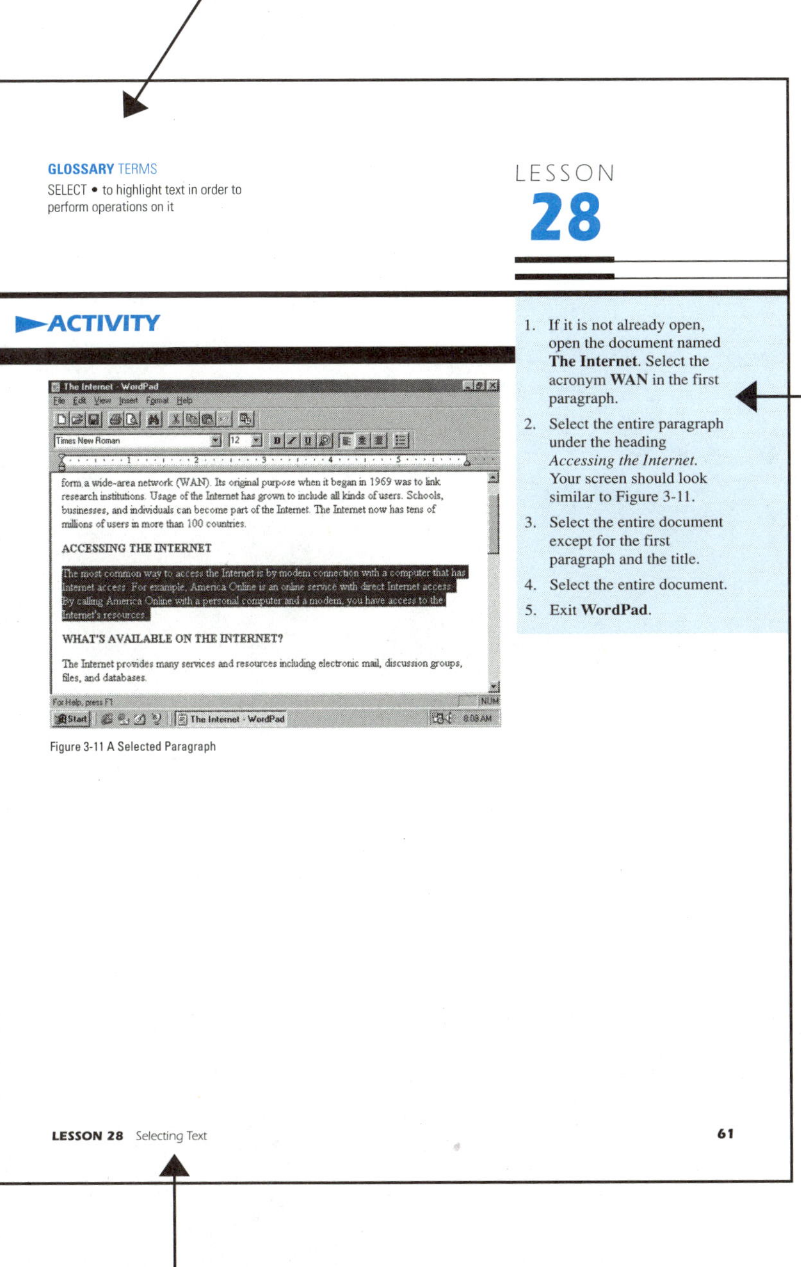

GLOSSARY TERMS

SELECT • to highlight text in order to perform operations on it

LESSON

28

►ACTIVITY

1. If it is not already open, open the document named **The Internet**. Select the acronym **WAN** in the first paragraph.
2. Select the entire paragraph under the heading *Accessing the Internet.* Your screen should look similar to Figure 3-11.
3. Select the entire document except for the first paragraph and the title.
4. Select the entire document.
5. Exit **WordPad**.

Figure 3-11 A Selected Paragraph

LESSON 28 Selecting Text 61

Activity Directions

Clear, concise directions to ensure success in applying learned skills.

Activity

An exercise to help you further develop the new skill and previously learned skills.

End of Unit Exercises

Most units end with:

- A Reinforcement Exercise that incorporates a review of previously learned skills.
- A Challenge Exercise that utilizes decision-making.

Preface

Microsoft Windows 98 is an easy-to-use operating system that provides many features of the most advanced operating systems, while retaining compatibility with existing software. Microsoft Windows 98 Simplified!: Tutorial and Applications is designed to make learning to use Windows 98 as easy as possible.

TEXT OVERVIEW

This text is designed to familiarize you with the features and user interface of Windows 98 in 128 lessons grouped into 12 units. Each lesson builds on what was learned in previous lessons, reinforcing the concepts already learned.

- Unit 1 introduces Windows 98 and covers the basics of starting Windows, using the Start button, using menus, and shutting down windows.
- Unit 2 covers the manipulation of windows on the desktop. The unit includes opening and closing windows, maximizing and minimizing windows, and moving and resizing windows.
- Unit 3 introduces WordPad, the simple word processor included with Windows 98.
- Unit 4 introduces the My Computer icon. Viewing, selecting, copying, and moving items are covered. The unit ends with creating folders, and opening and printing documents from an icon.
- Unit 5 introduces the Internet and the basic features of the Internet Explorer. The unit also shows how the My Computer window can double as a Web browser.
- Unit 6 presents the Windows Help system. Searching for help by contents, index, and using find are covered. Obtaining help with button names and menu commands is also covered.
- Unit 7 presents more desktop features including deleting files and folders, saving a document to the desktop, using the documents menu, and arranging the desktop. The unit also includes shortcuts and customizing the taskbar.
- Unit 8 covers the Explorer. In addition to browsing folders and copying and moving items, the unit covers formatting and copying disks and other file features.
- Unit 9 covers the Find command. Finding by name, location, date modified, file type, file size, and the text in a file are all covered.
- Unit 10 introduces Paint. The unit covers drawing lines and shapes, using colors, erasing, and adding text to paintings. Students will learn how to copy graphics created in Paint to other applications and how to capture images on the screen.
- Unit 11 presents some of the other Windows accessories and multimedia features. The Calculator, Notepad, and media player are covered. The unit also covers system maintenance features and running DOS programs.
- Unit 12 covers the Control Panel. Accessing the Control Panel, using the Hardware Wizard, and adding and removing programs are covered. The Control Panel is used in Unit 12 to change display settings, add desktop wallpaper, turn on a screen saver, change mouse settings, and set the system date and time.
- Appendix A presents networking concepts.
- Appendix B presents more detailed information about the Internet and the World Wide Web.

[1] Windows and Microsoft are registered trademarks of Microsoft Corporation.

Preface

- Appendix C describes the Windows 98 accessibility options for disabled computer users or those who need assistance when interacting with the computer.
- Appendix D introduces Outlook Express. Outlook Express allows you to send and receive e-mail and read Internet newsgroups.
- Appendix E provides an overview of the Windows Tune-Up Wizard and the Task Scheduler.
- The Instructor's Manual provides teaching suggestions and solutions to the book's activities.

ACKNOWLEDGMENTS

I owe thanks to many people who have contributed to this book. I especially thank Stephen Collings for many hours of hard work on the manuscript of this book and Radiant Design for creating the video clip used to demonstrate the media player.

Todd Knowlton

Contents

How to Use This Book iv
Preface vii
Contents ix
New Features xi
Start-up Checklist 1

UNIT 1
Windows Basics

1 Your Computer's Hardware 2
2 Software and Operating Systems 4
3 Introducing Windows 98 6
4 Starting Windows 8
5 Using the Mouse 10
6 Using the Keyboard 12
7 The Start Button 14
8 Switching Between Programs Using the Taskbar 16
9 Using Menus 18
10 Exiting a Program 20
11 Shutting Down Windows 22
Reinforcement Exercise 1 24
Challenge Exercise 1 25

UNIT 2
Working with Windows

12 The Elements of a Window 26
13 Opening and Closing Windows 28
14 Maximizing and Restoring a Window 30
15 Minimizing a Window 32
16 Moving a Window 34
17 Resizing a Window 36
18 Switching Between Windows 38
19 Arranging Windows 40
20 Scrolling 42
Reinforcement Exercise 2 44
Challenge Exercise 2 45

UNIT 3
Introduction to WordPad

21 Starting WordPad 46
22 Dialog Boxes 48
23 Opening a Document 50
24 Using Page Setup 52
25 Printing a Document 54
26 Closing a Document and Exiting WordPad 56
27 Creating a New Document 58
28 Selecting Text 60
29 Editing Text 62
30 Saving a Document 64
31 Copying Text 66
32 Moving Text 68
Reinforcement Exercise 3 70
Challenge Exercise 3 71

UNIT 4
My Computer

33 Storage Devices and Organization 72
34 Opening Drives and Folders 74
35 Web and Classic Clicking 76
36 Customizing Clicking 78
37 Navigating with the Toolbars 80
38 View Options 82
39 Arranging and Sorting Items 84
40 Selecting Items 86
41 Copying and Moving Items Among Folders 88
42 Copying and Moving Items to Another Disk 90
43 Renaming Documents and Folders 92
44 Undoing File and Folder Operations 94
45 Creating a New Folder 96
46 Opening and Printing a Document from Its Icon 98
Reinforcement Exercise 4 100
Challenge Exercise 4 101

UNIT 5
The Internet

47 The Internet 102
48 Opening Internet Explorer 104
49 Entering an Address and Clicking Links 106
50 Moving Between a Web Page Using Back and Forward 108
51 Saving and Printing a Web Page 110
52 Searching the Internet 112
53 Favorites on the Internet 114
54 History 116
55 Browsing the Internet with My Computer 118
Reinforcement Exercise 5 120
Challenge Exercise 5 121

UNIT 6
Help

56 Using Help Topics by Contents 122
57 Using Help Topics by Index 124
58 Using Search 126
59 Help Buttons 128
60 Printing Help Topics 130
61 Help with Button Names 132
62 Help with Menu Commands 134
63 Dialog Box 136
Reinforcement Exercise 6 138
Challenge Exercise 6 139

UNIT 7
More Desktop Features

64 Deleting a File or Folder 140
65 Restoring Deleted Items and Emptying the Recycle Bin 142
66 Copying and Saving to the Desktop 144
67 The Documents Menu 146
68 Arranging the Desktop 148
69 Creating a Shortcut 150
70 Creating a Printer Shortcut 152
71 Shortcut Properties 154
72 Closing a Minimized Program or Window 156
73 Positioning the Taskbar 158
74 Adding Toolbars to the Taskbar 160
75 Address Toolbar 162
76 Active Desktop 164
77 Customizing Active Desktop 166
Reinforcement Exercise 7 168
Challenge Exercise 7 169

Contents

UNIT 8
Using the Explorer

78 Starting the Windows Explorer 170
79 Expanding and Collapsing Folders 172
80 Browsing a Disk 174
81 Arranging Icons and Sorting Files 176
82 Selecting Objects 178
83 Creating Folders 180
84 Moving and Copying Files and Folders 182
85 Deleting a File or Folder 184
86 Formatting a Floppy Disk 186
87 Copying a Floppy Disk 188
88 Viewing MS-DOS Filename Extensions and Paths 190
89 Viewing Hidden Files and Folders 192
90 Customizing Folders 194
Reinforcement Exercise 8 196
Challenge Exercise 8 197

UNIT 9
Using Find

91 Starting Find 198
92 Finding Files and Folders by Name and Location 200
93 Finding Files and Folders by Date Modified 202
94 Finding Files by File Type and Size 204
95 Finding Files by the Text Contained in the Files 206
96 Saving Search Criteria and Results 208
Reinforcement Exercise 9 210
Challenge Exercise 9 211

UNIT 10
Painting

97 Introducing Paint 212
98 Opening a Drawing 214
99 Drawing Lines 216
100 Saving and Printing a Painting 218
101 Drawing Shapes 220
102 Using Colors 222
103 Erasing and Using Undo 224
104 Using the Selection Tools 226
105 Adding Text 228
106 Using Paintings in Other Applications 230
107 Capturing Screens and Windows 232
Reinforcement Exercise 10 234
Challenge Exercise 10 235

UNIT 11
Other Applications and Multimedia Features

108 Using the Calculator 236
109 Using the Notepad 238
110 Playing a Music CD 240
111 Using the Media Player 242
112 Recording Sounds 244
113 Using the Run Command 246
114 Startup Applications 248
115 Using the Disk Defragmenter 250
116 Using ScanDisk 252
117 Checking the Properties of a Storage Device 254
118 Running MS-DOS Programs 256
119 Copying Between MS-DOS and Windows Programs 258

UNIT 12
Control Panels and More About Printing

120 Introduction to the Control Panel 260
121 Using the Hardware Wizard 262
122 Adding and Removing Programs and Windows Components 264
123 Display Settings and Appearance 266
124 Adding Desktop Wallpaper 268
125 Using a Screen Saver 272
126 Changing Mouse Settings 274
127 Changing Date and Time 276
128 Viewing Fonts 278

Appendix A 281
Appendix B 285
Appendix C 289
Appendix D 292
Appendix E 294
Glossary 296
Index 298
Progress Record 303

New Features

WINDOWS 98 INCLUDES THE FOLLOWING NEW FEATURES:

- Powerful Web integration capabilities that let you access and store Web resources quickly.
- Easy access to Internet Explorer, Windows 98's Web browser. You can launch the browser from the Start menu. Or, simply click the Internet Explorer icon on the desktop or the Internet Explorer button on the Quick Launch toolbar, and you're ready to surf the Net.
- A Channel bar that enables you to receive information regularly from your favorite Web sites. By subscribing to a channel, information from a particular Web site is downloaded automatically to your computer at specified intervals. You don't even have to be connected to the Web!
- An Active Desktop option that displays the Channel bar and other "active" content from Web sites directly on your desktop.
- Navigation buttons and an Address bar in My Computer and Windows Explorer that help you move among your system's files, folders, and resources, as well as sites on the World Wide Web.
- A Links toolbar in My Computer and Windows Explorer that displays buttons for your favorite Web sites. Simply click a button to open the Web page.
- Outlook Express, Windows 98's e-mail program that you can access directly through Internet Explorer.
- A new Help system that's structured like the World Wide Web. Help topics and key terms are underlined and in a different color, closely resembling links on a Web page that you can click to quickly access additional information.
- Powerful system tools and utilities designed to keep your computer running smoothly.
- ActiveMovie Control, a new accessory that enables you to play movies and other multimedia files from your computer, a network, or the Internet.
- Display options that let you connect several monitors to your computer, thus expanding your desktop area.

Start-up Checklist

HARDWARE

- ☑ An IBM or IBM-compatible PC
- ☑ An 80486 DX2/66 processor or higher; Pentium processors provide significantly improved performance.
- ☑ 8 MB of RAM memory minimum; 16MB will be optimum for most users, but 32MB gives a noticeable performance boost to 32-bit applications.
- ☑ One hard disk (300MB or larger) with at least 110MB of free hard disk space. The amount of free hard disk space required by the Windows 95 to Windows 98 upgrade is determined by the cluster size of the target partition and the number of components already installed in Windows. Windows 98 requires at least 110MB of free hard disk space with the smallest cluster size and minimum installed components. This number can be as large as 243MB to install to a clean partition with the largest cluster size and all components selected. If Windows 98 stops the setup due to a lack of available free hard disk space, you can do the following to free additional hard disk space: Empty the Recycle Bin, empty the WWW Cache folder: delete **.tmp** and **.bak files**, or backup and move off the partition any MS/DOS programs.
- ☑ At least one $3\frac{1}{2}$-inch disk drive.
- ☑ A display adapter.
- ☑ An enhanced keyboard.
- ☑ A mouse or pen pointer.
- ☑ A printer that is supported by Windows 98, if you want to print with Windows.

SOFTWARE

- ☑ Microsoft Windows 98

UNIT 1

LESSON 1

Your Computer's Hardware

In this lesson, you will learn about the components that make up a computer.

CONCEPT LESSON

The Parts of a Computer System

A computer system is made up of devices that are collectively called *hardware*. Typically, these devices include:

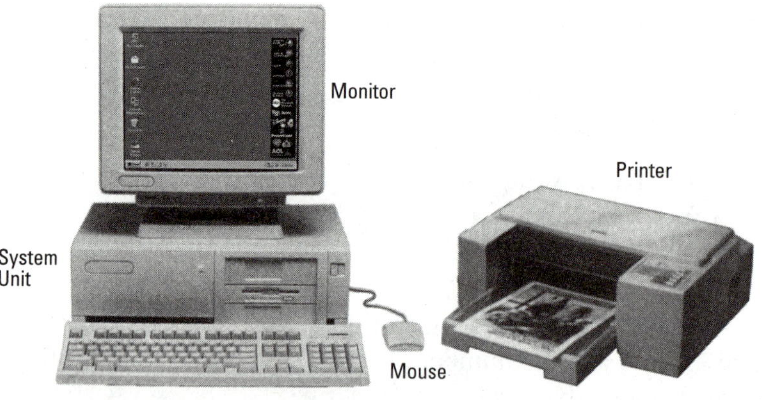

Figure 1-1 Parts of a Computer System

> **NOTE** The term *central processing unit* (or CPU) is sometimes used to describe the entire system unit, not just the processor in the system unit.

The *system unit* is the case that contains the processing and storage devices of the computer. The *monitor* is the primary output device. The images on the monitor's screen are how the computer provides most information to the user. The *keyboard* and *mouse* are the major input devices. The keyboard accepts text and numbers, and the mouse is used to work with the images on the screen. The mouse is what the user of a computer uses to choose most commands and answer questions the computer asks. The *printer* is the output device used to put information on paper. Some printers are connected directly to a single computer. Other printers are shared by many computers over a connection called a *network*.

Inside the system unit is the brain of the computer (called a *processor* or *central processing unit*). The system unit also houses the computer's temporary storage, called *RAM* (*random access memory*), and the more permanent storage of floppy disk drives and hard disk drives.

Many computer systems also include a *fax modem* for going online and communicating by fax, a *CD-ROM drive* for accessing information on compact disc, and speakers for quality sound output.

GLOSSARY TERMS

HARDWARE • the devices that make up a computer system

SYSTEM UNIT • the case that holds the processing and storage devices of the computer

MONITOR • the computer's video display

KEYBOARD • the device used to input text and numbers into the computer

MOUSE • a hand-held input device that allows you to point to and select items on the screen

LESSON

1

ACTIVITY

1. What devices are found in the system unit?

2. What is the computer's primary output device?

3. What device puts information on paper?

4. RAM is an acronym for:

5. List two input devices.

   a. ______________________________

   b. ______________________________

MORE GLOSSARY TERMS

PRINTER • an output device that puts text and images on paper

NETWORK • two or more computers connected by a communications link

CENTRAL PROCESSING UNIT (CPU) • the device that is the brain of the computer

RANDOM ACCESS MEMORY (RAM) • a computer's temporary storage

FAX MODEM • a device that allows computers to communicate and send and receive faxes via telephone lines

CD-ROM DRIVE • a device that allows computers to access data stored on compact disc

UNIT 1

LESSON 2

Software and Operating Systems

In this lesson, you will learn about the instructions that make a computer work.

CONCEPT LESSON

Software

As you learned in the previous lesson, a computer is a collection of devices that work together to process and store information and interact with the user. Computers, however, must be told what to do. The instructions a computer follows are known as *software*.

A word processor, spreadsheet program, or game is a type of software called *application software*. Application software performs the tasks you want the computer to do. For example, application software is what you use to produce a document or balance your checkbook. It takes more than application software, however, to make a computer run. Application software relies on another type of software, called *system software,* to control the hardware.

System software coordinates the interaction of the hardware devices, controls the input and output, and loads application software into memory so that you can run the programs you want to run. The system software required to run your computer is most often packaged together and called an *operating system*.

Operating Systems

In computing today, knowing the operating system a computer is using is more important than knowing the manufacturer of the computer itself. Application software is generally categorized by the operating system on which it runs. For example, a program may be categorized as an MS-DOS program, a Windows 98 program, an OS/2 program, or a MacOS program. All of these are operating systems that run on personal computers.

The operating system serves as a foundation for the application software, and application software inherits characteristics from the operating system. For example, if an operating system allows you to name files with long descriptive names, then the application software may also allow long filenames.

NOTE Some computers are capable of running more than one type of operating system. Many computers, however, support only one type of operating system.

GLOSSARY TERMS

SOFTWARE • the instructions a computer follows

APPLICATION SOFTWARE • the programs that perform useful tasks for the user

SYSTEM SOFTWARE • the software needed to control the hardware and load application software

OPERATING SYSTEM • the system software required to run an entire computer system

LESSON 2

ACTIVITY

1. Give two examples of types of application software.

   a. ______________________________

   b. ______________________________

2. Why is system software necessary?

3. List four operating systems.

   a. ______________________________

   b. ______________________________

   c. ______________________________

   d. ______________________________

UNIT 1

LESSON 3

Introducing Windows 98

In this lesson, you will learn about the Windows 98 operating system.

CONCEPT LESSON

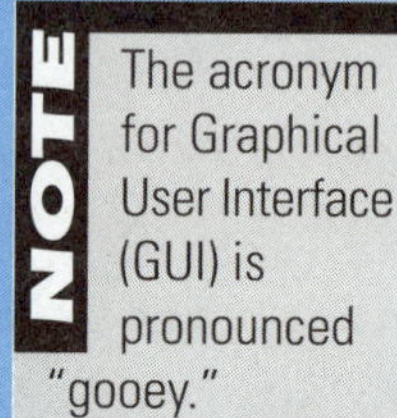

Graphical User Interface

Windows 98 is an operating system that communicates with the user through a *graphical user interface (GUI)* that makes the computer easy to use. A GUI displays buttons, icons, menus, and other controls on the screen. Using the mouse, the user can operate the computer by interacting with the images on the screen. Like other operating systems, Windows 98 includes the system software your computer needs to run. In addition, Windows 98 includes convenient accessories and programs that help you maintain your computer system and make the computer more useful.

Windows 98 makes it easy to start programs. You can even run more than one program at a time. You can switch between programs and transfer information between programs. Windows 98 also includes features that allow you to network computers together, use a fax modem to communicate with other computers over telephone lines, access the Internet, and send and receive faxes.

Organizing files is made easier with a GUI operating system. Tiny pictures, called *icons*, are used to represent the files stored on the computer's disks. A system of drives and folders is used to organize the files. Copying and deleting files can be accomplished without using the keyboard to enter a command.

The graphical abilities of Windows 98 make it a good operating system for *multimedia applications*. You can play sound files and video clips, record sounds, and play compact discs. Windows 98 also includes programs to help with common tasks, such as a calculator, a calendar, a notepad, a word processor, a painting program, and a card file.

GLOSSARY TERMS

GRAPHICAL USER INTERFACE (GUI) • a way of interacting with a computer through graphic images and controls

ICONS • tiny pictures used to represent files and to identify controls

MULTIMEDIA APPLICATIONS • programs that combine text, graphics, and sound

LESSON 3

ACTIVITY

1. What kind of user interface does Windows 98 provide?

2. What device is used to interact with the images on a graphical user interface?

3. What is an icon?

4. List two of Windows 98's multimedia features.

   a. ______________________________

   b. ______________________________

5. List three of the programs included with Windows 98 to perform common tasks.

   a. ______________________________

   b. ______________________________

   c. ______________________________

UNIT 1

LESSON 4

Starting Windows

In this lesson, you will learn how to start Windows 98.

SKILL PRACTICE

Starting Windows

1. After the computer performs its startup tests, Windows 98 will begin to load. After Windows loads, you may be presented with a Welcome message, called a *dialog box*.
2. If you received the Welcome dialog box, press the Enter key to close the dialog box. The Windows *desktop* appears. Your screen should appear similar to Figure 1-2.

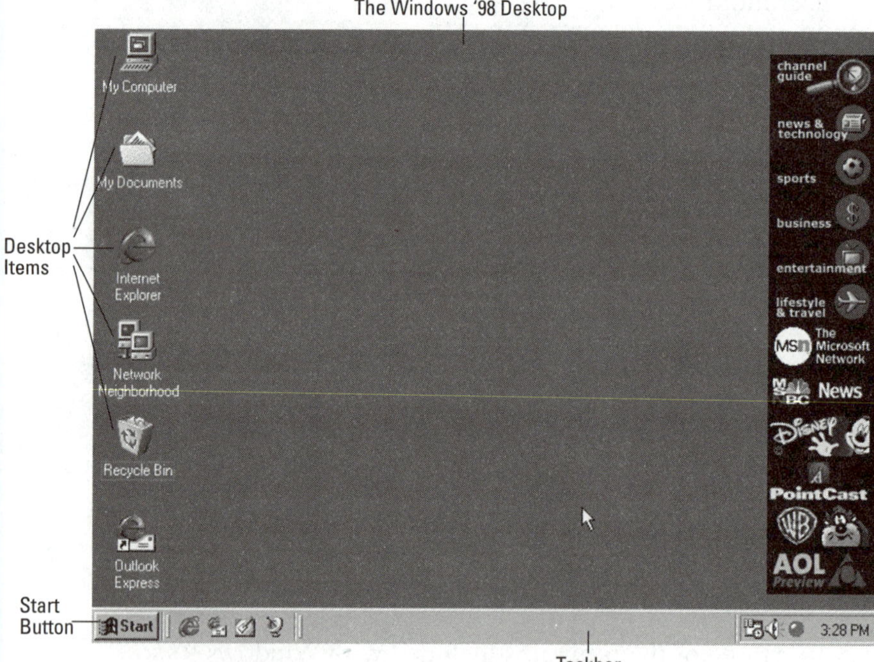

Figure 1-2 The Windows Desktop

The important parts of the Windows desktop are the desktop items, the taskbar, and the Start button. You will learn about these parts of the desktop in other lessons in this unit.

TIP You can prevent the Welcome dialog box from appearing on startup by clearing the check box near the bottom left corner of the dialog box.

GLOSSARY TERMS

DIALOG BOX • a window that gives information or requests input from the user

DESKTOP • the background against which the windows and icons appear

LESSON 4

ACTIVITY

Match the terms in the list below to the appropriate definition.

a. icons

b. system software

c. network

d. system unit

e. graphical user interface

f. operating system

g. dialog box

h. mouse

____ 1. A hand-held input device that allows you to point to and select items on the screen.

____ 2. A window that gives information or requests input from the user.

____ 3. A way of interacting with a computer by way of graphic images and controls.

____ 4. The case that holds the processing and storage devices of a computer.

____ 5. The software needed to control the hardware and load application software.

____ 6. The system software required to run an entire computer system.

____ 7. Two or more computers connected by a communication line.

____ 8. Tiny pictures used to represent files and to identify controls.

UNIT 1

LESSON 5

Using the Mouse

In this lesson, you will learn the mouse operations.

SKILL PRACTICE

The basic mouse operations are point, click, right-click, double-click, and drag.

Point

1. Position the mouse on the desk or mouse pad.
2. Move the mouse on the desk or mouse pad and watch the corresponding movement of the pointer on the screen.
3. Position the pointer over the time in the lower right corner of the screen. Do not press or click either mouse button. After a short delay, the day and date appear. This operation is called *pointing*.

> **NOTE** The pointer is the small arrow that moves across the screen with the movement of the mouse. The appearance of the pointer changes depending on the area or type of object it is pointing at.

Click

4. Point to the **My Computer** icon.
5. Quickly press and release the left mouse button one time. The My Computer icon changes color to indicate that it had been selected. This operation is called *clicking*.
6. Point to the **Recycle Bin** icon and click. The Recycle Bin is now selected.

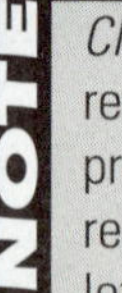

> **NOTE** *Clicking* refers to pressing and releasing the left mouse button. Some Windows operations will require you to click the right mouse button. This will be referred to as *right-clicking*.

Double-Click

7. Point to the **My Computer** icon.
8. Quickly press and release the left mouse button twice. The My Computer icon will open and display a window of additional icons. This operation is called *double-clicking*.
9. Click the **X** (called the Close button) in the upper right corner of the My Computer window. The window closes.

Drag

10. Point to the **My Computer** icon.
11. Press and hold down the left mouse button while the pointer is over the My Computer icon.
12. With the button held down, move the mouse to the right slightly. An image of the My Computer icon follows your pointer.
13. Move the pointer until it is approximately in the middle of the screen and release the mouse button. The icon moves to the new position. This operation is called *dragging*.

GLOSSARY TERMS

POINT • to position the mouse pointer on an icon or control on the screen

CLICK • to quickly press and release the left mouse button

RIGHT-CLICK • to quickly press and release the right mouse button

DOUBLE-CLICK • to quickly press and release the mouse button twice in rapid succession

DRAG • to press and hold the mouse button while moving the mouse pointer

LESSON 5

ACTIVITY

Click Here to Close

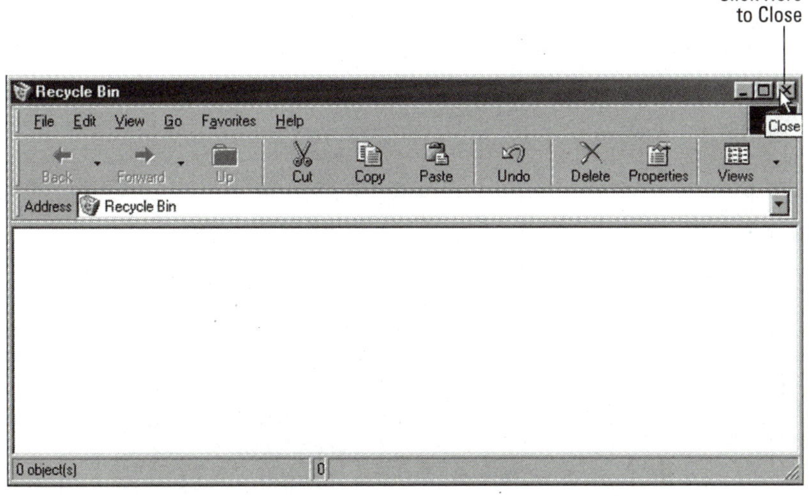

Figure 1-3 The Recycle Bin Window

1. Point to the **Start** button in the lower left corner of the screen. The words *Click here to begin* appear. Do not click the mouse.
2. Point to the **Recycle Bin** icon.
3. Click the **Recycle Bin** icon to select it.
4. Point to the **My Computer** icon in the middle of the screen.
5. Click the **My Computer** icon to select it.
6. Click in a blank area next to the My Computer icon to deselect it.
7. Double-click the **Recycle Bin** to open the Recycle Bin window.
8. Click the **X** (the Close button) in the upper right corner of the Recycle Bin window to close the window, as shown in Figure 1-3.
9. Drag the **My Computer** icon back to its original position at the upper left corner of the desktop.

UNIT 1

LESSON 6

Using the Keyboard

In this lesson, you will learn to use the keyboard with Windows.

SKILL PRACTICE

NOTE

Many commands have keyboard shortcuts that are accessible by using keys together. To use the shortcuts, you usually will use the Ctrl or Alt key in combination with some other key. These shortcuts are usually indicated with a +. For example, Alt+S indicates holding down Alt and pressing S.

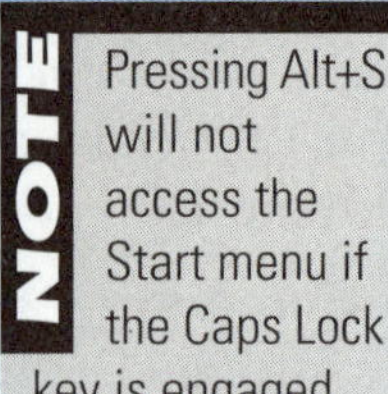

NOTE

Pressing Alt+S will not access the Start menu if the Caps Lock key is engaged.

TIP

The Escape key is used to cancel an operation.

Locating Important Keys

1. Using Figure 1-5 as a guide, identify the functions keys, Ctrl key, Alt key, Esc key, Shift key, and Enter key on your keyboard.
2. Identify the *cursor* control keys on your keyboard (see Figure 1-4).

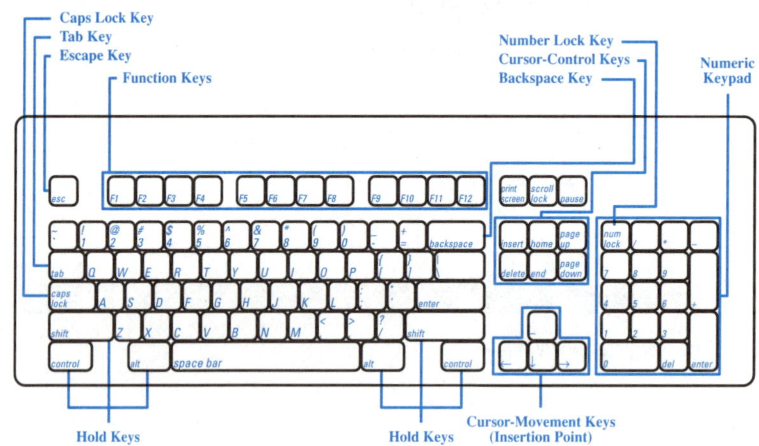

Figure 1-4 The Keyboard

Using Keys Together

3. Hold down the **Alt** key.
4. With the **Alt** key held down, press and release the **S** key. The Start menu opens.
5. Press **Esc** to close the Start menu.

GLOSSARY TERMS

CURSOR • the blinking vertical line that indicates the position at which the next character keyed will appear

LESSON 6

ACTIVITY

1. Press **Alt+S** to open the Start menu.
2. Press the **down arrow** to highlight the first item in the menu.
3. Press the **right arrow** to access a submenu, as shown in Figure 1-5.
4. Press **Esc** to close the submenu.
5. Press **Esc** again to close the Start menu.

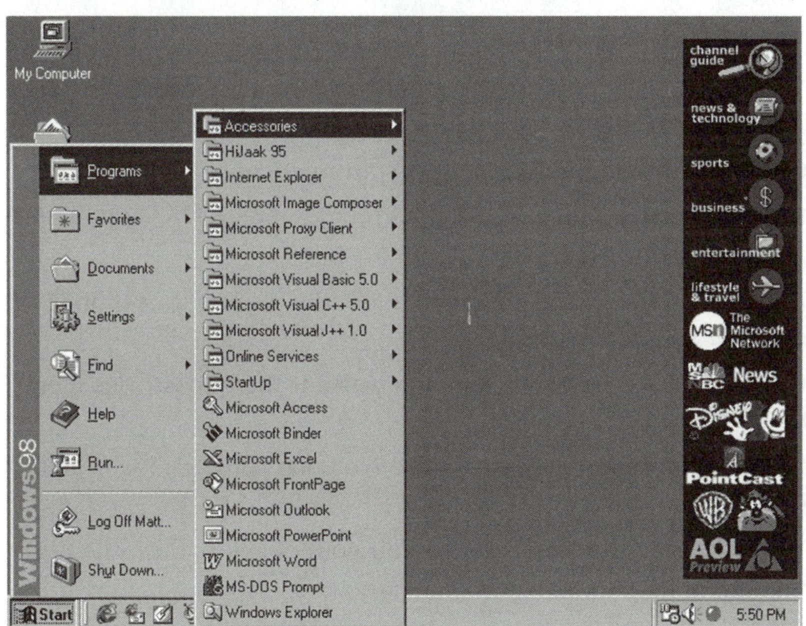

Figure 1-5 The Programs Submenu

UNIT 1

LESSON 7

The Start Button

In this lesson, you will learn how to use the Start button to start programs.

SKILL PRACTICE

TIP If you allow the pointer to rest on an item that displays an arrow to the right of its description, or click on such an item, a submenu appears to provide more options. Multiple-level menus are often called cascading menus.

NOTE Windows 98 allows more than one program to run at the same time.

To Start Programs

1. With the mouse, point to the **Start** button at the lower left corner of the screen.
2. Click the left mouse button. The Start menu appears.
3. Move the pointer up and down within the menu. Notice how the item under the arrow is highlighted.
4. Point to the **Programs** item and allow the pointer to rest on it until the submenu appears.
5. Point to the **Accessories** item and wait for the Accessories menu to appear.
6. Click the **Notepad** accessory. The Notepad program loads and runs.
7. While leaving the Notepad open on your desktop, click the **Start** menu.
8. Click the **Programs** item.
9. Click the **Accessories** item.
10. Choose **Paint** from the **Accessories** menu. The Paint program loads and runs. The Notepad is moved to the background.

LESSON

7

ACTIVITY

1. Open the **Start** menu.
2. Click the **Programs** item.
3. Click the **Accessories** item.
4. Start the **Calculator**. The other programs are moved to the background, as shown in Figure 1-6.
5. Leave the programs open and go on to Lesson 8.

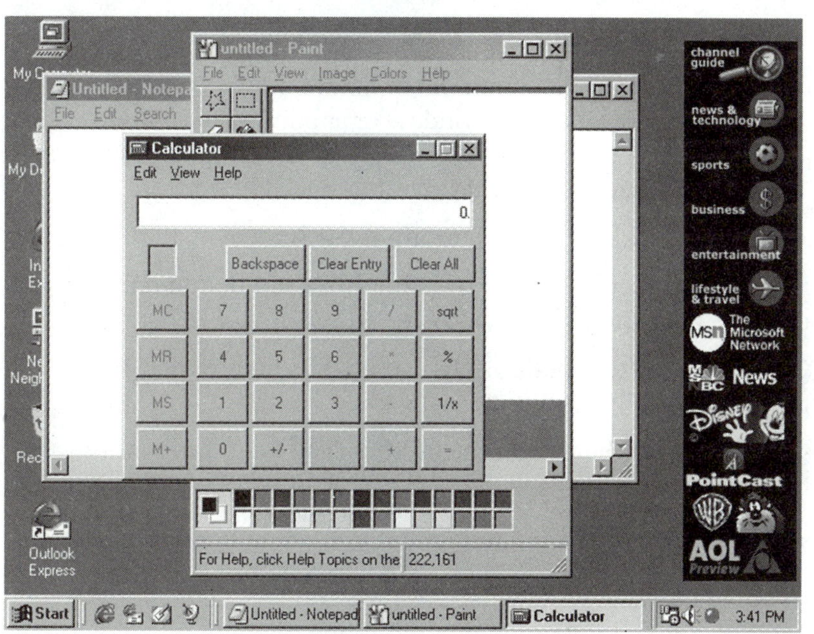

Figure 1-6 The Calculator

UNIT 1

LESSON 8

Switching Between Programs Using the Taskbar

In this lesson, you will learn to use the taskbar to switch between programs.

SKILL PRACTICE

NOTE The taskbar appears at the bottom of the screen by default. It can, however, be moved to any edge of the screen.

TIP If any portion of the window of another program is visible, you can click on the other program's window to quickly switch to the program.

To Switch Between Programs

In addition to being the location of the Start button, the *taskbar* displays buttons for each open window or application (see Figure 1-7). An application or window can be brought to the front and activated by clicking the corresponding taskbar button.

1. Analyze the taskbar at the bottom of the screen.
2. Position the mouse pointer over the **Notepad** button on the taskbar. The button will read *Untitled - Notepad.*
3. Click the **Notepad** button. The Notepad becomes the active program.
4. Click the **Paint** button on the taskbar. The Paint program becomes active.

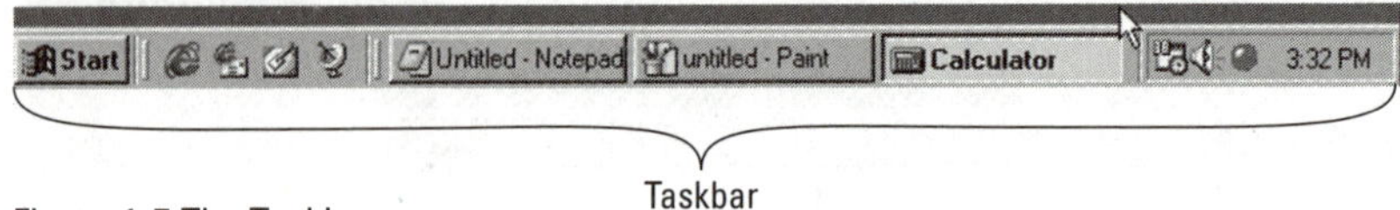

Figure 1-7 The Taskbar

GLOSSARY TERMS

TASKBAR • the bar that displays the Start button, as well as buttons for each open program and window

LESSON 8

▶ACTIVITY

1. Use the taskbar to switch to the **Calculator**.
2. Switch to the **Paint** program.
3. Switch to the **Notepad**. Your screen should appear similar to Figure 1-8. The sizes of your windows may vary from those in the figure.
4. Leave the **Calculator**, **Paint**, and **Notepad** open for the next lesson.

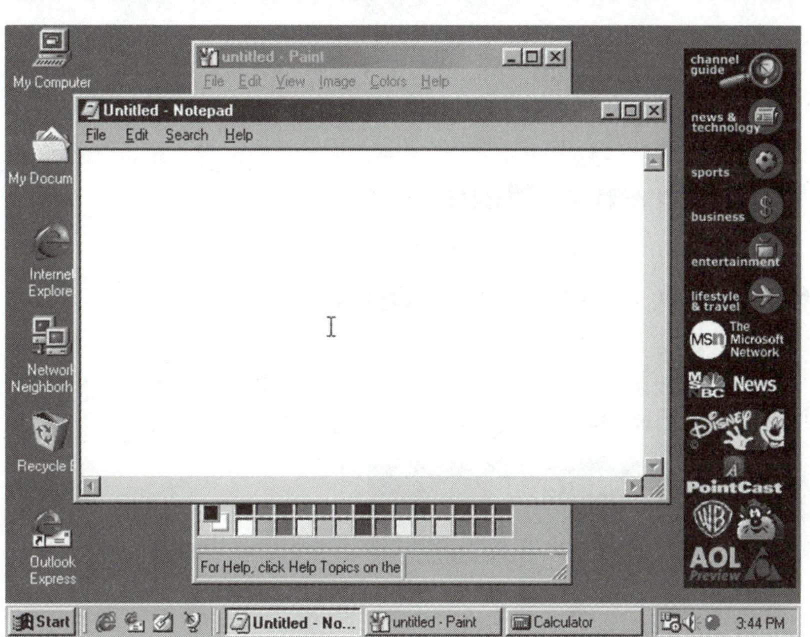

Figure 1-8 The taskbar allows you to switch quickly among programs.

UNIT 1

LESSON 9

Using Menus

In this lesson, you will learn how to pull down a menu and choose a command.

SKILL PRACTICE

Most commands in Windows programs are organized in menus that pull down from a program's menu bar. The *menu bar* is the row of menu names that appears below the title bar of most applications and windows.

To Pull Down a Menu

The Notepad should be the active program on your screen.

1. Click **File** on the menu bar (see Figure 1-9).
   Or
   Press **Alt+F**.

   Notepad's File menu drops down.

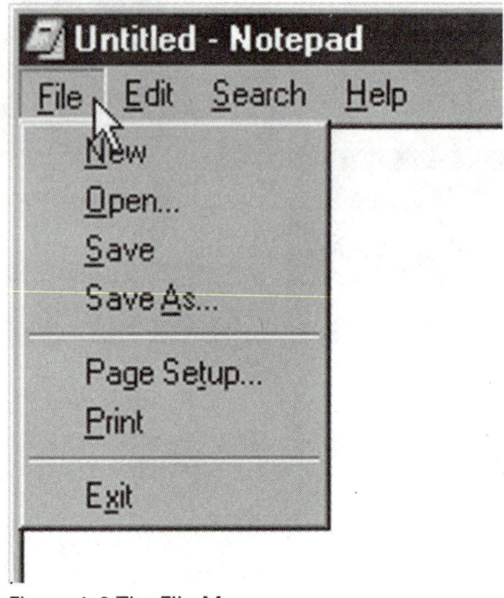

Figure 1-9 The File Menu

To Close a Menu Without Choosing a Command

2. Click somewhere outside the menu on the Notepad's work area.
   Or
   Press **Esc** (located at the top left corner of your keyboard). The File menu will close.

(continued on next page)

TIP: Notice that menus on the menu bar have an underlined character. If you hold down the Alt key and press the letter that corresponds to the underlined letter on the menu bar, the menu can be accessed without the mouse.

TIP: Once you have clicked to pull down a menu, you can move the mouse to other menus to pull them down without clicking again.

GLOSSARY TERMS

MENU BAR • the bar below the title bar from which menus pull down

LESSON

9

►ACTIVITY

1. Choose the **New** command from the **File** menu. A message appears asking if you want to save the changes to the current text.
2. Click the **No** button. The Notepad is cleared, as shown in Figure 1-10.
3. Leave the currently open applications open for the next lesson.

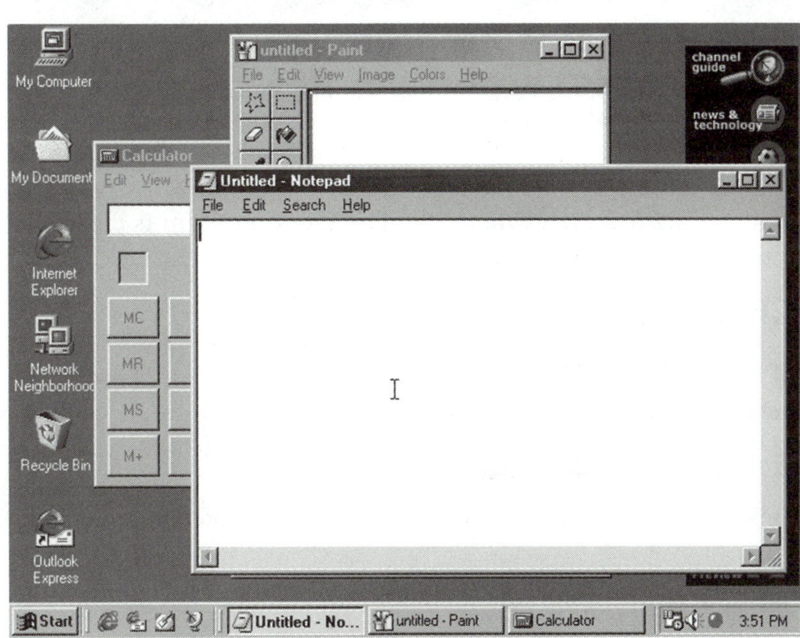

Figure 1-10 The New command cleared the Notepad.

***Skill Practice** (continued)*

To Choose a Command

3. Pull down the **Edit** menu.
4. Move the pointer over the commands in the menu. Notice how each command is highlighted as the pointer passes over it.
5. Click the **Time/Date** command. The time and date appear in the Notepad.

LESSON

10

Exiting a Program

In this lesson, you will learn to exit programs.

►SKILL PRACTICE

NOTE The Calculator does not have an Exit command or a File menu. However, clicking a program's close button can be used in place of the Exit command.

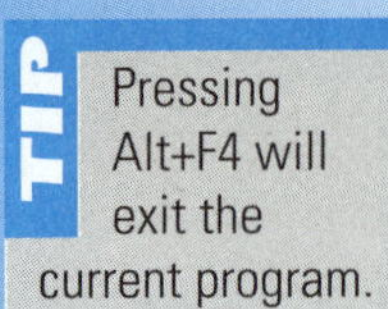

TIP Pressing Alt+F4 will exit the current program.

To Exit the Paint Program

1. Click the **Paint** button on the taskbar. The Paint program becomes active.
2. Click the **File** menu.
3. Choose **Exit** from the **File** menu. The Paint program is closed. Notice that the Paint button no longer appears on the taskbar.

To Close the Calculator

4. Click the **Calculator** button on the taskbar.
5. Click the Calculator's Close button.

To Exit the Notepad

6. Click anywhere in the Notepad window. The Notepad becomes active.
7. Choose **Exit** from the **File** menu.

LESSON

10

ACTIVITY

1. Start the **Notepad**.
2. Choose **Time/Date** from the **Edit** menu.
3. Start the **Calculator**. Your screen should look similar to Figure 1-11.
4. Use the taskbar to switch to the **Notepad**.
5. Exit the **Notepad**. Do not save changes.
6. Close the **Calculator**.

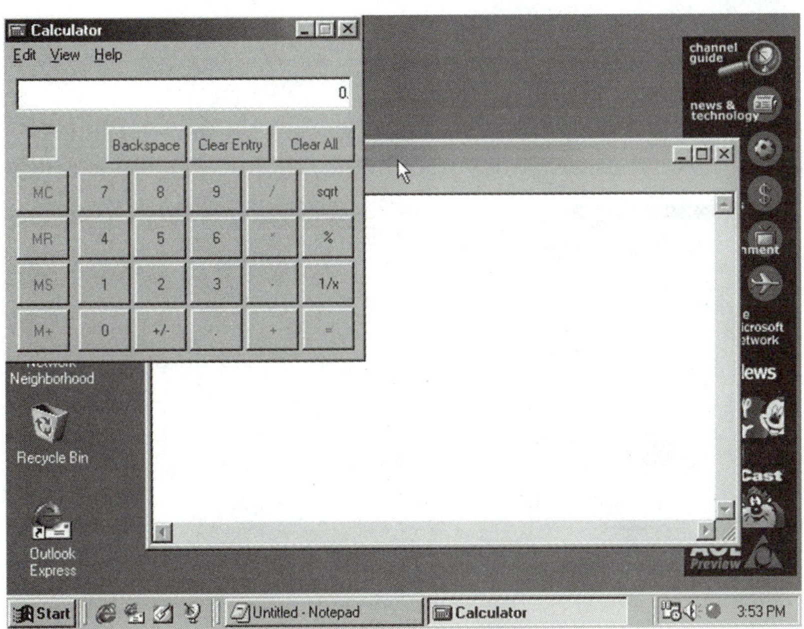

Figure 1-11 The Calculator appears on top of the Notepad.

UNIT 1

LESSON 11

Shutting Down Windows

In this lesson, you will learn to shut down Windows 98.

SKILL PRACTICE

To Shut Down Windows

1. Access the **Start** menu.
2. Choose **Shut Down** from the **Start** menu. The Shut Down dialog box appears, as shown in Figure 1-12.

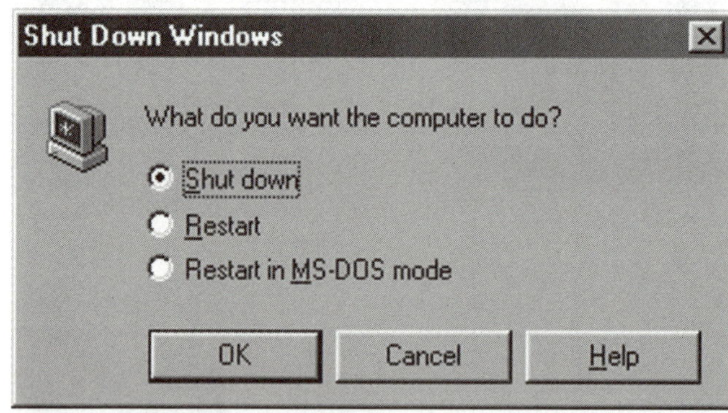

Figure 1-12 The Shut Down Dialog Box

3. Click **OK** to shut down Windows 98.
4. When the message *It's now safe to turn off your computer* appears, turn off the computer.

NOTE The Shut Down dialog box gives you the option to shut down the computer, restart, or restart the computer in MS-DOS. To choose one of the other options, click on the round button to the left of the desired option to select it.

TIP If you are on a network, click the Log off **User...** option on the Start menu to close all programs and log on as a different user.

LESSON

11

►ACTIVITY

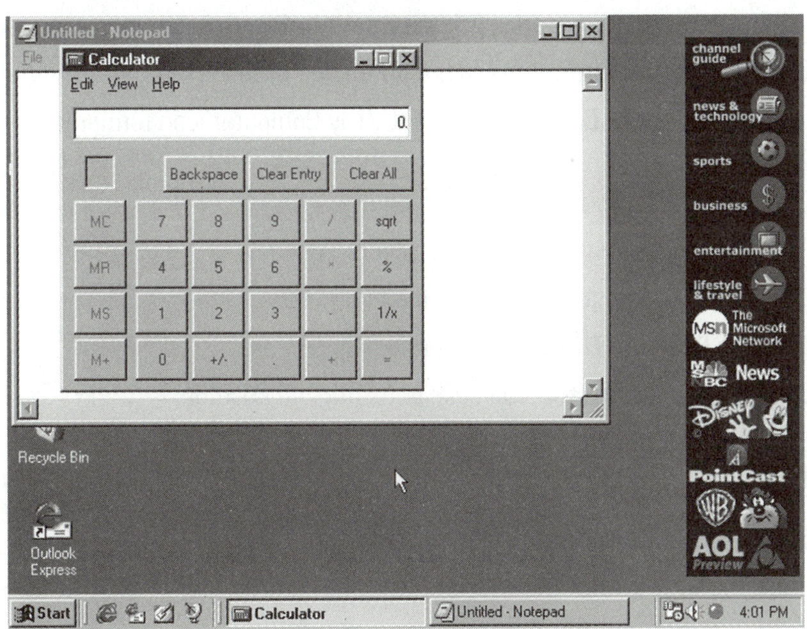

Figure 1-13 The Notepad and Calculator are running.

1. Turn on the computer.
2. After Windows 98 starts, start the **Notepad**.
3. Start the **Calculator**. Your screen should appear similar to Figure 1-13.
4. Exit the **Notepad**.
5. Close the **Calculator**.
6. Shut down Windows 98.
7. Turn off the computer.

Reinforcement Exercise

1. Turn on the computer. Wait for Windows 98 to start.
2. If necessary, close the Welcome dialog box.
3. When the desktop appears, click the **Recycle Bin** to select it.
4. Drag the **My Computer** icon to the right edge of the screen.
5. Drag the **Recycle Bin** to the space the My Computer icon formerly occupied.
6. Double-click the **Recycle Bin** to open it.
7. Pull down the **File** menu in the Recycle Bin window.
8. Choose the **Close** command from the Recycle Bin window's File menu.
9. Drag the **Recycle Bin** back to its original position.
10. Drag the **My Computer** icon back to its original position.
11. Start the **Calculator**.
12. Start the **Notepad**.
13. Switch to the **Calculator** using the taskbar.
14. Close the **Calculator**.
15. Exit the **Notepad**.
16. Choose **Shut Down** from the **Start** menu.
17. Choose the **Restart** option.
18. Click **OK**. The computer restarts and Windows 98 restarts.

Challenge Exercise

Match the terms in the list to the appropriate definitions.

___ 1. Hardware

___ 2. Application Software

___ 3. System Software

___ 4. Operating System

___ 5. Central Processing Unit

___ 6. Random Access Memory

___ 7. Software

___ 8. Graphical User Interface

___ 9. Icons

___ 10. Desktop

___ 11. Dialog Box

___ 12. Mouse

___ 13. Cursor

___ 14. Taskbar

___ 15. Menu Bar

a. The brain of the computer.
b. The background against which the windows and icons appear.
c. The bar that displays the Start button, as well as buttons for each open program and window.
d. The software needed to control the hardware and to load application software.
e. The programs that perform useful tasks for the user.
f. The blinking vertical line that indicates the position at which the next character keyed will appear.
g. The devices that make up a computer system.
h. The system software required to run an entire computer system.
i. A computer's temporary storage.
j. The instructions a computer follows.
k. A hand-held input device that allows you to point to and select items on the screen.
l. A way of interacting with a computer by way of graphic images and controls.
m. A window that gives information or requests input from the user.
n. The bar below the title bar from which menus pull down.
o. Tiny pictures used to represent files and to identify controls.

UNIT 2

LESSON 12

The Elements of a Window

In this lesson, you will learn the parts of windows.

►SKILL PRACTICE

> **NOTE** The elements shown in Figure 2-1 are not unique to the My Computer window. Most windows have the same controls.

Parts of Windows

1. Double-click the **My Computer** icon.
2. Compare the window on your screen with Figure 2-1. The contents of the window will vary, depending on the configuration of your computer system.

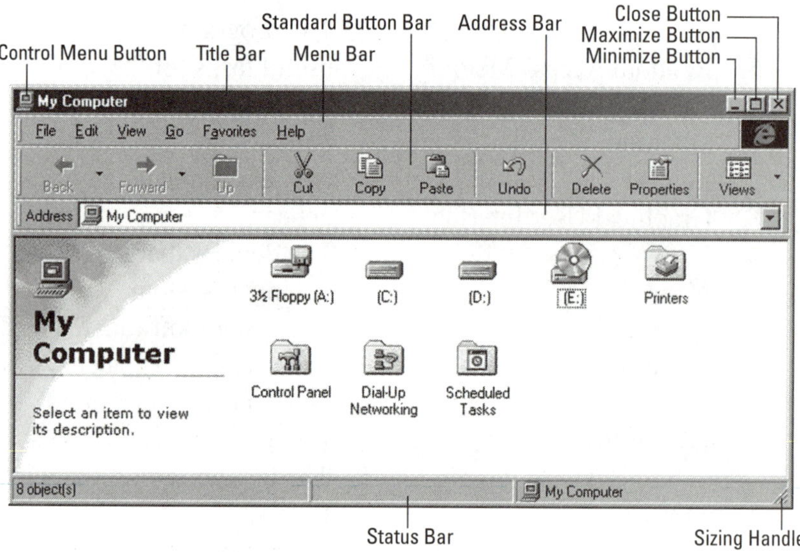

Figure 2-1 The Elements of a Window

Title bar - gives the name of the window or application

Menu bar - provides the menus for the commands available for working with an application or the contents of a window

Address bar - provides the name or address of the location viewed in the window

Standard button bar - provides buttons which serve as shortcuts to commonly used commands

Status bar - provides additional information about a command or highlighted object

Minimize button - removes a window from the desktop. The window is not closed and is still available from the taskbar.

Maximize button - enlarges a window to its maximum size

Close button - closes the window

Control menu button - accesses the control menu, which provides other window commands

Sizing handle - drag to resize the window manually

3. Leave the My Computer window open for the next lesson.

LESSON

12

ACTIVITY

1. What button enlarges a window to its maximum size?

2. What window element gives you the name of the window?

3. What button closes a window?

4. What window element allows you to resize a window manually?

5. What button removes a window from the desktop without closing it?

UNIT 2

LESSON 13

Opening and Closing Windows

In this lesson, you will learn how to open and close windows.

► SKILL PRACTICE

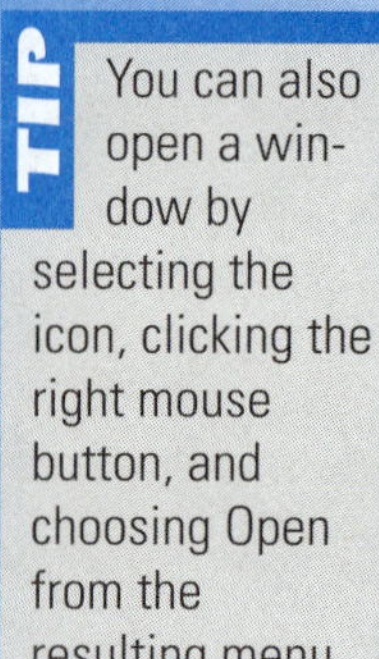

TIP You can also open a window by selecting the icon, clicking the right mouse button, and choosing Open from the resulting menu.

TIP You can also close a window by clicking the window's Control Menu button and choosing Close from the resulting menu.

To Open a Window

You can open a window by double-clicking its icon.

1. Double-click the **Recycle Bin**. The Recycle Bin window opens.

To Close a Window

Close a window by clicking the window's Close button.

2. Click the Recycle Bin's **Close button**, as shown in Figure 2-2.
3. Click the My Computer window's **Close button**.

Click here to close

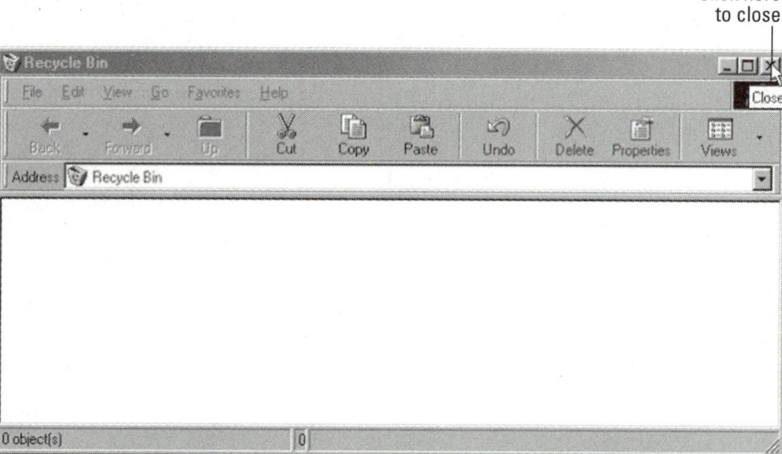

Figure 2-2 The Close Button

LESSON

13

► ACTIVITY

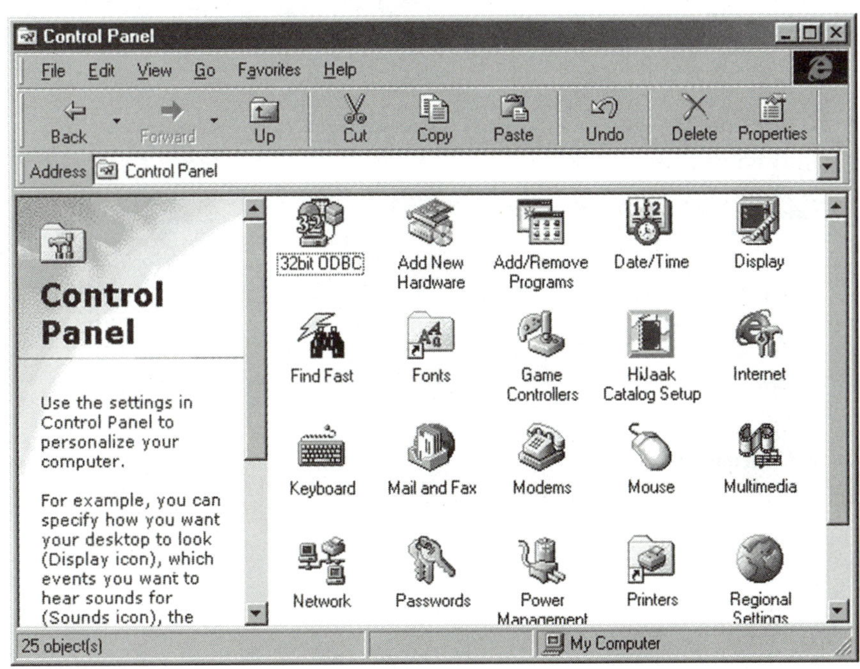

Figure 2-3 The Control Panel Window

1. Open the **My Computer** window.
2. Double-click the **Control Panel** folder icon in the My Computer window. The Control Panel window appears, as shown in Figure 2-3.
3. Close the **Control Panel** window.
4. Close the **My Computer** window.

UNIT 2

LESSON 14

Maximizing and Restoring a Window

In this lesson, you will learn how to maximize and restore a window.

SKILL PRACTICE

To Maximize a Window

1. Open the **My Computer** window.
2. Click the *Maximize button.* The window fills the screen, as shown in Figure 2-4.

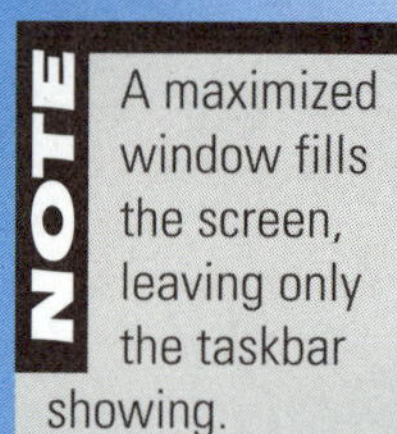

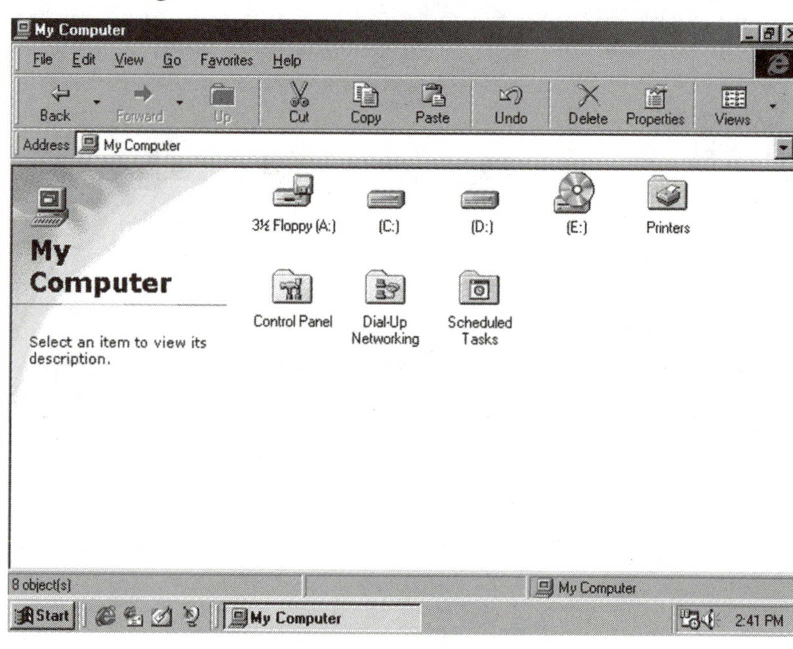

Figure 2-4 A Maximized Window

To Restore a Window

When a window is maximized, the Maximize button becomes a *Restore button*, as shown in Figure 2-5.

Restore Button

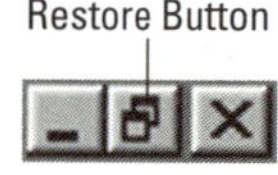

Figure 2-5 The Restore Button

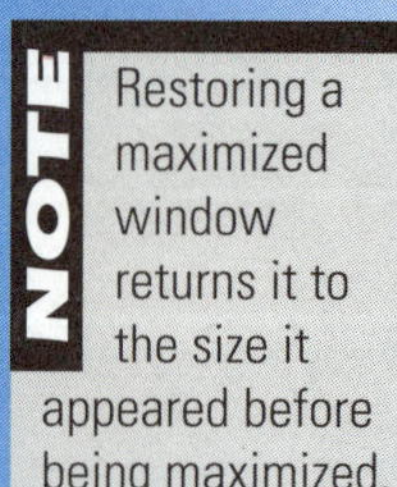

3. Click the **Restore** button on the My Computer window.
4. Close the **My Computer** window.

GLOSSARY TERMS

MAXIMIZE BUTTON • expands a window to fill the screen

RESTORE BUTTON • returns a maximized window to the size it was before being maximized

LESSON 14

ACTIVITY

1. Open the **Recycle Bin** window.
2. Maximize the **Recycle Bin** window. Your screen should appear similar to Figure 2-6.
3. Restore the **Recycle Bin** window. Your screen should appear similar to Figure 2-7.

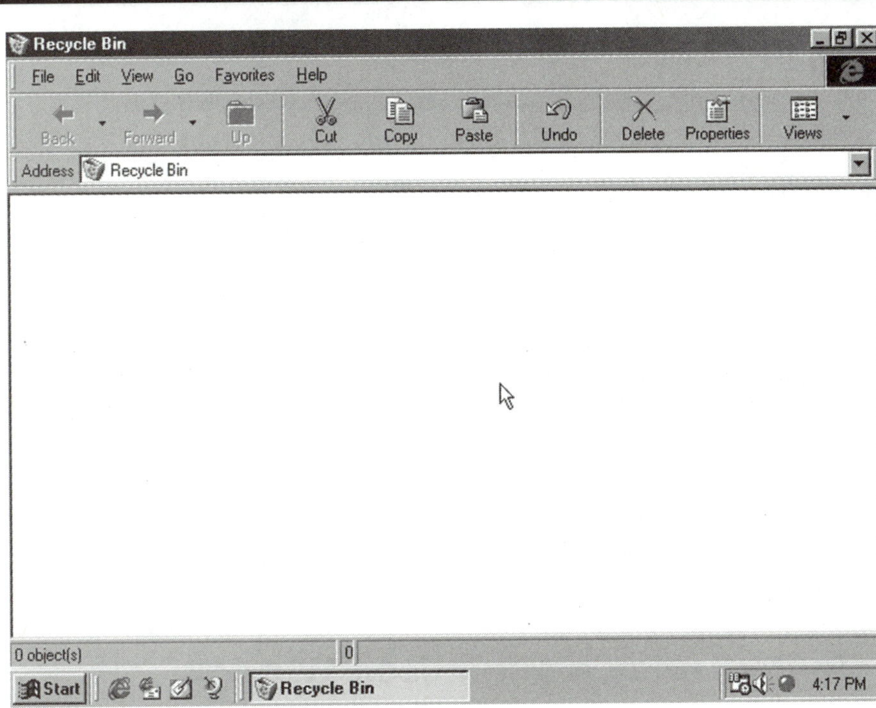

Figure 2-6 Maximized Recycle Bin

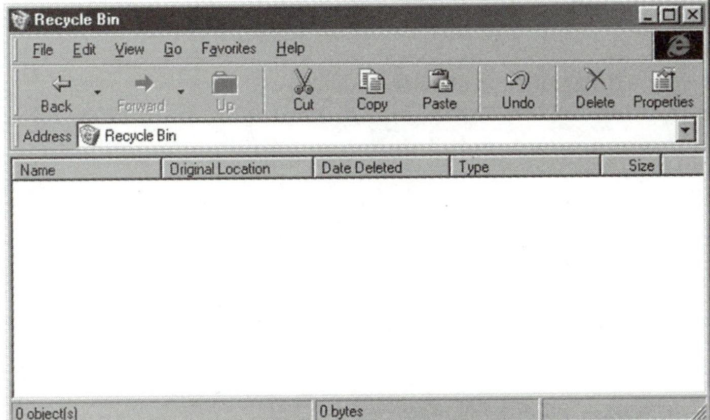

Figure 2-7 The Recycle Bin has been restored.

UNIT 2

LESSON 15

Minimizing a Window

In this lesson, you will learn how to minimize and redisplay a window.

SKILL PRACTICE

To Minimize a Window

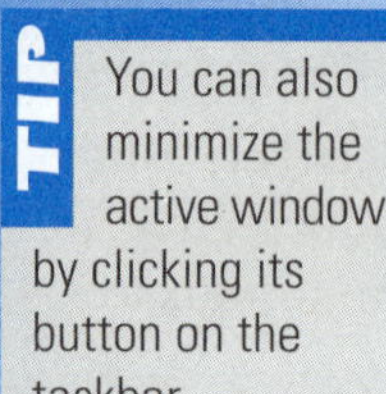

TIP You can also minimize the active window by clicking its button on the taskbar.

To temporarily remove a window from the desktop, you can minimize it.

1. Open the **My Computer** window.
2. Click the **Minimize** button, as shown in Figure 2-8. The window disappears. The window's name, however, still appears in the taskbar.

Figure 2-8 The Minimize Button

TIP You can minimize all open windows by positioning the pointer over an empty area of the taskbar, clicking the right mouse button, and choosing Minimize All Windows from the resulting menu.

To Redisplay a Minimized Window

To redisplay a minimized window, click the window's button in the taskbar.

3. Click the **My Computer** button on the taskbar. The window reappears.
4. Close the **My Computer** window.

LESSON

15

ACTIVITY

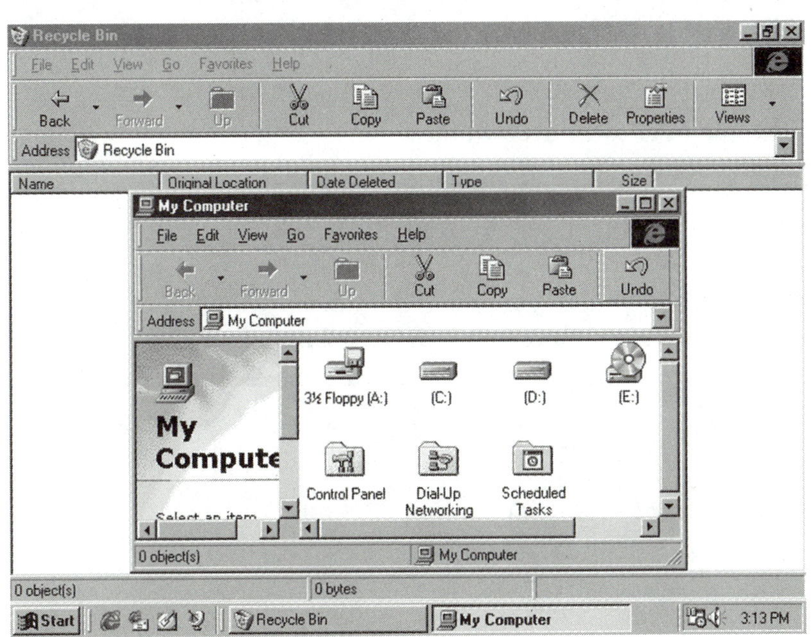

Figure 2-9 The windows are redisplayed.

1. Open the **Recycle Bin** window.
2. Maximize the **Recycle Bin** window.
3. Minimize the **Recycle Bin** window.
4. Open the **My Computer** window.
5. Minimize the **My Computer** window.
6. Redisplay the **Recycle Bin** window.
7. Redisplay the **My Computer** window (see Figure 2-9).
8. Restore the **Recycle Bin** window.
9. Close both windows.

UNIT 2

LESSON 16

Moving a Window

In this lesson, you will learn how to move windows.

►SKILL PRACTICE

TIP When moving a window, do not drag from the top border of the title bar. If you do, you may accidentally resize the window rather than move it. You will learn how to resize windows in the next lesson.

To Move a Window

To move a window, drag its title bar.

1. Open the **My Computer** window.
2. Point to the **title bar**, as shown in Figure 2-10.

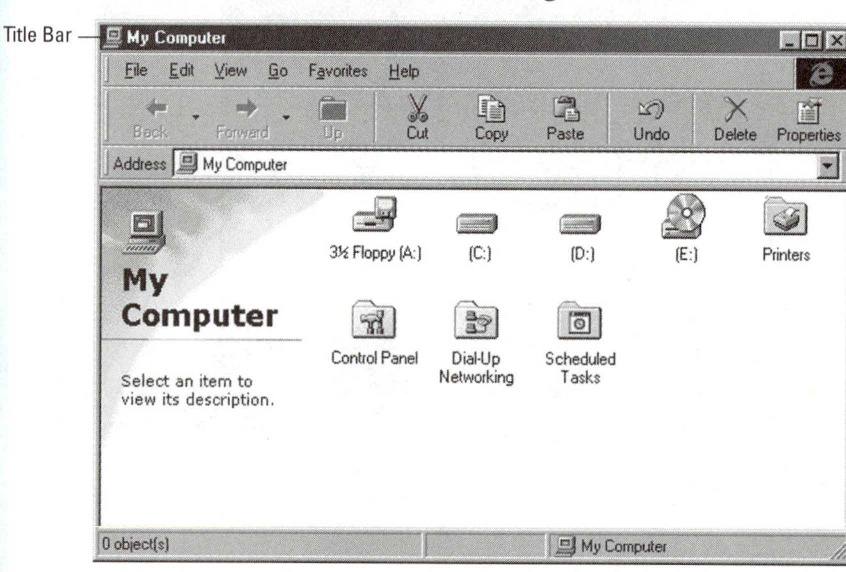

Figure 2-10 Move a window by dragging its title bar.

3. With the pointer on the **title bar**, press and hold the left mouse button.
4. With the mouse button held down, move the pointer to the right about 1 inch. You should see the window repositioned on your screen.
5. Release the mouse button.
6. Close the **My Computer** window.

LESSON
16

►ACTIVITY

1. Open the **Recycle Bin** window.
2. Maximize the **Recycle Bin** window.
3. Restore the **Recycle Bin** window.
4. Open the **My Computer** window.
5. If necessary, move the **My Computer** window over the **Recycle Bin** window (see Figure 2-11).
6. Move the **My Computer** window back to its original position.
7. Close both windows.

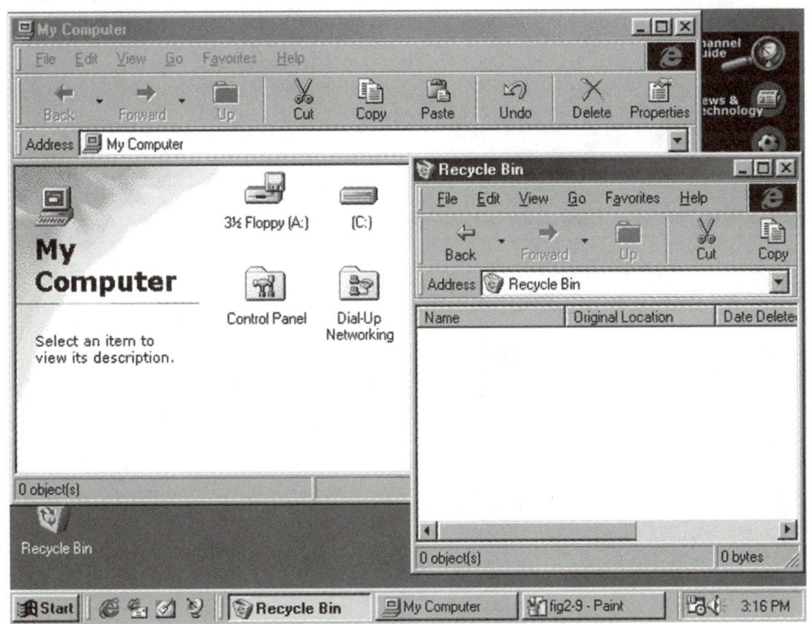

Figure 2-11 Windows may overlap each other.

UNIT 2

LESSON 17

Resizing a Window

In this lesson, you will learn how to resize windows.

►SKILL PRACTICE

To resize a window, drag one of the window's edges or drag the sizing handle in the bottom right corner of the window.

To Make a Window Wider

1. Open the **Recycle Bin** window.
2. Move the window to the center of the screen.
3. Position the pointer on the right edge of the window. The pointer becomes a double-headed arrow, as shown in Figure 2-12.

Figure 2-12 Positioning the pointer on an edge allows you to resize the window.

4. Drag the right edge of the window until it is about 1 inch from the right edge of the screen.
5. Drag the right edge of the window back approximately to its original position.

To Make a Window Taller

6. Position the pointer on the top or bottom edge of the window.
7. Drag the edge up or down slightly to make the window taller.

(continued on next page)

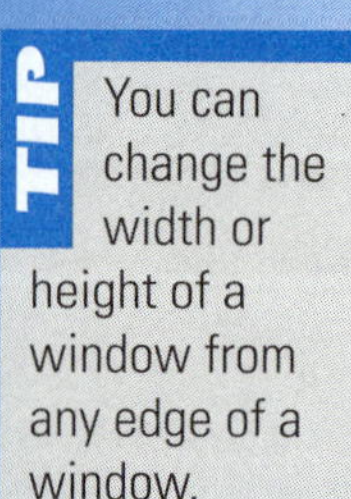

TIP You can change the width or height of a window from any edge of a window.

LESSON

17

ACTIVITY

Figure 2-13 Moving and resizing windows allows you to place windows on the screen in a convenient arrangement.

1. Open the **My Computer** window.
2. Move and size the windows to make your screen closely match Figure 2-13.
3. Close both windows.

Skill Practice (continued)

To Change Height and Width at the Same Time

8. Position the pointer on the sizing handle in the bottom right corner of the window.
9. Drag the sizing handle down and to the right. The window becomes larger.
10. Drag the sizing handle up and to the left until the window is approximately its original size.

TIP

Any corner of the window can be used to resize the window. The bottom right corner, however, is the easiest to use because the pointer can be positioned correctly more easily.

UNIT 2

LESSON 18

Switching Between Windows

In this lesson, you will learn how to switch between windows.

SKILL PRACTICE

TIP Be careful when clicking in a window to switch to a window. If you click on a control of an inactive window, such as the Close button, the control will be activated when the window becomes active.

NOTE Operations are always performed in the active window.

To switch between windows, click on the window you want to become active or click the window's button on the taskbar.

Clicking to Switch Between Windows

1. Open the **Recycle Bin** window.
2. Open the **My Computer** window.
3. Click the **Recycle Bin** window's title bar or anywhere in the window. The Recycle Bin becomes the active window.
4. Click the **My Computer** window's title bar. The My Computer window becomes the active window.

Using the Taskbar to Switch Between Windows

5. Click the **Recycle Bin** button on the taskbar. The Recycle Bin becomes the active window.
6. Click the **My Computer** button on the taskbar. The My Computer window becomes the active window.
7. Close both windows.

LESSON

18

▶ACTIVITY

1. Open the **My Computer** window.
2. Start the **Notepad**.
3. Maximize the **Notepad**.
4. Click the **My Computer** button on the taskbar. The My Computer window appears over the Notepad, as shown in Figure 2-14.
5. Click in the **Notepad** window. The Notepad becomes active.
6. Exit the **Notepad**.
7. Close the **My Computer** window.

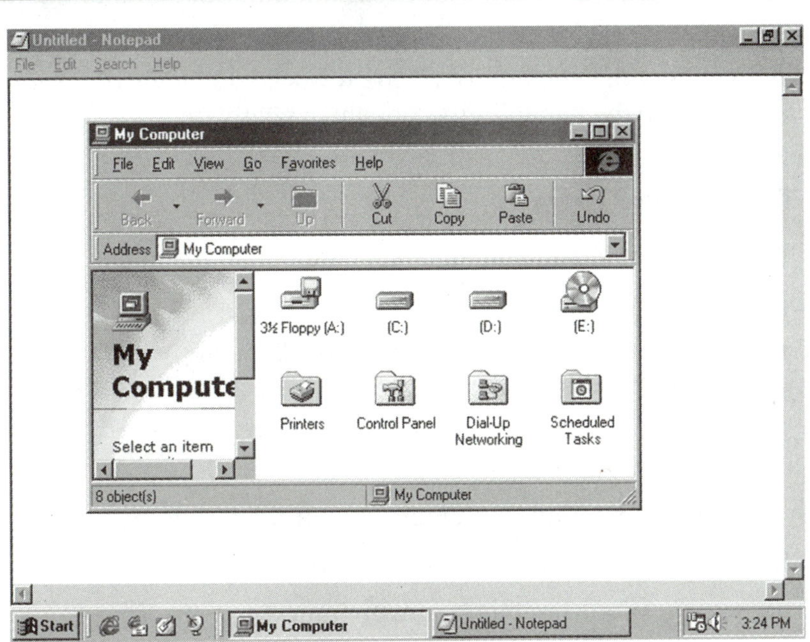

Figure 2-14 The Notepad is moved to the background.

UNIT 2

LESSON 19

Arranging Windows

In this lesson, you will learn how to tile and cascade windows.

SKILL PRACTICE

When several windows are open at the same time, you can *tile* the windows to allow the contents of all the windows to be visible. You may also *cascade* the windows to stack them neatly on top of each other.

NOTE: The Tile Windows Horizontally command makes the windows tend to be wide. The Tile Windows Vertically command makes the windows tend to be tall.

To Tile Windows

1. Open the **Recycle Bin** window.
2. Open the **My Computer** window.
3. Open the Control Panel folder in the My Computer window. You may need to *scroll* or resize the window to see the Control Panel folder.
4. Start the **Notepad**.
5. Position the pointer over an empty area of the taskbar.
6. Click the right mouse button. A menu appears.
7. Choose **Tile Windows Horizontally** from the menu. The windows are tiled.

NOTE: Tiling and cascading resizes the windows involved. To return the windows to their original sizes, you must resize them manually.

To Cascade Windows

8. Click the right mouse button on an empty area of the taskbar.
9. Choose **Cascade Windows** from the menu. The windows are cascaded.
10. Close all the windows.

GLOSSARY TERMS

TILE • to arrange and resize windows in such a way as to make all of the windows fully visible at the same time

CASCADE • to arrange and resize windows in such a way as to stack them neatly on top of each other with the title bars showing

SCROLL • to move the contents of a window within the bounds of the window's size

LESSON 19

ACTIVITY

1. Open the **My Computer** window.
2. Start the **Notepad**.
3. Tile the windows vertically. Your screen should appear similar to Figure 2-15.
4. Cascade the windows.
5. Tile the windows horizontally.
6. Click in the **Notepad** window.
7. Exit the **Notepad**.
8. Close the **My Computer** window.

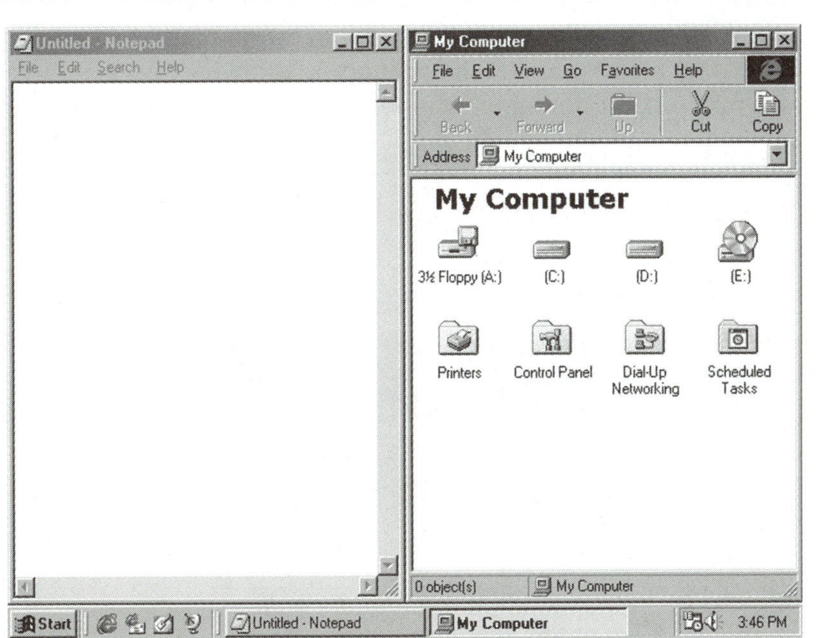

Figure 2-15 These windows are tiled vertically.

UNIT 2

LESSON 20

Scrolling

In this lesson, you will learn how to scroll the contents of windows.

SKILL PRACTICE

When a window has more contents than can be displayed in the window at its current size, scroll bars appear, allowing you to *scroll*, or move the contents within the window.

To Scroll Window Contents

1. Open the **My Computer** window.
2. Resize the window as shown in Figure 2-16. At least one scroll bar should appear when the window becomes too small for the contents.

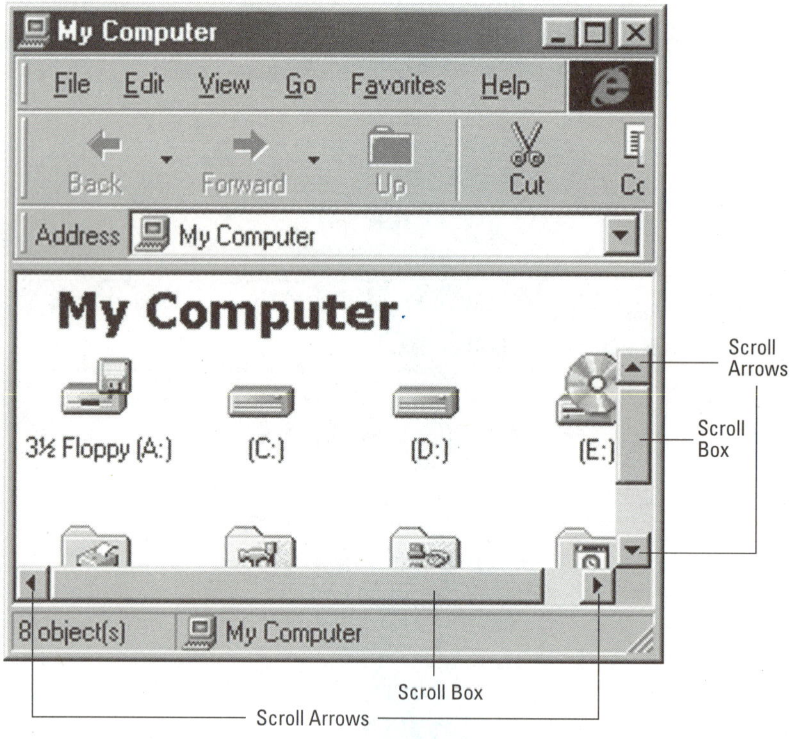

Figure 2-16 Scroll bars appear when a window is too small to display all of its contents.

TIP You can press and hold the mouse button on a scroll arrow to scroll continuously.

3. Click one of the scroll arrows to scroll the contents slightly.
4. Drag one of the scroll boxes from one end of the scroll bar and then to the other.
5. Resize the window to make it large enough so that the scroll bars disappear.
6. Close the window.

GLOSSARY TERMS

SCROLL BARS • graphic elements which allow you to scroll the contents of a window

LESSON 20

ACTIVITY

1. Open the **My Computer** window.
2. Open the **Control Panel** folder in the My Computer window.
3. Resize the **Control Panel** window until the vertical and horizontal scroll bars appear.
4. Practice using the scroll bars to view the contents of the window.
5. Resize the **Control Panel** window to its original size.
6. Close both windows.

UNIT 2

Reinforcement Exercise

1. Open the **Recycle Bin** window.
2. Open the **My Computer** window.
3. Switch to the **Recycle Bin** window using the taskbar.
4. Switch to the **My Computer** window by clicking in the My Computer window. Move the Recycle Bin window if necessary.
5. Maximize the **My Computer** window.
6. Switch to the **Recycle Bin** window using the taskbar.
7. Minimize the **Recycle Bin** window.
8. Restore the **My Computer** window.
9. Move the **My Computer** window to a the lower right corner of the screen.
10. Move the **My Computer** window back to its original position.
11. Resize the **My Computer** window to the smallest possible size.
12. Expand the **My Computer** window to be about 2 inches square.
13. Scroll the contents of the **My Computer** window to the left by clicking the right scroll arrow.
14. Resize the **My Computer** window to a size that accommodates all its contents. You may have to scroll back to the left to display all the icons.
15. Redisplay the **Recycle Bin** window.
16. Tile the windows vertically.
17. Cascade the windows.
18. Tile the windows horizontally.
19. Start the **Calculator**.
20. Cascade the windows.
21. Close the **Calculator** and the other windows.

Challenge Exercise

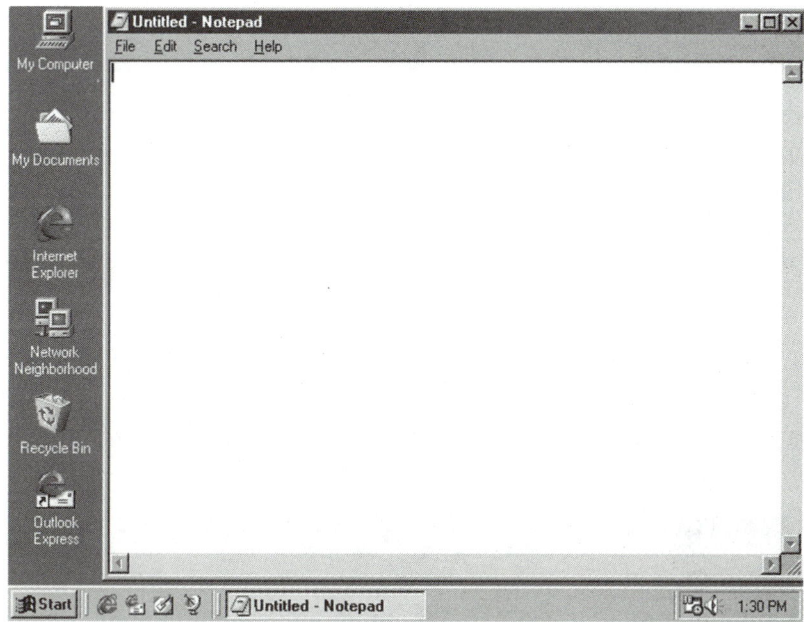

Figure 2-17 You can move and resize a window to occupy whatever area you choose.

1. Start the **Notepad**.
2. Resize and move the **Notepad** to appear as shown in Figure 2-17.
3. Maximize the **Notepad**.
4. Minimize the **Notepad**.
5. Open the **My Computer** window.
6. Redisplay the **Notepad**.
7. Restore the **Notepad**.
8. Cascade the windows.
9. Close the **My Computer** window.
10. Exit the **Notepad**.

UNIT 3

LESSON 21

Starting WordPad

In this lesson, you will learn how to start WordPad.

SKILL PRACTICE

WordPad is a simple word processor that can be used to create basic documents such as letters and reports.

TIP If your screen does not include the toolbar, format bar, or ruler, you can activate them from the View menu.

To Start WordPad

1. Click the **Start** button.
2. Open the **Programs** menu and then the **Accessories** menu.
3. Click **WordPad** in the Accessories menu. WordPad starts. Your screen should appear similar to Figure 3-1.
4. If WordPad does not appear maximized, maximize the window.

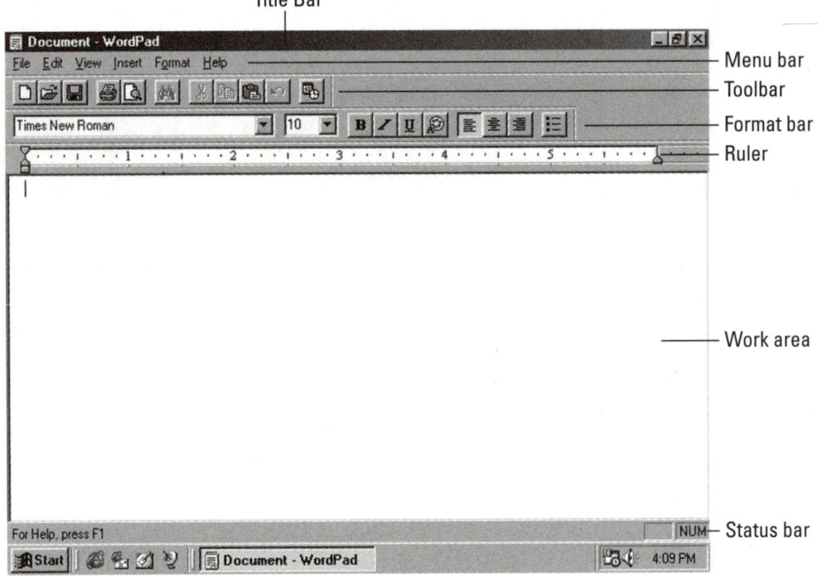

Figure 3-1 WordPad

Title bar - provides the name of the current document
Menu bar - provides the commands available in WordPad
Toolbar - contains icons that provide shortcuts to WordPad commands
Format bar - contains shortcuts for formatting text
Ruler - used to set indents and margins
Work area - area where the document is entered and displayed
Status bar - provides information about the current command

(continued on next page)

LESSON
21

ACTIVITY

1. Briefly describe the steps required to start WordPad.

2. What is the purpose of the ruler?

3. What is the purpose of the toolbar?

4. In what portion of the WordPad window does the document appear?

5. Where does the document name appear?

Skill Practice *(continued)*

5. Familiarize yourself with the parts of the WordPad screen as identified in Figure 3-1.
6. Leave WordPad open for the lessons that follow.

UNIT 3

LESSON 22

Dialog Boxes

In this lesson, you will learn about dialog boxes.

SKILL PRACTICE

TIP If you encounter a dialog box that you did not intend to access or that you would like to close without making changes, click the Cancel button.

Dialog Boxes

A *dialog box* provides information to the user or asks the user to supply more information. A dialog box is a lot like other windows except it contains controls that allow you to communicate with the program. Figure 3-2 shows the features of a typical dialog box.

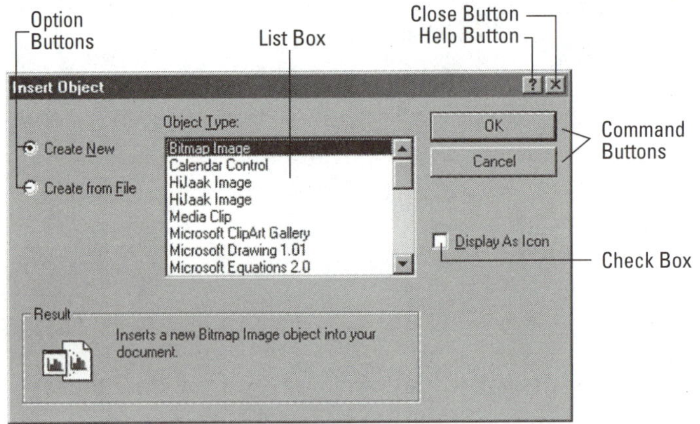

Figure 3-2 A Dialog Box

Dialog boxes can have several kinds of controls. The most common are command buttons, check boxes, option buttons, list boxes, and text boxes.

Command buttons are buttons that carry out a command when clicked. Many dialog boxes have OK and Cancel buttons. *Check boxes* allow you to select one or more of a group of options. A check mark or X appears when the option is activated. *Option buttons* allow you to choose only one of a group of options. Only one option in the group can be active at a time. A *list box* allows you to choose an item from a scrolling list. A *text box* allows you to key text in response to a question the dialog box is asking.

Most dialog boxes include some common controls, such as a Close button and a Help button. You can click the Help button and then click one of the controls in the dialog box for an explanation of that control.

GLOSSARY TERMS

DIALOG BOX • a window which provides information to the user or asks the user to supply more information

COMMAND BUTTONS • buttons which carry out commands

CHECK BOX • a dialog box control which allows you to choose one or more of a group of options

OPTION BUTTONS • a dialog box control which allows you to choose only one of a group of options

LESSON 22

ACTIVITY

1. What makes a dialog box different from other windows?

2. What are the most common dialog box controls?

3. How does a check box differ from an Option button?

4. What type of control allows you to choose an item from a scrolling list?

5. Describe how to use the Help button in a dialog box.

MORE GLOSSARY TERMS

LIST BOX • a dialog box control which allows you to choose an item from a scrolling list

TEXT BOX • a dialog box control which allows you to key text in response to a question

UNIT 3

LESSON 23

Opening a Document

In this lesson, you will learn how to open a document.

►SKILL PRACTICE

To Open a Document

Before beginning the steps below, make sure WordPad is running and active on your screen.

1. Place your work disk in the appropriate floppy disk drive.
2. Choose **Open** from the **File** menu. The Open dialog box appears.
3. Click the **down arrow** in the Look in drop down list box, as shown in Figure 3-3.

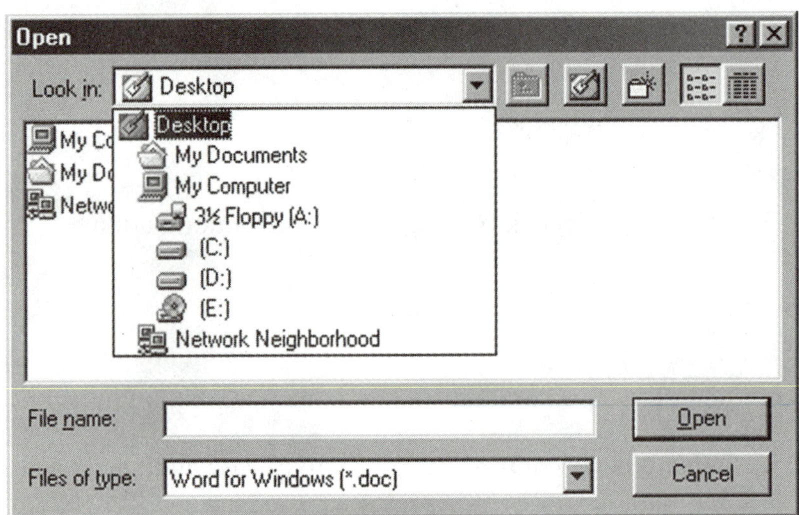

Figure 3-3 The Open Dialog Box

4. Choose the item that identifies the floppy disk drive that holds your work disk. You may need to scroll up or down the list. The files and folders on the work disk appear in the Open dialog box.
5. Click on the document named **United Nations**.
6. Click the **Open** button. The United Nations document opens.

TIP The Open dialog box can also be accessed with the keyboard shortcut Ctrl+O.

NOTE If your work disk files are on hard disk or a network, your instructor may need to help you locate the files.

NOTE WordPad allows only one document to be open at a time. Opening a document automatically closes any other document that may have been open.

LESSON
23

ACTIVITY

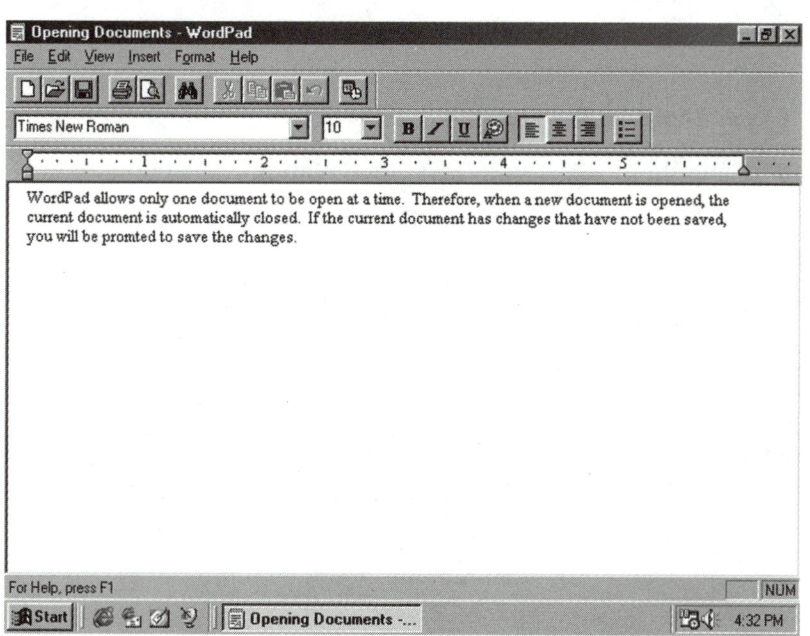

Figure 3-4 An Open Document

1. Open the document named **Opening Documents** from your work disk. The United Nations document closes and the new document appears, as shown in Figure 3-4.
2. Open the **United Nations** document again.

UNIT 3

LESSON 24

Using Page Setup

In this lesson, you will learn to use the Page Setup command.

SKILL PRACTICE

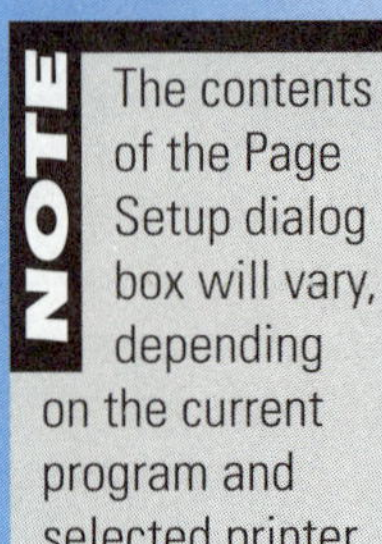

The Page Setup command allows you to choose paper size, page orientation, and page *margins*.

To Use Page Setup

WordPad should be open with the United Nations document open.

1. Choose **Page Setup** from the **File** menu. The Page Setup dialog box appears, as shown in Figure 3-5.

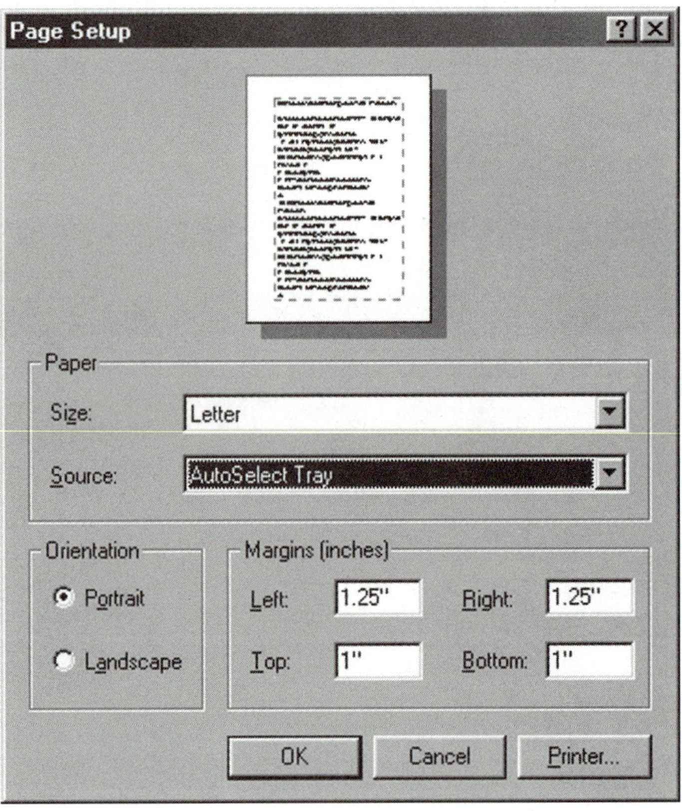

Figure 3-5 Page Setup Dialog Box

2. Click the *Portrait Orientation* option if it is not already selected.
3. Press **Tab** repeatedly until the highlight appears in the Left Margin text box.
4. Key **1.5** and press **Tab**.

(continued on next page)

GLOSSARY TERMS

MARGIN • the space between the edge of the page and the printed text

PORTRAIT ORIENTATION • printing text upright on the page, in the normal reading position

LESSON 24

ACTIVITY

1. Use **Page Setup** to set the margins of the United Nations document as follows:

   Left Margin: **1"**

   Right Margin: **1"**

   Top Margin: **1.75"**

   Bottom Margin: **1.5"**

2. Compare the Page Setup dialog box on your screen with Figure 3-6.
3. Click **OK** to apply the new margins to your document. The dialog box will close.

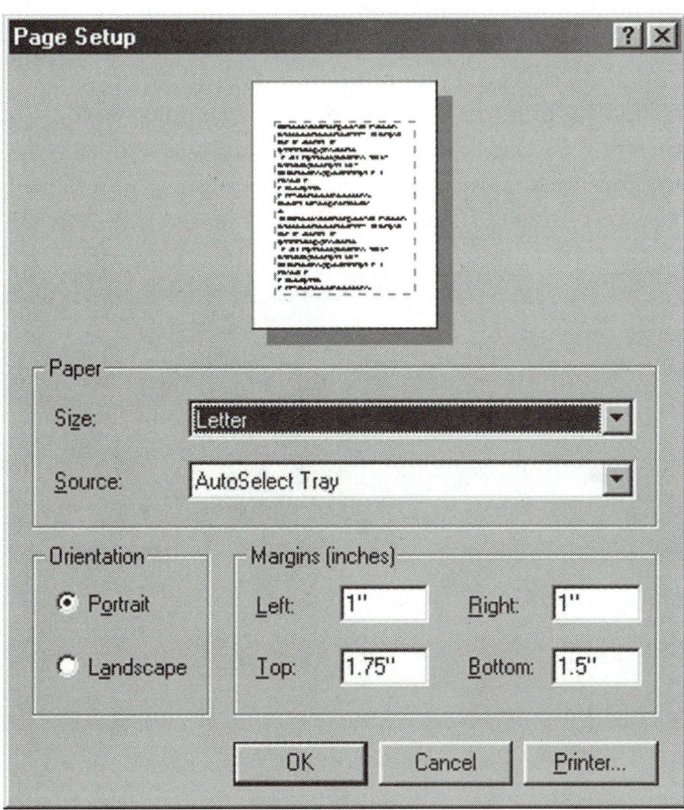

Figure 3-6 New Margins

***Skill Practice** (continued)*

5. Key **1.5** in the Right Margin text box and press **Tab**. Notice that the margins of the sample page in the dialog box change as you enter new values.
6. Key **1.5** in the Top Margin text box and press **Tab**.
7. Key **2** in the Bottom Margin text box.
8. Click **OK** to close the dialog box and apply the new settings to the document.

TIP Pressing Tab highlights the text in the next text box. When you key new text, the existing text is replaced.

UNIT 3

LESSON 25

Printing a Document

In this lesson, you will learn to print a document.

►SKILL PRACTICE

TIP You may print a document using the Print button on the toolbar. Using the Print button, however, skips the Print dialog box and begins printing immediately with the default settings.

NOTE The Print dialog box gives you the option to choose a printer, select a range of pages to print, and enter the number of copies you wish to print. Depending on the chosen printer and current program, the Print dialog box may have more or fewer options.

To Print a Document

1. With the United Nations document open in WordPad, choose **Print** from the **File** menu. The Print dialog box appears, as shown in Figure 3-7. Your Print dialog box may vary slightly from the one in Figure 3-7.
2. Click **OK**. The document prints.

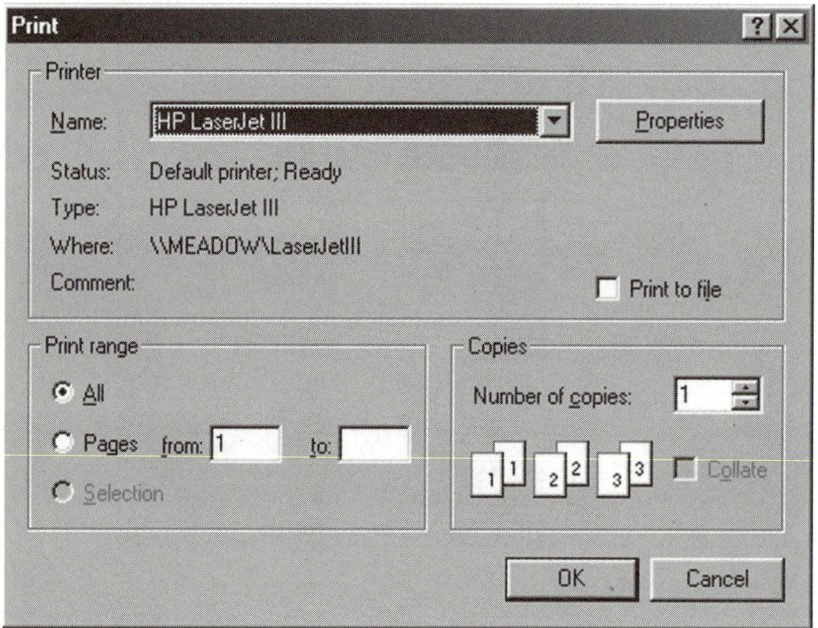

Figure 3-7 Print Dialog Box

LESSON

25

ACTIVITY

1. Choose **Print** from the **File** menu.
2. Specify to print only page 2. (Hint: Click the Pages option and enter from 2 to 2 as the range.)
3. Print the page.

UNIT 3

LESSON 26

Closing a Document and Exiting WordPad

In this lesson, you will learn to close a document and exit WordPad.

SKILL PRACTICE

TIP To close a document without exiting WordPad, open a new document or choose New from the File menu.

NOTE Most word processors allow more than one document to be open at a time. Most word processors also allow documents to be closed without requiring that another document be opened or created.

To Close a Document and Exit WordPad

1. With the United Nations document open in WordPad, choose **Exit** from the **File** menu. WordPad may ask if you want to save changes to the document.

Figure 3-8 Save Changes Dialog Box

2. If necessary, click **No**. WordPad closes, and you are returned to the Windows desktop.

LESSON
26

►ACTIVITY

1. Start **WordPad**.
2. Open the document named **Opening Documents** from your work disk. Your screen should appear similar to Figure 3-9.
3. Exit **WordPad**.

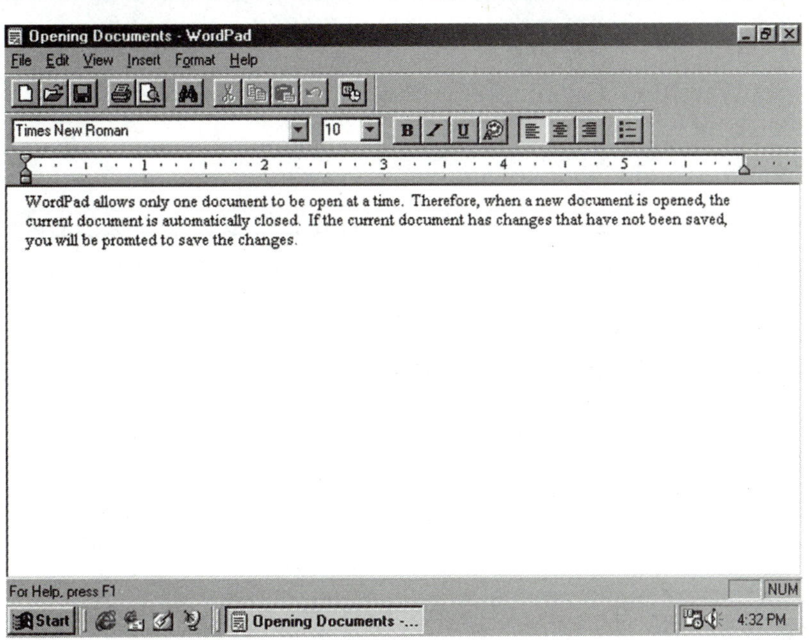

Figure 3-9 WordPad with an Open Document

UNIT 3

LESSON 27

Creating a New Document

In this lesson, you will learn how to create a new document and how to key text.

SKILL PRACTICE

To Start WordPad and Begin a Document

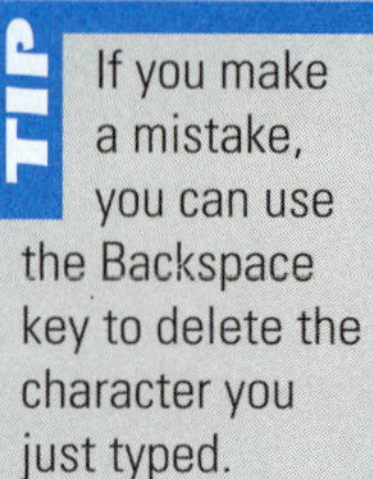

1. Start **WordPad**. Opening WordPad automatically creates a new document.
2. Enter the following text with the keyboard:

   You can create a new document in WordPad by simply keying text after WordPad starts.

To Create a New Document

3. Choose **New** from the **File** menu.

   Or

   Click the **New** button on the toolbar.

   The New dialog box appears, as shown in Figure 3-10, asking what type of document you want.

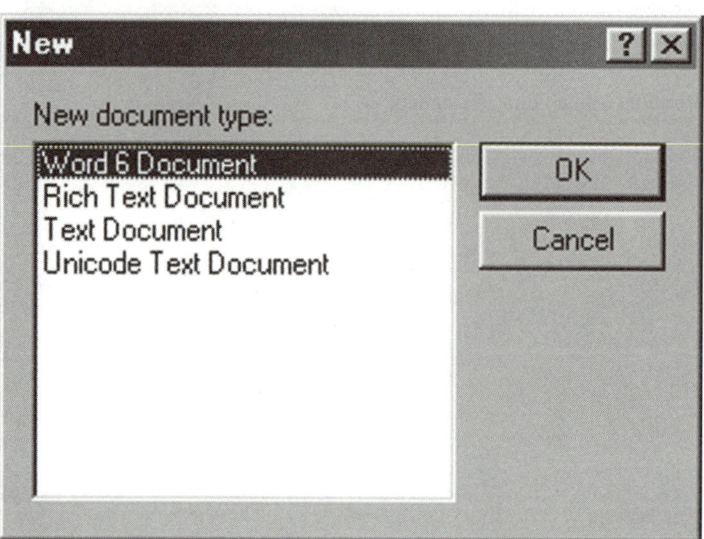

Figure 3-10 New Dialog Box

4. Choose **Word 6 Document** and click **OK**. A message box appears, asking if you want to save the current document.
5. Click **No**. A new document appears.

LESSON

27

ACTIVITY

1. Enter the following sentences into a new WordPad document.

   To create a new document, choose New from the File menu. You will be prompted to save the current document.

2. Create a new document without saving the current document and key in the paragraph at left.
3. Print the document.
4. Exit **WordPad** without saving the new document.

If you want to communicate over the Internet with a large group of people with common interests, Newsgroups are a great way to learn and express thoughts about almost any subject. You can join a newsgroup about local news, travel, or music -- there is something on almost every subject. Newsgroups are easy to join, and often prove very interesting and helpful.

UNIT 3

LESSON

28

Selecting Text

In this lesson, you will learn how to select text in a document.

►SKILL PRACTICE

Before performing an operation on text, you must select the text which you want to effect.

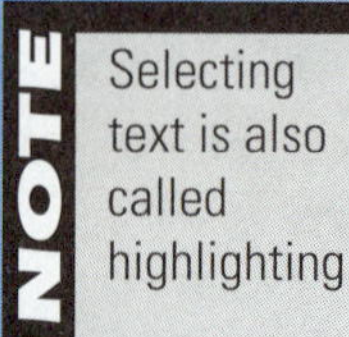

To Select a Word

To *select* one word, you can double-click on the word you wish to select.

1. Start **WordPad**.
2. Choose **Open** from the **File** menu.

   Or

   Click the **Open** button in the toolbar.
3. Open the document named **The Internet** from your work disk.
4. Position the pointer on the word **institutions** in the first paragraph and double-click. The word *institutions* is selected.

To Select an Entire Paragraph

To select a paragraph, you can triple-click anywhere in the paragraph you wish to select.

5. Position the pointer anywhere in the first paragraph and triple-click. The paragraph is selected.

To Select Any Amount of Text

To select any amount of text, click at the beginning of the selection and drag to the end of the text you wish to highlight.

6. Position the pointer at the beginning of the first word of the second paragraph.
7. Drag the pointer to the end of the sentence. The entire sentence is selected.

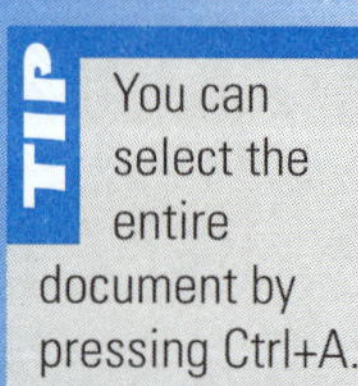

To Select All Text

8. Choose **Select All** from the **Edit** menu. The entire document is selected.
9. Click anywhere in the document to deselect the text.

GLOSSARY TERMS

SELECT • to highlight text in order to perform operations on it

LESSON 28

ACTIVITY

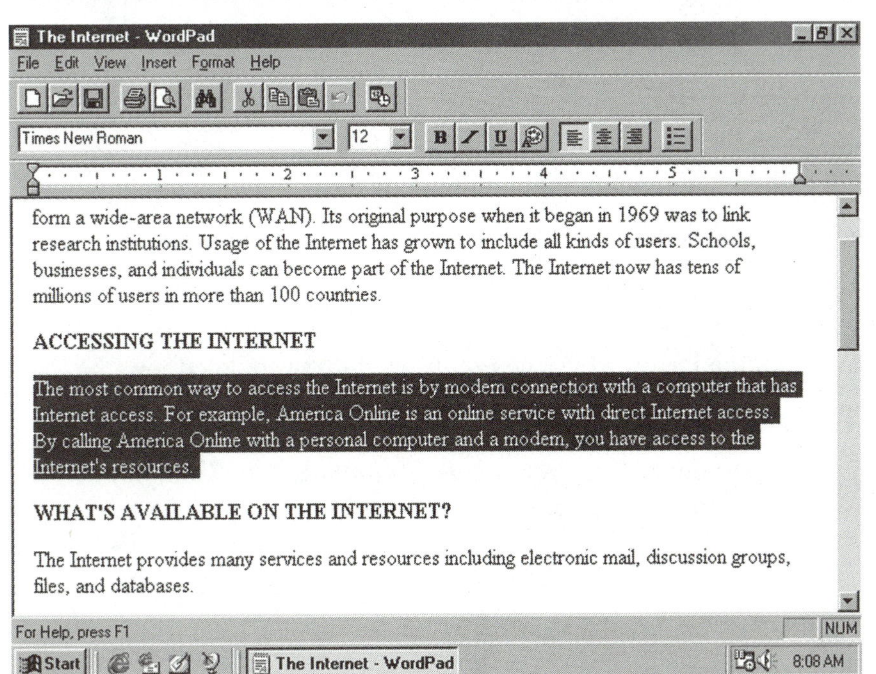
The Internet - WordPad

File Edit View Insert Format Help

Times New Roman 12

form a wide-area network (WAN). Its original purpose when it began in 1969 was to link research institutions. Usage of the Internet has grown to include all kinds of users. Schools, businesses, and individuals can become part of the Internet. The Internet now has tens of millions of users in more than 100 countries.

ACCESSING THE INTERNET

The most common way to access the Internet is by modem connection with a computer that has Internet access. For example, America Online is an online service with direct Internet access. By calling America Online with a personal computer and a modem, you have access to the Internet's resources.

WHAT'S AVAILABLE ON THE INTERNET?

The Internet provides many services and resources including electronic mail, discussion groups, files, and databases.

For Help, press F1

NUM

Start

The Internet - WordPad

8:08 AM

Figure 3-11 A Selected Paragraph

1. If it is not already open, open the document named **The Internet**. Select the acronym **WAN** in the first paragraph.
2. Select the entire paragraph under the heading *Accessing the Internet*. Your screen should look similar to Figure 3-11.
3. Select the entire document except for the first paragraph and the title.
4. Select the entire document.
5. Exit **WordPad**.

UNIT 3

LESSON 29

Editing Text

In this lesson, you will learn how to delete and insert text.

SKILL PRACTICE

NOTE The Delete key erases the character to the right of the cursor. The backspace key erases characters to the left of the cursor.

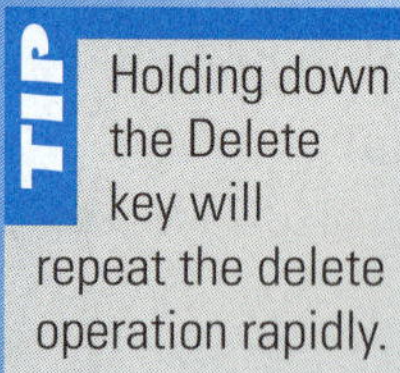

TIP Holding down the Delete key will repeat the delete operation rapidly.

To Delete Text

1. Start **WordPad**.
2. Open the document named **The Internet**.
3. Move the cursor to the beginning of the title *The Internet.*
4. Press the **Delete** key until the entire title is deleted.
5. Select the word **all** in the sentence that begins *Usage of the Internet.*
6. Press the **Delete** key. The highlighted text is deleted.

To Insert Text

7. With the cursor between the words *include* and *kinds*, key the word **many** and a space, as shown in Figure 3-12.

her to form a wide-area ne
969 was to link research in
lude many kinds of users
of the Internet. The Interr
)0 countries.

Figure 3-12 Inserting Text

LESSON

29

▶ACTIVITY

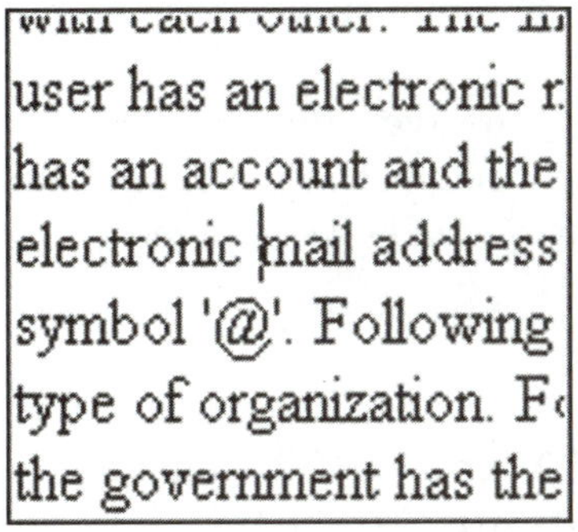

1. Delete all the headings in the document.
2. In the paragraph about electronic mail, position the cursor in the sentence that begins *In an e-mail address*.
3. Edit the sentence to begin *In an electronic mail address*, as shown in Figure 3-13.
4. Exit **WordPad** without saving.

user has an electronic r
has an account and the
electronic mail address
symbol '@'. Following
type of organization. F
the government has the

Figure 3-13 Edited Text

UNIT 3

LESSON 30

Saving a Document

In this lesson you will learn how to save your documents to a disk.

SKILL PRACTICE

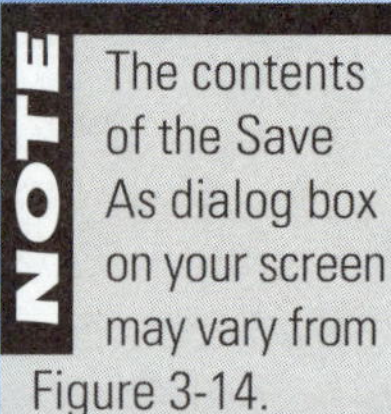

To Save a Document

Use the Save As command the first time you save a document or if you want to give an existing document a new name. Use the Save command to save changes to a document that has already been named.

1. Start **WordPad**.
2. Enter the following paragraph:

   In the period between 1910 and 1920, more than 30 million people (about 30% of Americans) lived on farms in the United States. By 1992, only about 2% (about 4.6 million) of the population lived on farms.

3. Choose **Save As** from the **File** menu. The Save As dialog box appears, as shown in Figure 3-14.

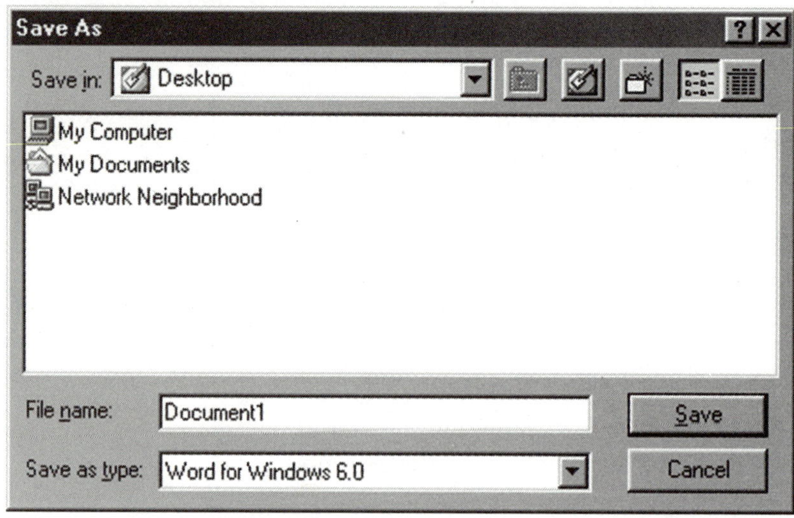

Figure 3-14 Save As Dialog Box

4. From the **Save in** pop-up list, choose the floppy disk drive that holds your work disk (probably the one labeled A:).
5. Click in the **File name** text box. The cursor appears in the text box.
6. Delete the existing name and key **Ag Population** as the filename.

(continued on next page)

LESSON

30

►ACTIVITY

1. Change the font of the paragraph to a font of your choice.
2. Set the font size to 18-point.
3. Set a first-line indent of 0.5 inches. Your screen should appear similar to Figure 3-15.
4. Save the document to your work disk as **Ag Population 2**.
5. Print the document and exit **WordPad**.

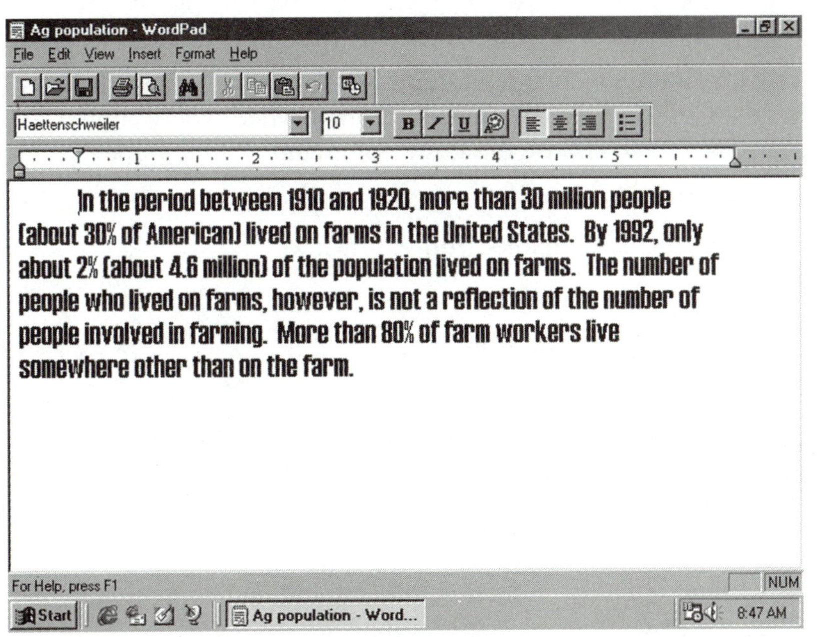

Figure 3-15 Paragraph After Font and Format Changes

***Skill Practice** (continued)*

7. Click the **Save** button. The document is saved, and the dialog box closes.

8. Add the following sentences to the end of the existing paragraph:

   The number of people who live on farms, however, is not a reflection of the number of people involved in farming. More than 80% of farm workers live somewhere other than on the farm.

9. Choose **Save** from the **File** menu.

   Or

   Click the **Save** button on the toolbar.

   The document is saved again.

10. Print the document.

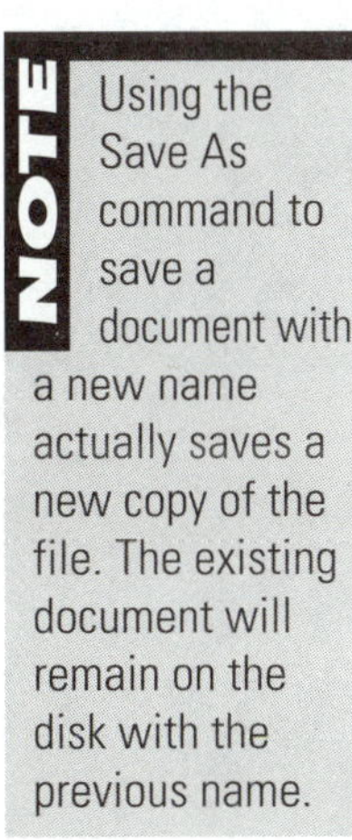

UNIT 3

LESSON

31

Copying Text

In this lesson, you will learn how to copy text within a document.

SKILL PRACTICE

NOTE Text that has been copied is held in an area of the computer's memory called the *Clipboard*. The text remains on the Clipboard until the computer is turned off or until something else is copied to the Clipboard.

TIP Text on the Clipboard can be pasted multiple times, which is convenient when more than one copy is needed.

To Copy Text

To copy text within a document, highlight the text you want to copy, choose the Copy command, place the cursor where you want the copy to appear, and choose the Paste command.

1. Start **WordPad**.
2. Open the document named **Job Interview**.
3. Highlight the first sentence.

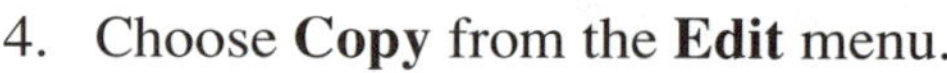

4. Choose **Copy** from the **Edit** menu.

   Or

   Click the **Copy** button on the toolbar.
5. Move the cursor to the end of the document.
6. Choose **Paste** from the **Edit** menu.

   Or

   Click the **Paste** button on the toolbar.

GLOSSARY TERMS

CLIPBOARD • the area in the computer's memory where text that has been cut or copied is held

LESSON 31

ACTIVITY

1. Select the first paragraph.
2. Copy the paragraph and paste it at the end of the document.
3. Paste the paragraph at the end of the document again.
4. Exit **WordPad** without saving.

UNIT 3

LESSON 32

Moving Text

In this lesson, you will learn how to move text within a document.

►SKILL PRACTICE

To Move Text

To move text, highlight the text you want to move, choose the Cut command, position the pointer where you want the text inserted, and choose the Paste command.

1. Start **WordPad** and open the document named **The Internet**.
2. Highlight the heading *ACCESSING THE INTERNET* and the paragraph that follows it. Include the blank line that follows the paragraph.
3. Choose **Cut** from the Edit menu.

   Or

   Click the **Cut** button on the toolbar.

   The selected text is removed.
4. Move the cursor to the end of the document.
5. Press **Enter** to create a blank line.
6. Click the **Paste** button on the toolbar.

NOTE Like the Copy command, the Cut command places text on the Clipboard. The difference is that the Cut command removes the text from its original position.

LESSON

32

ACTIVITY

1. Open the document named **The Internet** if it is not already open.
2. Cut the *World Wide Web* heading and the paragraph that follows it.
3. Paste it above the *Electronic Mail* heading.
4. Save the document as **The Internet 2**.
5. Print the document.
6. Exit **WordPad**.

Reinforcement Exercise

1. Start **WordPad**.
2. Key the text shown at right into a blank document.
3. Select the entire second paragraph.
4. Select the last sentence of the document.
5. Edit the end of the first sentence of the document to read as follows:
   When working with computers, you will often see file sizes and memory sizes referred to using terms like byte, kilobyte, megabyte, gigabyte, and terabyte.
6. Add the following sentence to the end of the last paragraph in the document.
   The next level of storage size, which is becoming more common, is the terabyte (1 trillion bytes).
7. Save the document as **Bytes**.
8. Copy the first paragraph and paste it between the second and third paragraphs.
9. Cut the paragraph you just pasted and paste it at the beginning of the document.
10. Delete the paragraph you just pasted and delete any extra or insert missing blank lines at the beginning of the document or between paragraphs.
11. Add the title **Measuring Memory and Storage** to the top of the document. Create one blank line between the title and the first paragraph.
12. Save the document again.
13. Print the document and exit **WordPad**.

When working with computers, you will often see file sizes and memory sizes referred to using terms like byte, kilobyte, megabyte, and gigabyte. Understanding these terms can make working with computers easier.

A byte is roughly enough memory or disk space to store one character of data. A double-spaced page of text requires approximately 1000 bytes of storage. To run Windows 98, you should have at least 16 million bytes of random access memory installed in your computer. To install Windows 98 on your hard disk requires approximately 45 million bytes of disk space.

Because the number of bytes required for many tasks is so large, prefixes from the metric system have been borrowed to describe storage sizes. A thousand bytes is referred to as a kilobyte. For example, a file may require 16 kilobytes of disk space (written as 16K or 16KB). A million bytes is referred to as a megabyte. A hard disk may store 850 megabytes (written as 850M or 850MB). Hard disks now are commonly measured in gigabytes (a billion bytes). For example, you may see a hard disk that stores 1.6 gigabytes (1.6G or 1.6GB).

Challenge Exercise

In reality, a kilobyte is not exactly a thousand bytes, a megabyte is not exactly a million bytes, a gigabyte is not exactly a billion bytes, and a terabyte is not exactly a trillion bytes. This is because, for technical reasons, computers count in a number system based on twos rather than tens. A kilobyte, for example, is actually 1024 bytes, which is 2 raised to the 10th power.

1. Start **WordPad**.
2. In a blank document, key the paragraph shown at left.
3. Save the document as **Byte Details**.
4. Select the entire document by using the Select All command.
5. Copy the text to the Clipboard.
6. Open the document you created in the Unit 3 Reinforcement Exercise (**Bytes**).
7. Paste the paragraph at the end of the document.
8. Adjust spacing between paragraphs if necessary.
9. Save the document as **Byte Complete**.
10. Print the document.
11. Exit **WordPad**.

UNIT 4

LESSON

33

Storage Devices and Organization

In this lesson, you will learn how files are organized on your computer's storage devices.

SKILL PRACTICE

Storage Devices

A computer system typically includes at least two storage devices: a hard drive and a floppy disk drive. Many computer systems include a second floppy disk drive and/or a CD-ROM drive. A key role of the operating system is to allow access to these storage devices. Applications software can access these devices by communicating with the operating system. The operating system must also provide a way for the computer user to access the storage devices of the system. Windows 98 provides access to the storage devices on your computer with the My Computer icon.

> **NOTE** A file can contain a document, a program, or data required by the operating system.

> **NOTE** Folders are sometimes called directories.

Double-clicking the My Computer icon displays a window that shows the storage devices on your computer system, similar to the one shown in Figure 4-1. The contents of each storage device is organized using a system of *folders* and *files*. Because a storage device may contain thousands of files, files are grouped and stored within folders. Folders can include other folders to further subdivide the files within a folder.

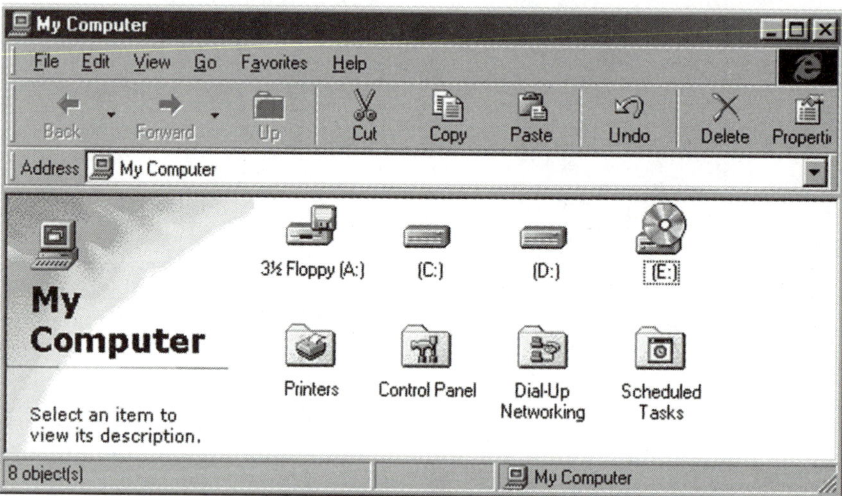

Figure 4-1 My Computer

GLOSSARY TERMS

FILE • a program or document stored on a computer's storage device

FOLDER • an item used to organize files into groups

ACTIVITY

1. What two types of storage devices are found on almost every computer?

2. Name a storage device that is optional but is part of many computer systems.

3. What is the role of the operating system in regard to storage devices?

4. What feature of Windows 98 allows you to access the storage devices of your computer?

5. What are used to organize the files on a storage device?

UNIT 4

LESSON 34

Opening Drives and Folders

In this lesson, you will learn how to use the My Computer icon to open drives and folders.

SKILL PRACTICE

TIP The drive letter assigned to each storage device is also displayed in the My Computer window under each icon to help you identify the storage devices.

NOTE By default, a new window is displayed each time a storage device or folder is opened. In the next lesson, you will learn how to browse through folders in one window rather than opening a new window with each folder. If, during this skill practice, only one window is used to display the contents of the folders, the option has been changed from the default.

Opening Drives

1. Double-click the **My Computer** icon. A window similar to Figure 4-2 appears. Your My Computer window will likely vary slightly from the figure.

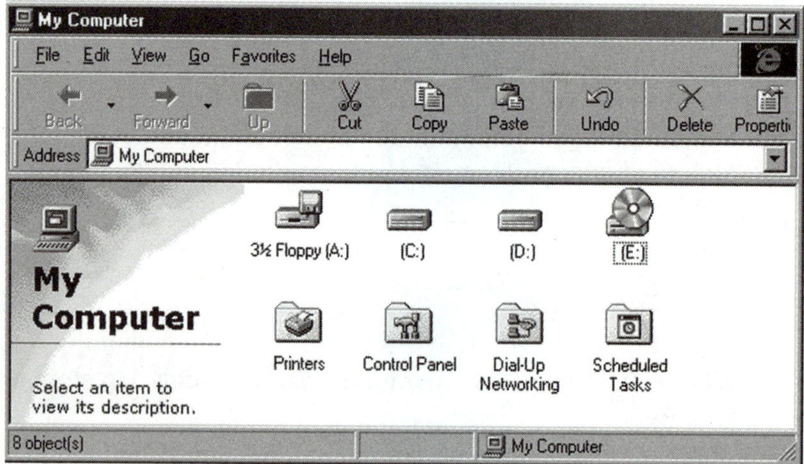

Figure 4-2 The My Computer Window

2. Double-click the icon that corresponds to your hard drive. If you have more than one hard drive icon, click the hard drive from which your computer starts (the C: drive).

Opening Folders

3. Double-click the **Windows** folder. You may need to scroll the contents of the window to find the Windows folder. The Windows folder opens.

4. Close all open windows.

LESSON
34

ACTIVITY

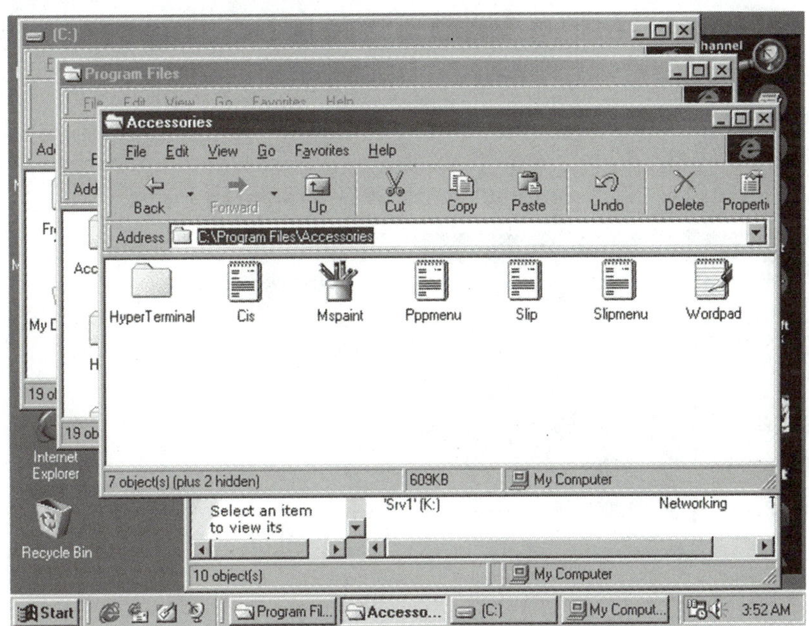

Figure 4-3 Browsing Using the My Computer Icon

1. Open the **My Computer** window.
2. Open the hard disk labeled with the drive letter C.
3. Open the folder named **Program Files**.
4. Open the folder named **Accessories**. Your screen should appear similar to Figure 4-3.
5. Close the **Accessories** window.
6. Close the **Program Files** window.
7. Open the **Windows** folder.
8. Close all open windows.

UNIT 4

LESSON 35

Web and Classic Clicking

In this lesson, you will learn how to browse through folders using both the Web and classic methods.

SKILL PRACTICE

NOTE: When browsing with the Web style feature, all the icons are underlined. The underline indicates that only a single click is required to open the file or folder.

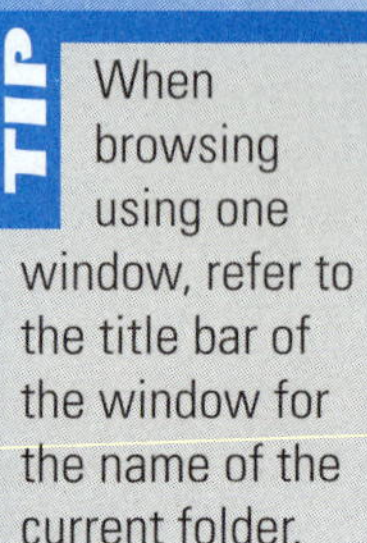

TIP: When browsing using one window, refer to the title bar of the window for the name of the current folder.

To Browse Using Web Style Clicking

1. Double-click the **My Computer** icon. The My Computer window opens.
2. Pull down the **View** menu from the menu bar which appears near the top of the My Computer window, as shown in Figure 4-4.

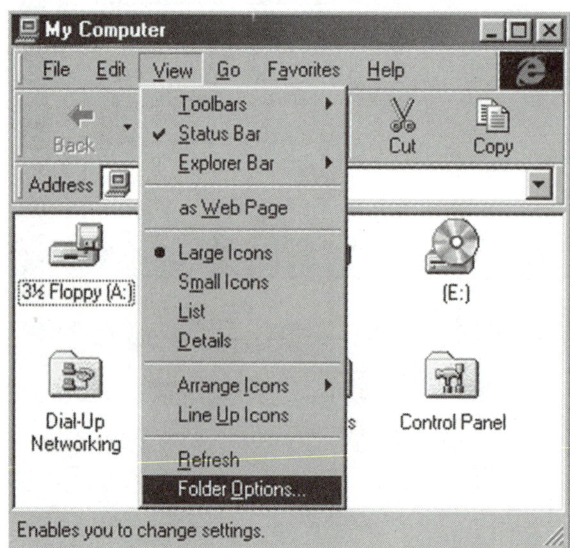

Figure 4-4 The View Menu

3. Choose **Folder Options** from the **View** menu. The Folder Options dialog box appears (see Figure 4-5).
4. If the General section is not already displayed, click the **General** tab of the Folder Options dialog box.
5. Choose the option labeled **Web style**.
6. Click **OK**. Then confirm you want to use Web style by clicking OK again.
7. Single click the **C:** drive icon. The current window changes to display the contents of the hard disk.
8. Single click the **Windows** folder. Again, the same window displays the requested contents.

(continued on next page)

LESSON

35

▶ACTIVITY

1. Open the **My Computer** window.
2. Open the hard disk labeled with the drive letter C.
3. Open the folder named **Program Files**.
4. Open the folder named **Accessories**.
5. Close all of the open windows except the My Computer window.
6. Set the option that causes browsing to occur in Web style.
7. Open **C:** drive again.
8. Open the folder named **Program Files**.
9. Open the folder named **Accessories**.
10. Close the **Accessories** window and open the **My Computer** window.
11. Set the option that causes browsing to occur in classic style.
12. Close the **My Computer** window.

Skill Practice *(continued)*

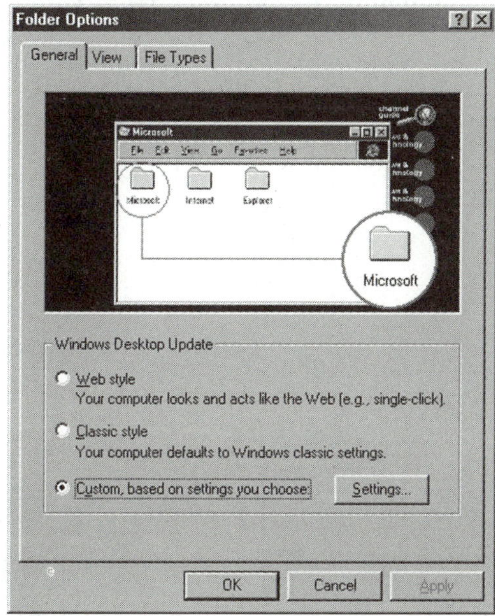

Figure 4-5 Go to a Different Folder Box.

To Browse Using Classic Style Clicking

9. With the Windows folder open, choose **Folder Options** from the **View** menu. The Folder Options dialog box appears.
10. Choose the option labeled **Classic style**.
11. Click **OK**.
12. Double click the **System** folder that is found in the Windows folder. A new window is created to display the contents of the System folder.
13. Close all open windows.

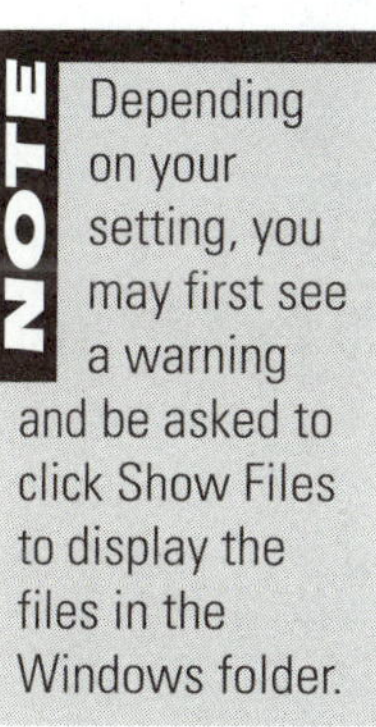

NOTE Depending on your setting, you may first see a warning and be asked to click Show Files to display the files in the Windows folder.

UNIT 4

LESSON 36

Customizing Clicking

In this lesson, you will learn how to customize the clicking style.

►SKILL PRACTICE

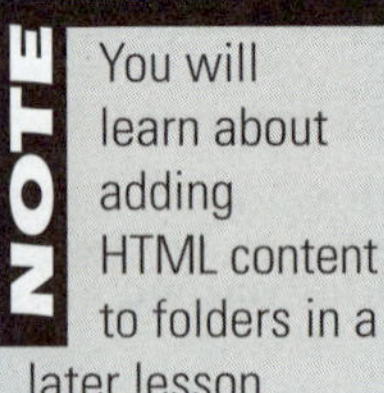

NOTE You will learn about adding HTML content to folders in a later lesson.

To Browse Using Web Style Clicking

1. Double-click the **My Computer** icon. The My Computer window opens.
2. Choose **Folder Options** from the **View** menu. The Folder Options dialog box appears.
3. If the General section is not already displayed, click the **General** tab of the Folder Options dialog box.
4. Choose the option labeled **Custom, based on settings you choose**.
5. Click the **Settings** button. The Custom Settings dialog box appears, as shown in Figure 4-6.

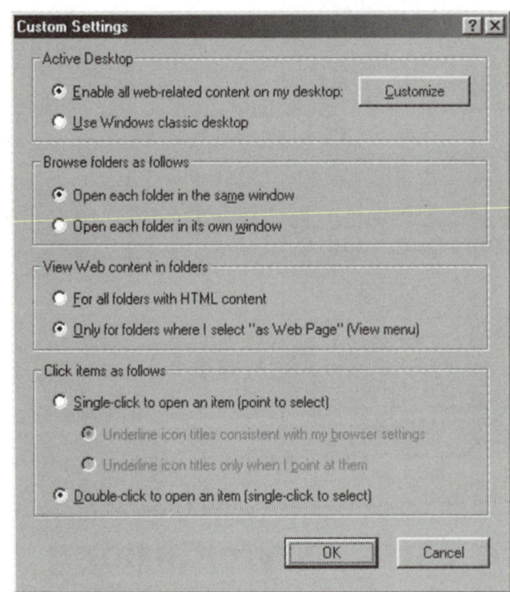

Figure 4-6 The Settings Dialog box

NOTE The Click items as follows option group toggles between single clicking and double clicking to open an icon. The single-click option can be set to underline all icons or just the icon that is under the cursor.

6. In the **Active Desktop** option group, click the **Use Windows classic desktop** option if it is not already selected. This category will be discussed further in a later lesson.
7. In the **Browse folders as follows** option group, click the **Open each folder in the same window** option.

(continued on next page)

LESSON

36

►ACTIVITY

1. Open the **My Computer** window.
2. Customize the clicking method to open folders in separate windows, show folders as web pages only when you choose, and open folders when single clicked with all icons underlined.
3. Open the hard disk labeled with the drive letter C.
4. Open the folder named **Windows**.
5. Open the folder named **Start Menu**.
6. Set the option that causes browsing to occur in the classic style.
7. Close all open windows.

Skill Practice *(continued)*

8. In the **View Web content in folders** option group, click the **Only for folders where I select "as Web Pages" (View menu)** option.
9. In the **Click items as follows** option group, click the **Double-click to open an item (single click to select)** option.
10. Click **OK**. The Custom Settings dialog box closes.
11. Click **Apply** if the Apply button is available.
12. Click **Close** or **OK**. The Folder Options dialog box closes.
13. Double-click the **C: drive** icon. Notice how the folder opens in the same window, even though the classic style clicking is in use.
14. Choose **Folder Options** from the **View** menu.
15. Click the **Classic style** clicking method.
16. Click **OK**.
17. Close the **My Computer** window.

UNIT 4

LESSON 37

Navigating with the Toolbars

In this lesson, you will learn to use the various toolbars in folder windows to navigate through folders.

SKILL PRACTICE

TIP The Text Labels option on the Toolbars submenu submenu adds text description to the icons on the toolbar.

To Display the Toolbars

1. Open the **My Computer** window.
2. Pull down the **View** menu and access the **Toolbars** submenu. Make sure the **Standard Buttons** and **Address Bar** options are checked. Select those toolbars if necessary. The My Computer window should look similar to Figure 4-7.

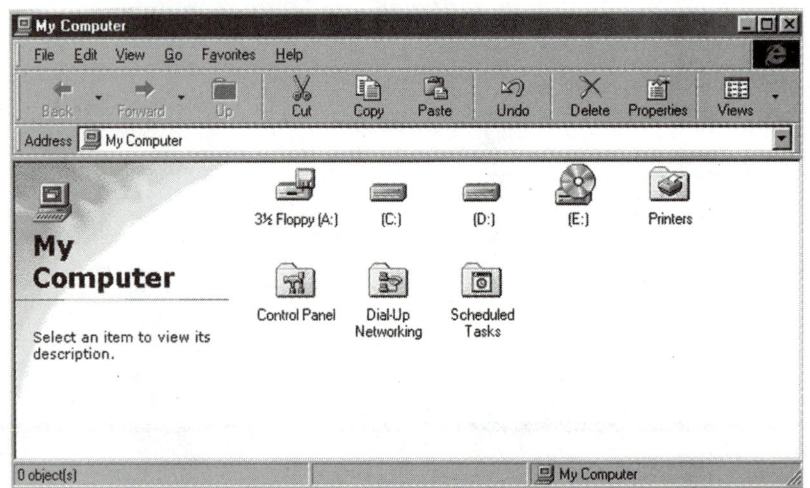

Figure 4-7 The Standard Buttons toolbar and Address Box toolbar

TIP You can right click on the empty part of the toolbar to select different toolbars.

3. If necessary, move and resize the window to display the entire toolbar.

Using the Toolbar to Back Up One Level

4. Set the option that causes browsing to occur using Web style clicking.
5. Open the **C:** drive window.
6. Open the **Windows** folder.

7. Click the **Up** button on the toolbar. The contents of the C: drive reappears.
8. Click the **Up** button again. The My Computer window appears.

(continued on next page)

LESSON

37

1. Open the **My Computer** window.
2. Hide the **Address Bar** toolbar if it is visible.
3. Open the **C:** drive.
4. Open the folder named **Program Files**.
5. Open the folder named **Accessories**.
6. Display both the **Address Bar** toolbar and the **Standard Buttons** toolbar.
7. Use the Up button to return to the **Program Files** window.
8. Use the **Address Bar** to return to the **My Computer** window.
9. Set the option that causes folders to be browsed using Classic style clicking.
10. Close the window.

Skill Practice *(continued)*

Using the Address Bar

9. Click the arrow at the end of the **Address Bar**, as shown in Figure 4-8. A list of devices and folders appears.
10. Choose **Recycle Bin** from the scrolling list. The window displays the contents of the Recycle Bin.

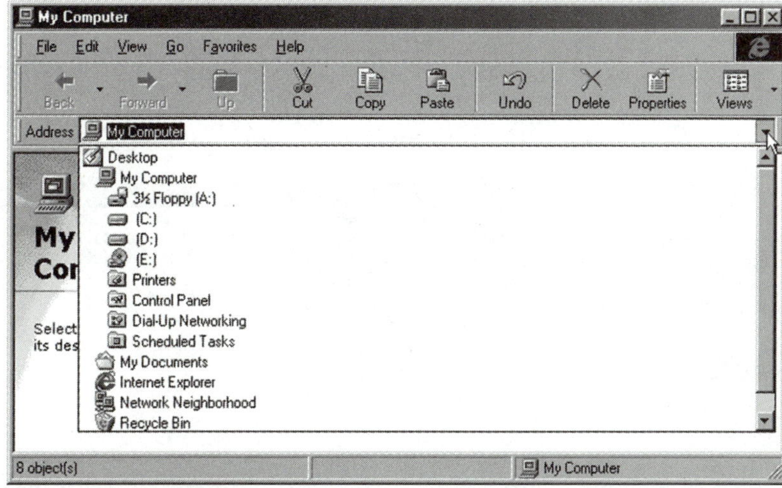

Figure 4-8 The Address Bar.

To Hide the Toolbar

11. Pull down the **View** menu and access the **Toolbars** submenu.
12. Click the **Standard Buttons** option to remove the checkmark. The Standard Buttons toolbar is hidden.
13. Close the **Recycle Bin** window.

UNIT 4

LESSON 38

View Options

In this lesson, you will learn to use the My Computer view options.

SKILL PRACTICE

To View by Small Icon

1. Open the **My Computer** window.
2. Choose **Small Icons** from the **View** menu. The contents are displayed with smaller icons.

To View by Large Icon

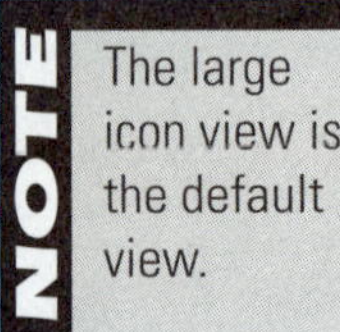

3. Choose **Large Icons** from the **View** menu. The contents are displayed using the standard, large icons.

To View in List Form

4. Choose **List** from the **View** menu. The contents appear in a list, displaying small icons.

To View Details

5. Choose **Details** from the **View** menu. The contents appear in a list, displaying additional information about the items in the list (see Figure 4-9).

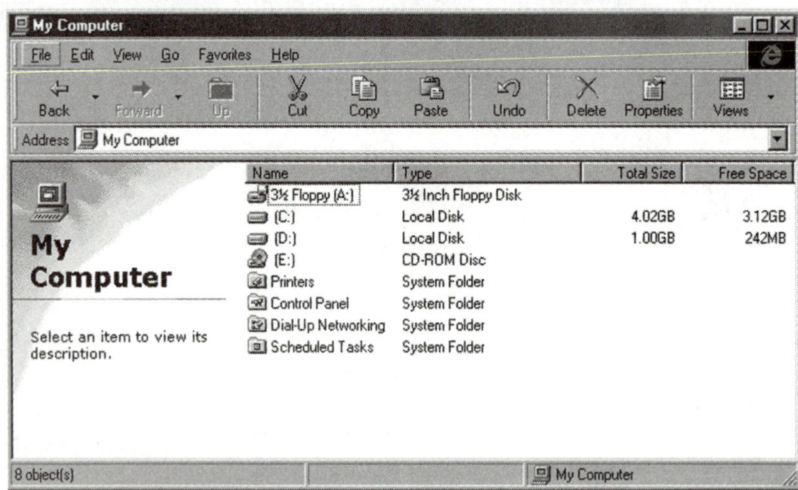

Figure 4-9 Details View

6. Open the **C:** drive window.
7. Open the **Windows** folder and maximize it.
8. If not already in Details view, choose **Details** from the **View** menu. The filename, type, size, and date modified are listed.

(continued on next page)

LESSON
38

►ACTIVITY

1. Open the **My Computer** window and maximize it.
2. Use the toolbar to switch among all four available views.
3. Switch to **Large Icons** view.
4. Place your work disk in the floppy drive and open the floppy drive's window.
5. Open the **More Documents** folder.
6. Maximize the **More Documents** window.
7. Use the **View** menu to view the documents in **List** view.
8. Use the **View** menu to switch to **Small Icons** view.
9. Switch to **Details** view. Your screen should appear similar to Figure 4-10.
10. Restore the **More Documents** window.
11. Close all windows except the **My Computer** window.
12. Restore the **My Computer** window and close it.

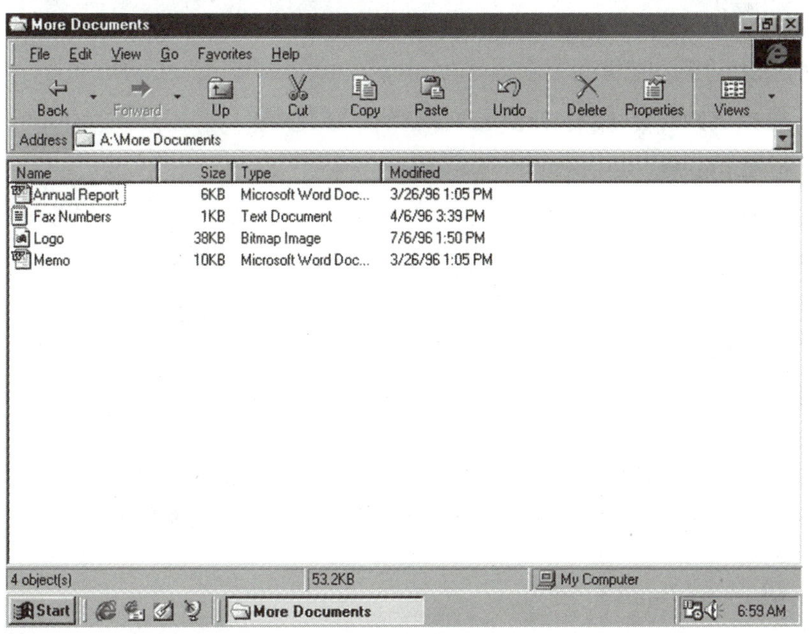

Figure 4-10 Details View

***Skill Practice** (continued)*

To Switch Views Using the Toolbar

9. Display the Standards Buttons toolbar.
10. Click the small arrow beside the Views button and choose **Small Icons**.
11. Use the Views button to choose **List**.
12. Use the Views button to choose **Details**.
13. Use the Views button to choose **Large Icons**.
14. Restore the window by clicking the Restore button on the title bar.
15. Close all windows.

UNIT 4

LESSON 39

Arranging and Sorting Items

In this lesson, you will learn to sort items in folders.

SKILL PRACTICE

In each view, you can arrange the icons or sort the list by name, size, type, and date.

To Arrange Items in Any View

1. Open the **My Computer** window.
2. Open the **C:** drive window.
3. Open the **Windows** folder and maximize the window.
4. If not already in large icon view, choose **Large Icons** from the **View** menu.
5. Pull down the **View** menu and access the **Arrange Icons** submenu.
6. Choose **by Date** from the **Arrange Icons** submenu. The items are arranged in date order, with the most recently added or modified files listed first.
7. Switch to small icon view.
8. Pull down the **View** menu and access the **Arrange Icons** submenu.
9. Choose **by Size** from the **Arrange Icons** submenu. The items are arranged in file size order, with the smallest files appearing first.
10. Switch to **List** view.
11. Pull down the **View** menu and access the **Arrange Icons** submenu.
12. Choose **by Name** from the **Arrange Icons** submenu. The items are sorted alphabetically by name.
13. Switch to **Details** view.
14. Pull down the **View** menu and access the **Arrange Icons** submenu.
15. Choose **by Type** from the **Arrange Icons** submenu. The items are sorted by type.

NOTE When items are arranged, folders are sorted first, followed by files.

(continued on next page)

LESSON
39

ACTIVITY

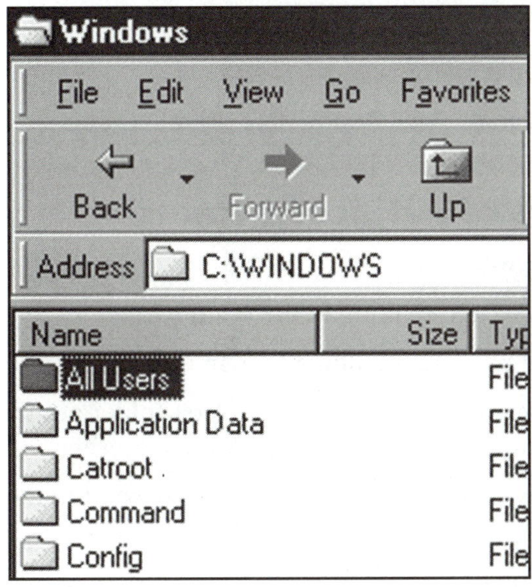

Figure 4-11 Category Headings

Skill Practice (continued)

To Sort Items Using Category Headings in Details View

16. Click the **Name** category heading, as shown in Figure 4-11. The items are sorted by name, from A to Z.
17. Click the **Name** category heading again. The items are sorted by name, from Z to A.
18. Click the **Size** category heading. The items are sorted from smallest to largest.
19. Switch to **Large Icons** view.
20. Restore the Windows window and close all windows.

1. Open the **My Computer** window.
2. Set the option that causes browsing to occur in a single window.
3. Open the **C:** drive window.
4. Open the **Windows** folder.
5. Open the **System** folder.
6. Maximize the window.
7. View the contents by **Details**.
8. Use the category headings to sort the items by date from oldest to newest.
9. Switch to **Large Icons** view.
10. Arrange the items by Name.
11. Restore the window.
12. Set the option that causes browsing to occur in multiple windows.
13. Close the window.

When you click any of the category headings a second time, the sort order is reversed.

UNIT 4

LESSON 40

Selecting Items

In this lesson, you will learn to select items in folders.

SKILL PRACTICE

To Select an Item

1. Open the **My Computer** window.
2. Click the icon that represents your floppy disk drive **A:**. The item is selected.

To Select a Group of Adjacent Items

3. Open the **C:** drive window.
4. Open the **Windows** folder and maximize the window.
5. View by large icons and arrange the items by name.
6. Position the pointer above and to the left of the first folder at the top of the window, as shown in Figure 4-12.
7. Begin a selection box by positioning the pointer above and to the left of the area you want to select.
8. Click and drag a selection box around the first two folders in the first two rows (see Figure 4-13). The actual folders selected is not important. All icons in the selection box will be selected.

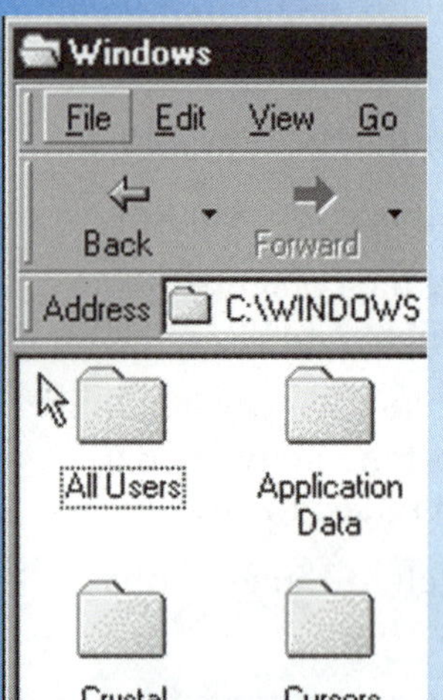

Figure 4-12 Position the Pointer

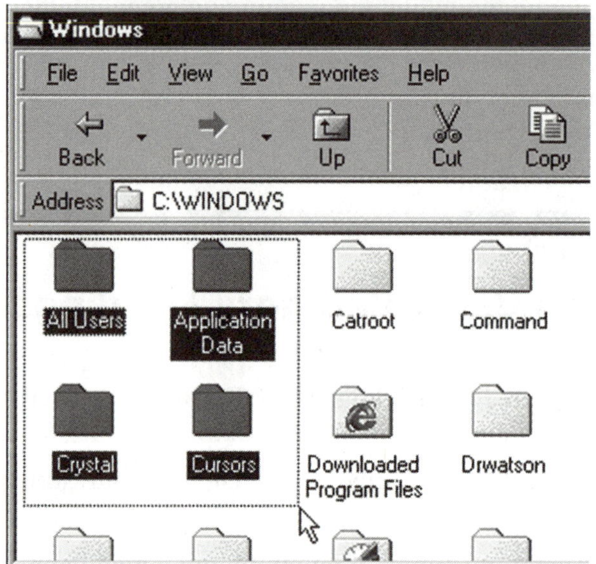

Figure 4-13 Click and Drag a Selection Box

(continued on next page)

LESSON

40

►ACTIVITY

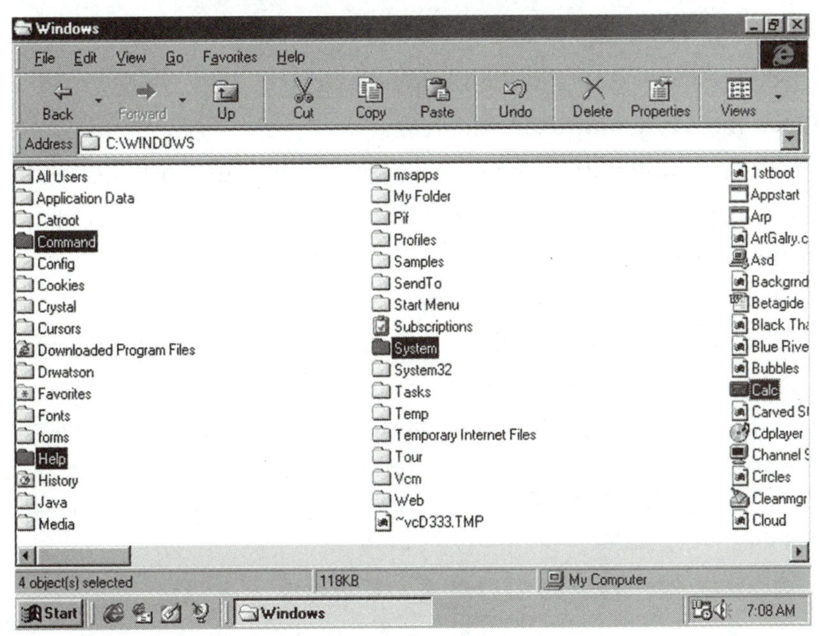

Figure 4-14 The Ctrl key allows you to select nonadjacent icons.

***Skill Practice** (continued)*

9. Click in a blank area of the window to deselect the items.
10. Drag another selection box. This time, select all the icons in the top three rows.

To Select Nonadjacent Items

11. Click in a blank area of the window again to deselect the items.
12. Click the **Command** folder to select it.
13. Hold down the **Ctrl** key and click the **Start Menu** folder.
14. Hold down the **Ctrl** key and click the **System** folder.
15. Hold down the **Ctrl** key and click the **Calc** icon.
16. Click a blank area of the window to deselect the items.
17. Restore the **Windows** window.
18. Close all open windows.

1. Open the **My Computer** window.
2. Open the **C:** drive window.
3. Open the **Windows** window and maximize it.
4. Switch the view to small icons and arrange the items by name.
5. Select the **Notepad** icon. You may have to scroll to find the Notepad icon.
6. Select the **Help** folder.
7. Select a group of about ten adjacent icons.
8. Select the entire second column of icons by dragging a selection box beginning at the top of the column. When the selection box reaches the bottom of the window, the contents will scroll until you reach the bottom of the column.
9. Select the following non-adjacent icons: the **System** folder, the **Calc** icon, the **Help** folder, and the **Command** folder (see Figure 4-14).
10. Restore the **Windows** window and close all open windows.

NOTE

Dragging a selection box to the edge of a window will cause the window to scroll.

UNIT 4

LESSON

41

Copying and Moving Items Among Folders

In this lesson, you will learn to copy and move items among folders.

SKILL PRACTICE

To Copy Items Using Copy and Paste

1. Place your work disk in the floppy disk drive.
2. Open the **My Computer** window.
3. Open the window that shows the contents of your work disk.
4. Open the **Letters** folder and the **Reports** folder and arrange the windows side-by-side.
5. Select the document named **Amy**.
6. Choose **Copy** from the **Edit** menu in the **Letters** folder window.
7. Click in the **Reports** window to make it the active window.
8. Choose **Paste** from the **Edit** menu in the **Reports** window. The Amy document is copied to the Reports window. You may see a dialog box that illustrates the copy process with animated flying paper.

TIP If the Standard Buttons toolbars is displayed, you can use the Copy and Paste buttons to copy files.

To Move Items Using Cut and Paste

9. Select the document named **Notes for Fall Convention** in the Reports window.
10. Choose **Cut** from the **Edit** menu or click the **Cut** button on the toolbar. The document's icon becomes dimmed to show that it is about to be moved.
11. Click in the **Letters** window to make it the active window.
12. Choose **Paste** from the **Edit** menu or click the **Paste** button on the toolbar. The document is moved to the Letters folder.

To Move Items by Dragging Their Icons

13. Verify that the **Letters** window and **Reports** window are both visible on the screen.
14. Position the pointer on the **Notes for Fall Convention** document and hold the left mouse button down.
15. Drag the icon from the **Letters** window to the **Reports** window and release the mouse button over the **Reports** window. The document is moved to the Reports folder.

(continued on next page)

LESSON 41

►ACTIVITY

1. Use Copy and Paste to copy the document named **Summer Convention** to the **Letters** folder.
2. Open the **My Computer** window (if it's not already open). Position the window in such a way that makes the My Computer window visible without covering the Letters or Reports windows. You screen should appear similar to Figure 4-15.
3. While holding down the **Ctrl** key, drag the document named **Kim** to the icon of the floppy drive that contains your work disk. The file is copied.
4. Open the window that shows the contents of your work disk. Locate the document named Kim that you copied.
5. Drag the document named **Kim** over the **Letters** folder and release the mouse button when the Letters folder is highlighted. A message will appear, alerting you that a document by the same name already exists in the Letters folder.
6. Click **Yes** to replace the document with the one you are moving.
7. Use Cut and Paste to move the **Casper** document from the Reports window to the Letters window.
8. Click **Yes** when prompted to replace the document in the Letters folder.
9. Arrange the icons in the **Letters** window by name.
10. Arrange the icons in the **Reports** window by name.
11. Close all open windows.

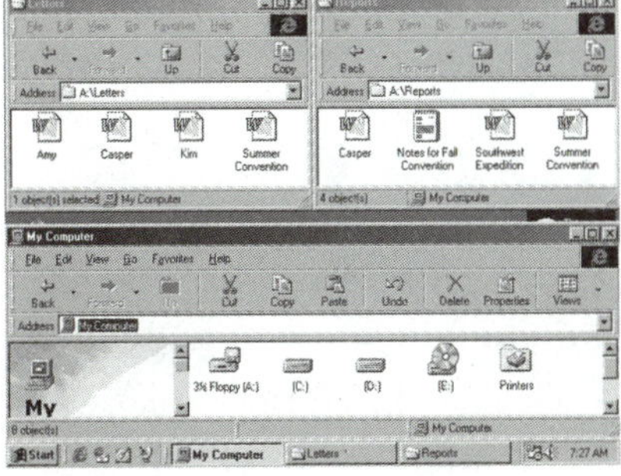

Figure 4-15 Files can be copied and moved by dragging them between folders.

TIP You can also drag an item to another folder using the right mouse button. When you release the mouse button, a menu appears from which you can choose to either move or copy the item.

TIP You can duplicate a file within the same folder by highlighting the icon, choosing Copy, and then choosing Paste. A copy of the file will appear in the same folder. The pasted file will have the same name as the original, but the name will begin with the words *Copy of.*

***Skill Practice** (continued)*

To Copy Items by Dragging Icons

16. Select the document named **Casper** in the Letters window.
17. While holding down the **Ctrl** key, drag the document to the **Reports** window.

UNIT 4

LESSON

42

Copying and Moving Items to Another Disk

In this lesson, you will learn to copy and move items among disks.

SKILL PRACTICE

To Copy an Item to Another Disk

When a file is dragged to a folder that exists on another disk drive or to the icon of another disk drive, the file will be copied by default with no need to hold down the Ctrl key.

1. Place your work disk in the floppy disk drive if it is not already there.
2. Open the **My Computer** window.
3. Open the window that shows the contents of your work disk.
4. Open the **Reports** folder and arrange the windows in such a way that the Reports and My Computer windows are both fully visible.
5. Drag the document named **Southwest Expedition** from the Reports folder to the **C:** drive icon in the My Computer window. The file is copied to the C: drive.
6. Make the **Reports** window active and display the toolbar if it is not already visible. You may have to resize the window to make the entire toolbar visible.

7. Select the document named **Summer Convention** in the Reports folder and click the **Copy** button on the toolbar.
8. Open the **C:** drive window and paste the document in the C: drive window. The document is copied to the C: drive.

To Move an Item to Another Disk

If you want to move a file to another disk drive by dragging, hold down the Shift key to override the default and cause the file to be moved rather than copied.

9. Locate the **Southwest Expedition** document in the C: drive window.
10. Position the windows in such a way that the **C:** drive window and the **Reports** window are both visible.
11. Select **the Southwest Expedition** document.

(continued on next page)

LESSON

42

ACTIVITY

1. Open the **More Documents** folder on your work disk.
2. Copy the document named **Memo** to the **C:** drive.
3. From the **C:** drive window, send the **Memo** document to the work disk in the floppy drive.
4. Using Cut and Paste, move the **Memo** document from the **C:** drive to the **Letters** folder on the floppy disk.
5. Close all open windows.

Skill Practice *(continued)*

12. While holding down the **Shift** key, drag the **Southwest Expedition** document from the **C:** drive window to the **Reports** window. A message will appear, asking if you want to replace the existing file.
13. Click **Yes**. The document moves from the C: drive to the Reports folder on the floppy disk.

To Send an Item to a Floppy Disk

A shortcut allows you to quickly copy a file to a floppy disk.

14. Make the **C:** drive window active.
15. Select the document named **Summer Convention**.
16. Right-click the document's icon. A shortcut menu appears, as shown in Figure 4-16.
17. From the **Send To** submenu, choose the floppy drive that contains your work disk. The document is copied to the work disk.
18. If it is not already selected, highlight the **Summer Convention** document in the C: drive window.
19. Choose **Cut** from the **Edit** menu.
20. Make the **Reports** window active and choose **Paste** from the **Edit** menu.
21. Click **Yes** when prompted to replace the existing file.
22. Close all open windows.

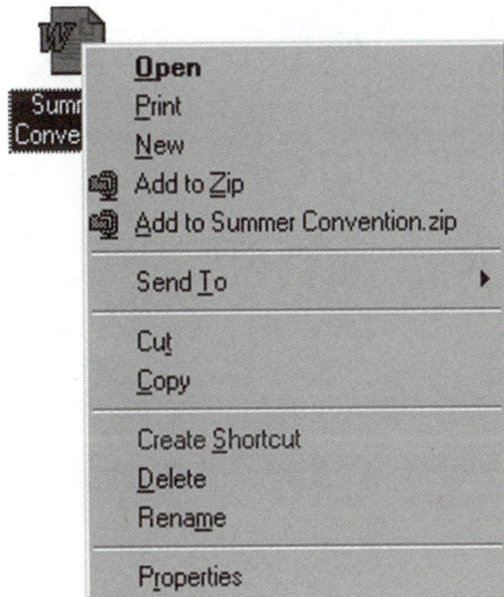

Figure 4-16 The shortcut menu allows you to easily send a file to a floppy disk.

UNIT 4

LESSON

43

Renaming Documents and Folders

In this lesson, you will learn to rename documents and folders.

SKILL PRACTICE

To Rename a Document or Folder

1. Open the window that shows the contents of your work disk.
2. Open the **More Documents** folder and view the contents by large icon.
3. Click the document named **Fax Numbers** to select it.
4. Pause a second or two and click once more directly on the name of the document. The name will become ready for editing.
5. Key **Fax List** as the new filename and press **Enter**.
6. Close the **More Documents** folder.
7. With the **More Documents** folder selected, click on the name of the folder to prepare it to be edited.
8. Press the **left arrow**. The highlight disappears, and a cursor is visible in the folder name.
9. Press the **left arrow** repeatedly until the cursor is to the left of the word *Documents*. The folder should appear similar to Figure 4-17.
10. Press **Backspace** until the word *More* is deleted.
11. Press **Enter**.

NOTE Click with care. If you click the second time too quickly, the document may open.

Figure 4-17 You can edit a document or folder name much as you edit other text.

LESSON

43

▶ACTIVITY

1. Open the folder you renamed Documents.
2. Change the name of the **Fax List** document back to **Fax Numbers**.
3. Close the window.
4. Change the name of the **Documents** folder back to **More Documents**.
5. Close all open windows.

UNIT 4

LESSON 44

Undoing File and Folder Operations

In this lesson, you will learn how to undo file and folder operations.

SKILL PRACTICE

To Undo an Operation

1. Open the window that shows the contents of your work disk.
2. Change the name of the **Reports** folder to your first name and press **Enter**.
3. Choose **Undo Rename** from the **Edit** menu.

   Or

   Click the **Undo** button on the toolbar.

   The original name is restored.

To Undo a Series of Operations

You can undo a series of file or folder operations by repeatedly choosing Undo.

4. Change the name of the **Reports** folder to your last name.
5. Open the **Letters** folder.
6. Select the document named **Kim** and choose **Copy** from the **Edit** menu.
7. Choose **Paste** from the **Edit** menu to duplicate the document.
8. Select the document named **Amy** and choose **Cut** from the **Edit** menu.
9. Open the **More Documents** folder and choose **Paste** from the **Edit** menu. The document named Amy is moved to the More Documents folder.
10. Choose **Undo Move** from the **Edit** menu. The document named Amy is moved back to the Letters folder.
11. Choose **Undo Copy** from the **Edit** menu. A message appears asking if you want to delete the copy of the file.
12. Click **Yes**.
13. Choose **Undo Rename** from the **Edit** menu. The Reports folder is renamed.

TIP When using Undo to undo a series of operations, you can use the Undo command from any of the windows' menu bars or toolbars.

LESSON

44

▶ACTIVITY

1. Change the name of the **Letters** folder to **My Letters**.
2. Copy the document named **Amy** from the **My Letters** folder to the **C:** drive.
3. Move the document named **Casper** from the **My Letters** folder to the **Reports** folder.
4. Change the name of the **Reports** folder to **My Reports**.
5. Undo the four actions taken in the steps above.
6. Close all open windows.

UNIT 4

LESSON 45

Creating a New Folder

In this lesson, you will learn how to create a new folder.

SKILL PRACTICE

> **TIP** You can only create a new folder from the File menu when no items in the window are selected.

To Create a New Folder

1. If your work disk is not in the floppy drive, insert it in the drive.
2. Open the work disk window.
3. Pull down the **File** menu.
4. Click **New** and then choose **Folder** from the New submenu. A new folder appears, ready to accept a name.
5. Key **My Folder** as the folder name and press **Enter**.
6. Open the **My Folder** folder.
7. Right-click in the **My Folder** window to access the shortcut menu, as shown in Figure 4-18.
8. Access the **New** submenu and choose **Folder**. A folder appears in the My Folder window.
9. Name the new folder **Nested Folder** and press **Enter**.

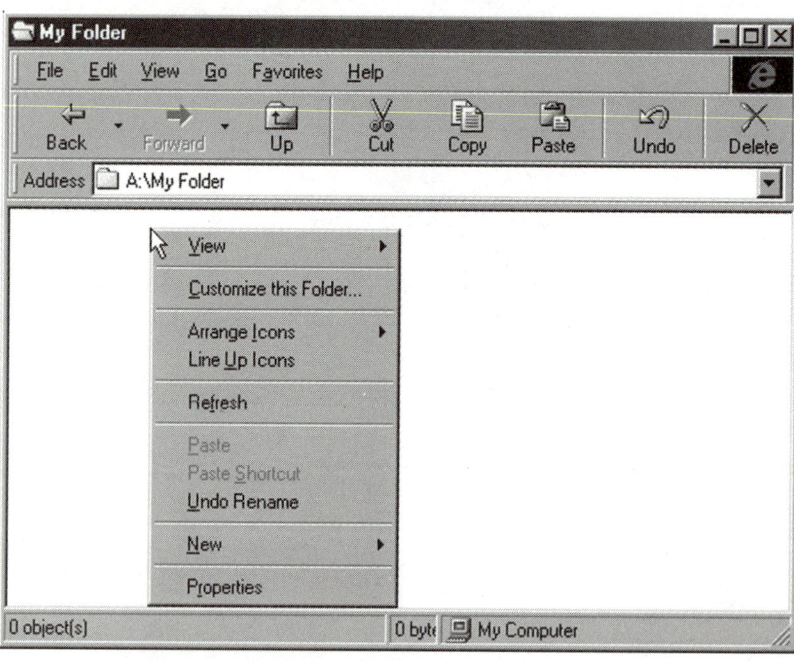

Figure 4-18 You can create a folder from a shortcut menu.

LESSON

45

ACTIVITY

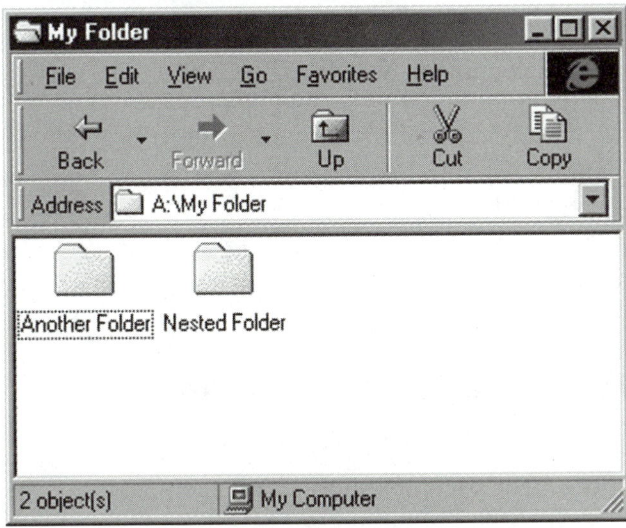

Figure 4-19 Folders can be created within folders.

1. Create a new folder named **Another Folder** in the **My Folder** window.
2. Arrange the folders in the **My Folder** window by name. The window should appear similar to Figure 4-19.
3. Close all open windows.

LESSON

46

Opening and Printing a Document from Its Icon

In this lesson, you will learn how to open a document by double-clicking its icon and how to print a document from a shortcut menu.

SKILL PRACTICE

NOTE If your computer system has Microsoft Word installed, Word may start instead of WordPad.

To Open a Document from its Icon

When you double-click a document, Windows loads the program that created the file and automatically loads the document.

1. If your work disk is not in the floppy drive, insert it in the drive.
2. Open the work disk window.
3. Double-click the icon of the document named **Letter of Application**. WordPad starts and loads the document.
4. Exit the program.

To Print a Document from its Icon

5. Select the document named **Printing from an Icon**.
6. Right-click the document's icon. A shortcut menu appears.
7. Choose **Print** from the shortcut menu. Notepad loads and the document prints. Notepad will automatically exit after sending the document to the printer.

LESSON

46

ACTIVITY

1. Open the document named **Printing from an Icon** by double-clicking the icon.
2. Exit **Notepad**.
3. Print the document named **Poster** from its icon.
4. Close all open windows.

Reinforcement Exercise

1. Open the **My Computer** window.
2. Verify that browsing will occur in separate windows.
3. Open the **C:** drive window.
4. Open the **Windows** folder.
5. Open the **System** folder.
6. Open any of the folders visible in the System folder.
7. Close all open windows except for the My Computer window.
8. Set the option that causes browsing to occur in a single window.
9. Open the same series of folders you opened in steps 3 through 6 above.
10. View the toolbar if it is not already visible.
11. Maximize the window.
12. Use the toolbar to switch among all four views.
13. Switch to Details view and sort by name.
14. Switch to Large Icons view and arrange by size.
15. Use the **Up One Level** button as many times as necessary to return to the **My Computer** window.
16. Set the option that causes browsing to occur in separate windows.
17. Open the **Windows** folder and select the **Start Menu** folder.
18. Switch to List view and select the first row of adjacent items.
19. Select the **Command** and **Help** folders.
20. Open the **Letters** folder on your work disk.
21. Use Copy and Paste to copy the document named **Kim** to the **More Documents** folder.
22. In the **More Documents** folder, change the name of **Kim** to **Kim 2**.
23. Move the document named **Kim 2** from the **More Documents** folder to the **Letters** folder.
24. Use Undo to undo the operations you performed in steps 23, 22, and 21.
25. Create a new folder on the work disk. Name the folder **Just for Practice**.
26. Open the **Just for Practice** folder and create a folder inside it named **Empty**.
27. Print the document named **Letter of Application** from its icon.
28. Close all open windows.

Challenge Exercise

1. Open the **My Computer** window.
2. View the contents in Details view.
3. On paper, record the names of each storage device in the **My Computer** window.
4. Also, record the type, total size, and free space reported in the window for each device.
5. View the contents by large icon.
6. Open the **Windows** folder on the **C:** drive.
7. View the contents by detail and sort by name in descending order.
8. View the contents by size from largest to smallest.
9. Select two of the smallest nonadjacent files from the **Windows** folder.
10. Use the **Send To** shortcut to send the files to your work disk.
11. View the contents of the **Windows** folder by large icon.
12. Open the work disk window.
13. Move the two files you copied from the **Windows** folder to the **Just for Practice** folder.
14. Close all open windows.

UNIT 5

LESSON 47

The Internet

In this lesson, you will learn about the history of the Internet and how it works.

SKILL PRACTICE

The History of the Internet

The Internet was developed by a Department of Defense (DOD) research project in 1969 to connect a number of networks that already existed into a single network, or a network of networks. This project was named ARPANET (Advanced Research Projects Agency Network). ARPANET was primarily used to link DOD research centers with their researchers in universities.

The Internet has exploded with growth since 1969, and now connects governments, schools, companies, and individuals around the world. There are tens of millions of people connected to the Internet in more than 100 countries.

Because the Internet is made up of many networks and every kind of computer in existence, some standard must exist in order for all of these varied computers and networks to successfully communicate with each other. This language of communications is called a protocol. The *protocol* used by the Internet is called TCP/IP.

Parts of the Internet

The Internet provides many different services, such as the ability to transfer files, send electronic mail, and connect to the World Wide Web. There are also databases that can be searched and a variety of ways in which information and messages can be shared.

The World Wide Web (WWW) is the fastest growing and probably the most exciting service of the Internet. The WWW is a form of client/server networking. Servers on the Internet run a *Web server* that communicates with client software (called a Web browser) on the user's computer. Information sent to the client is in a special form called *hypertext markup language* (HTML).

Web pages also have unique addresses that allow users to access the page. An address on the WWW is called a *uniform resource locator* (URL). An example of a URL is http://www.thomson.com. Each part of URL means something. First, http:// means that the document being retrieved is to use a special protocol called *hypertext transfer protocol* (HTTP). The www means that this is a WWW page. The name thomson.com is the domain name. The domain name follows the *Domain Name System* (DNS). This system allows each particular page to have its own individual name.

GLOSSARY TERMS

PROTOCOL • the language of communication between computers

WEB SERVER • a program that communicates with a Web browser

HYPERTEXT MARKUP LANGUAGE (HTML) • the format in which information is sent from a Web server to a client's Web browser

UNIFORM RESOURCE LOCATOR (URL) • an address on the World Wide Web

LESSON 47

ACTIVITY

1. What was the name of the project that began the Internet?

2. Name two types of organizations that use the Internet.

3. Name two services that the Internet provides.

4. What is an address on the WWW called?

5. Why is the DNS used on the Internet?

MORE GLOSSARY TERMS

HYPERTEXT TRANSFER PROTOCOL (HTTP) • the protocol used to retrieve Web pages

DOMAIN NAME SYSTEM (DNS) • the system that allows each WWW site to have its own individual name, and gives it the ability to be accessed by users throughout the world

UNIT 5

LESSON
48

Opening Internet Explorer

In this lesson, you will learn how to start Internet Explorer.

►SKILL PRACTICE

Opening Drives

1. Click the **Start** button.
2. Position your cursor arrow on the **Programs** menu.
3. From the **Internet Explorer** menu, click **Internet Explorer**. The Internet 4. Explorer will open as shown in Figure 5-1.
4. Choose **Close** from the **File** menu. Internet Explorer closes.

Figure 5-1 Internet Explorer

To Start Internet Explorer from the Desktop

5. Double click the **Internet Explorer** icon on the desktop. The Internet Explorer starts.
6. Close **Internet Explorer** with the **Close** button.

To Start Internet Explorer from the Taskbar

7. Click the **Launch Internet Explorer Browser** button in the Quick Launch toolbar on the taskbar. Internet Explorer starts.
8. Close **Internet Explorer**.

LESSON
48

ACTIVITY

1. Start **Internet Explorer** from the **Start Menu**.
2. Close **Internet Explorer**.
3. Start **Internet Explorer** from the **Desktop**.
4. Close **Internet Explorer**.
5. Start **Internet Explorer** from the **Taskbar**.
6. Close **Internet Explorer**.

UNIT 5

LESSON 49

Entering an Address and Clicking Links

In this lesson, you will learn how to enter a URL and browse the Internet using hyperlinks.

SKILL PRACTICE

TIP Pressing **Ctrl+Enter** after typing the domain of the URL will automatically add the beginning **http:\\www.** and the ending **.com** to the URL.

NOTE When the cursor is over the hyperlink, the URL will be shown in the status bar.

NOTE Pointing the mouse at the Back or Forward buttons will display the address of the page the button will open.

To Enter an Internet Address

1. Open **Internet Explorer** with the Quick Launch button on the taskbar.
2. Click the **Address bar**. The current URL will be highlighted.
3. Enter the URL **www.knowlton.net/win98** into the Address bar and press enter. The screen should look similar to Figure 5-2.

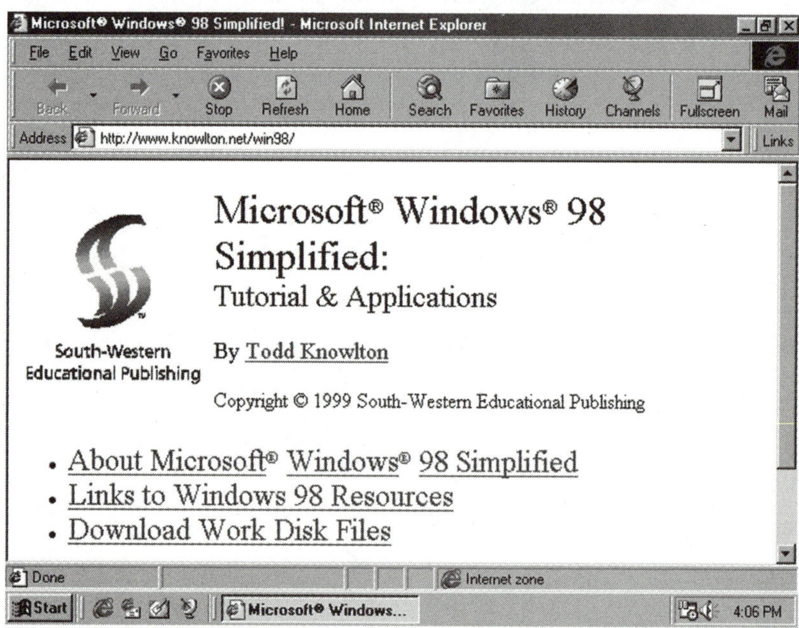

Figure 5-2 Internet Explorer shows the URL entered in the address bar.

To Browse the Internet Using Hyperlinks

Within many Web pages are hyperlinks. *Hyperlinks* are the way pages are linked allowing a user to jump from one page to another by clicking objects and text on the screen. Hyperlinks are usually a different color than the rest of the text and are underlined. They can also be in the form of an icon. The mouse cursor will change into a pointing hand when it is over a hyperlink.

4. With the Web page still open, click the hyperlink **About Microsoft® Windows® 98 Simplified**. A new Web page appears on the screen.

(continued on next page)

GLOSSARY TERMS

HYPERLINKS • the way pages are linked allowing a user to jump from one page to another by clicking objects and text on the screen

LESSON 49

ACTIVITY

1. Open the Web page **www.mainfunction.com**
2. Click the hyperlink for the current issue of MainFunction.
3. Click one of the current articles from the list.
4. Return to the MainFunction home page by using the down arrow on the address bar.
5. Close all open windows.

***Skill Practice** (continued)*

To View Previously Opened Pages

5. Open the Web site for MainFunction at **www.mainfunction.com**.
6. Click the down arrow on the right side of the address bar. A list of the last 25 pages that were opened appears.
7. Click the address for **Microsoft® Windows® 98 Simplified.** The Microsoft® Windows® 98 Simplified now appears on the screen.
8. Leave **Internet Explorer** open for the next activity.

UNIT 5

LESSON

50

Moving Between a Web Page Using Back and Forward

In this lesson, you will browse previously loaded Web pages using the back and forward buttons.

SKILL PRACTICE

To View a Previously Opened Page

1. Start **Internet Explorer**.
2. Type **www.knowlton.net/win98** into the address bar, and press **Enter**. The Microsoft® Windows® 98 Simplified home page is loaded on the screen.
3. Click the **Links to Windows 98 Resources** hyperlink.

4. After the page has been loaded, click the **Back** button. The Microsoft® Windows® 98 Simplified Web page is displayed on the screen.

5. Click the **Forward** button. The Links to Windows 98 Resources page appears on the screen.

To Stop a Web Page from Loading

6. Click the **Back** button. The home page appears on the screen.
7. Click the **About Microsoft® Windows® 98 Simplified** hyperlink.
8. Click the picture of the book that is on the screen.

9. Once the picture begins to load, press the **Stop** button. The stop button terminates the transfer between the computers, and the picture is only partially loaded.

To Refresh a Web Page

10. Click the **Refresh** button. After a few seconds the page is reloaded and the full picture appears on the screen.

LESSON

50

▶ACTIVITY

1. Open South-Western's page at **www.swep.com**.
2. Click on one of the hyperlinks.
3. Click the **Back** button to return to the previous page.
4. Click the **Forward** button.
5. Open Disney's Web page at **www.disney.com**.
6. Click a hyperlink on the home page and then press the stop button before the page completely loads.
7. Click the **Refresh** button to reload the page.
8. Close **Internet Explorer**.

UNIT 5

LESSON 51

Saving and Printing a Web Page

In this lesson, you will learn how to save an HTML file and print it.

►SKILL PRACTICE

Saving Web pages is different from saving an ordinary text file. Internet Explorer can only save the text from a page and leave empty boxes to replace the pictures.

Saving an HTML Document

1. Open **Internet Explorer**.
2. Type **www.mainfunction.com** into the address bar.
3. Place your work disk in the floppy disk drive.
4. Choose **Save As** from the **File** menu. The Save As dialog box appears, as shown in Figure 5-3.

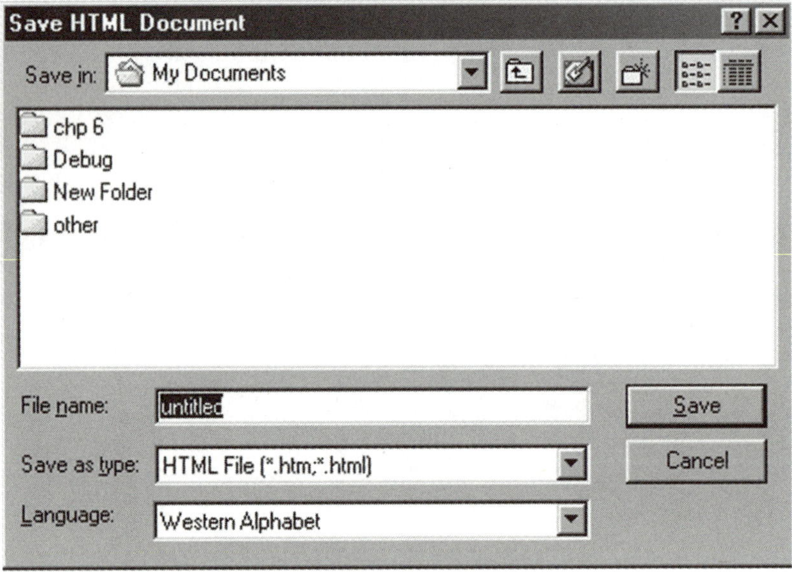

Figure 5-3 Save As Dialog Box

5. Click the **Save in** box and select the drive that contains your work disk.
6. Type **Mainfunction** in the **File name** box.
7. Click **Save**.
8. After the file has been saved, close **Internet Explorer** and use **My Computer** to view the contents of your work disk.

(continued on next page)

LESSON

51

1. If not already displayed, open **www.mainfunction.com** from **Internet Explorer**.
2. Click the hyperlink for the current issue of MainFunction.
3. Click the hyperlink of an article hyperlink looks interesting.
4. Save the page on your work disk using the name of the article as the filename.
5. Print the document.
6. Close **Internet Explorer**.

Skill Practice *(continued)*

9. Double click the file **Mainfunction**. Internet Explorer will open and display the file you have just saved. Notice that the file contains only the text and is missing the graphics from the original page.

Printing an HTML Document

10. Return to the MainFunction home page at **www.mainfunction.com**.
11. Choose **Print** from the **File** menu. The Print dialog box appears, as in Figure 5-4.

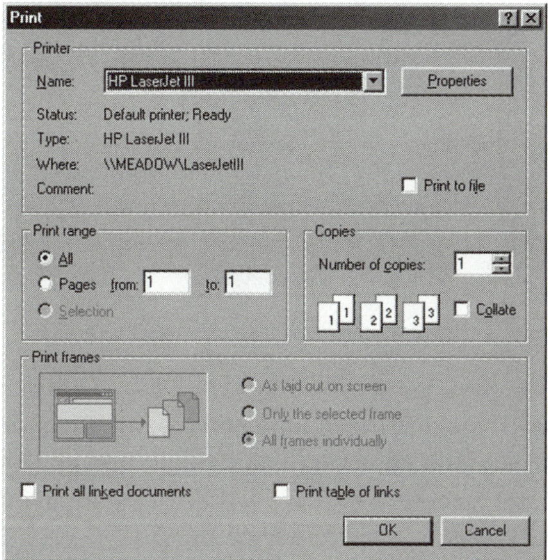

Figure 5-4 Print Dialog Box

12. Click **OK**.
13. Leave **Internet Explorer** open for the next activity.

UNIT 5

LESSON 52

Searching the Internet

In this lesson, you will use search engines to find different sites on the Internet.

SKILL PRACTICE

To Use a Search Engine

1. Open **Internet Explorer**.
2. Type **www.knowlton.net/win98** into the address bar.
3. Click the **Search** button on the toolbar. A search window appears from the left side of Internet Explorer.

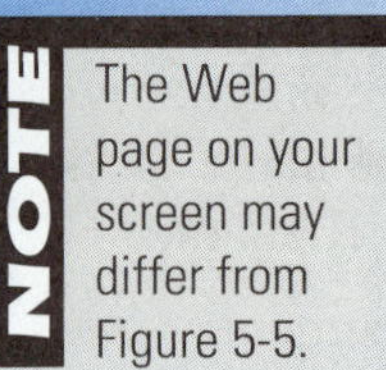

NOTE The Web page on your screen may differ from Figure 5-5.

4. Change the **Choose Provider** box at the top of the search window to **Infoseek**. The screen should appear similar to Figure 5-5.

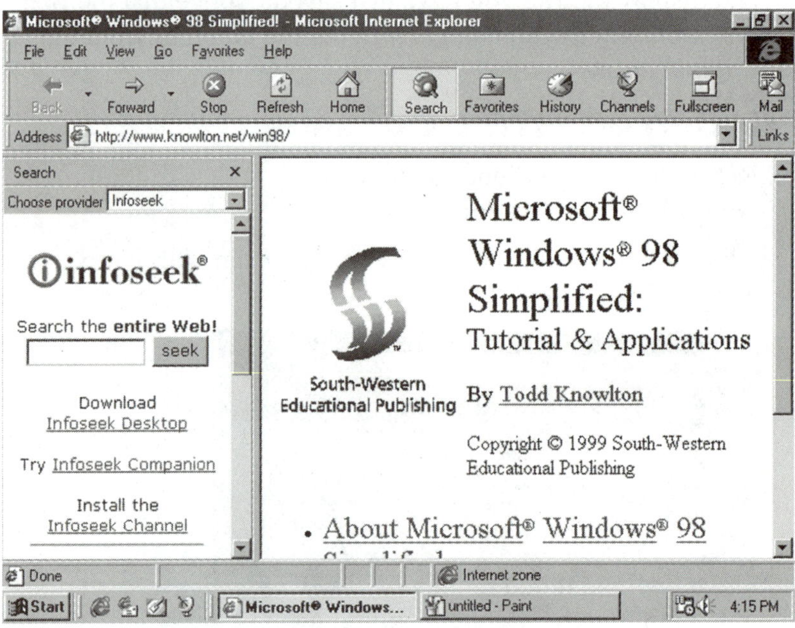

Figure 5-5 The Search button extends a search window from the left side of Internet Explorer.

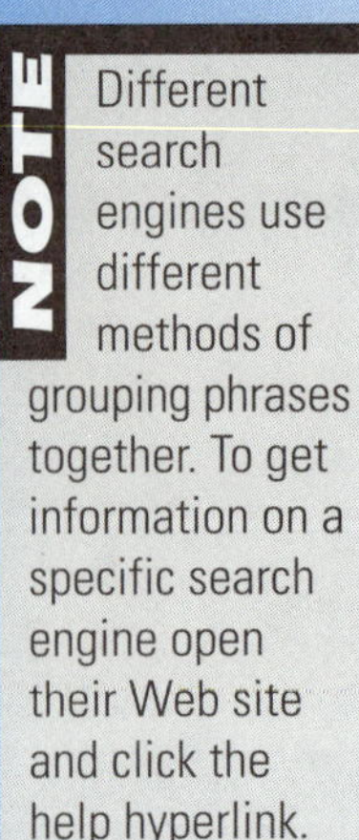

NOTE Different search engines use different methods of grouping phrases together. To get information on a specific search engine open their Web site and click the help hyperlink.

5. Type "**Windows 98**" (include the double quotes) into the search box. The quotes around the phrase tell Infoseek to find all the cases where the word Windows and number 98 appear adjacent to one another. Press **Enter**. The number of results and the list of results appears under the search box.
6. Scroll down and click the hyperlink for the first search result. Internet Explorer displays that site and leaves the search window on the screen.

(continued on next page)

LESSON

52

ACTIVITY

1. Open **Internet Explorer**.
2. Open the **Search Window**.
3. Change the **Search Engine** to **Infoseek**.
4. Search for the phrase "**Computer Education**."
5. Click the first hyperlink.
6. Close the **Search** window.
7. Close **Internet Explorer**.

***Skill Practice** (continued)*

7. Click the **close** button in the search window. The search window closes and the search result fills the screen.
8. Close **Internet Explorer**.

LESSON

53

Favorites on the Internet

In this lesson, you will learn to use Favorites to browse the Web.

►SKILL PRACTICE

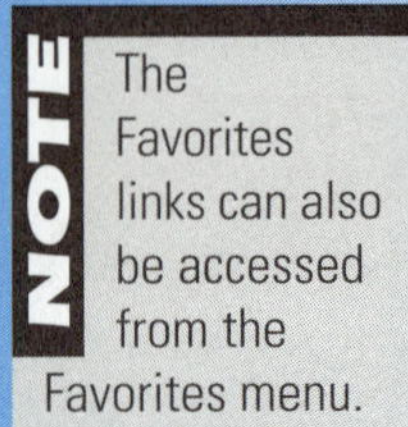

To Open Web Pages in the Favorites Folder

1. Open **Internet Explorer**.
2. Click the **Favorites** button on the toolbar. The Favorites window opens from the left side of Internet Explorer with a list of folders and Web sites.
3. Click the **Links** folder to open it. A list of Web sites appears under the folder, as shown in Figure 5-6.

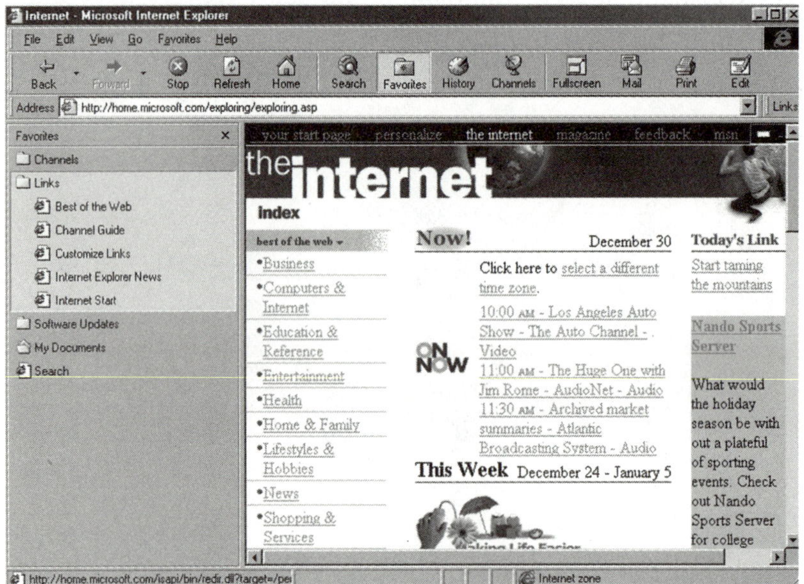

Figure 5-6 The Links folder opens from the Favorites window.

4. Click the link named **Best of the Web**. Internet Explorer now has a page from Microsoft on the screen.
5. Close the **Favorites** window.

To Add More Favorites

6. Type **www.mainfunction.com** in the address bar and press **Enter**. The MainFunction page appears on the screen.
7. Click **Add to Favorites** from the **Favorites** menu. A dialog box appears, as shown in Figure 5-7.

(continued on next page)

LESSON

53

ACTIVITY

1. Open **Internet Explorer**.
2. Use the **Favorites** menu to open MainFunction's home page.
3. Click the link that accesses the current issue of MainFunction.
4. Add this page to your favorite links in the **Links** folder.
5. Save the page as **Current Issue of MainFunction.**
6. Open the Links menu from the **Favorites** menu.
7. Delete the **Current Issue of MainFunction and MainFunction Home Page** links.
8. Close **Internet Explorer**.

Skill Practice *(continued)*

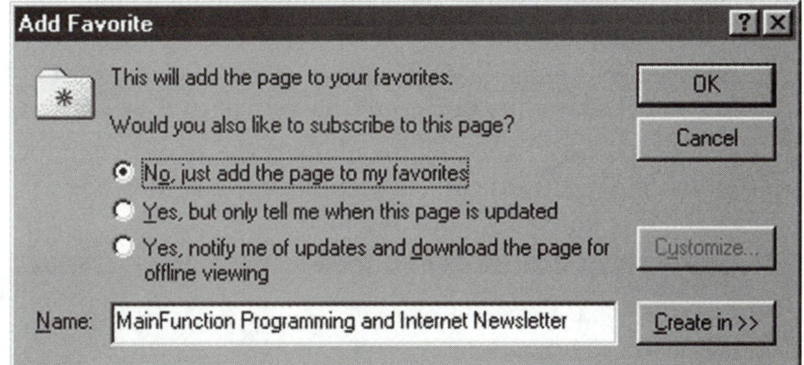

Figure 5-7 Add to Favorites Dialog Box

8. In the **Name** box, type **MainFunction Home Page** if it does not already appear.
9. Click the **Create in** button. A list of the Favorites folders extends from the bottom of the Add to Favorites dialog box.
10. Click the **Links** folder.
11. Click **OK**. The MainFunction home page has been added to the Favorites menu.
12. Close **Internet Explorer**.
13. Click the **Start** button.
14. Open the **Favorites** menu and then the **Links** menu.
15. Click the **MainFunction Home Page** link. The MainFunction home page is now on the screen.

To Delete a Link from the Favorites Folder

16. Open the **Links** menu from the **Favorites** menu.
17. Right click the **MainFunction Home Page** link. A shortcut menu appears.
18. Click **Delete**. The **Confirm File Delete** dialog box appears.
19. Click **No** to keep the link for the next activity.
20. Close **Internet Explorer**.

UNIT 5 LESSON 54

History

In this lesson, you will learn to use the history button to retrace previous sites visited on the Internet.

►SKILL PRACTICE

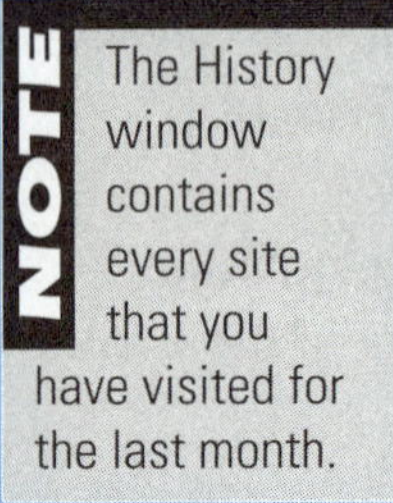

NOTE The History window contains every site that you have visited for the last month.

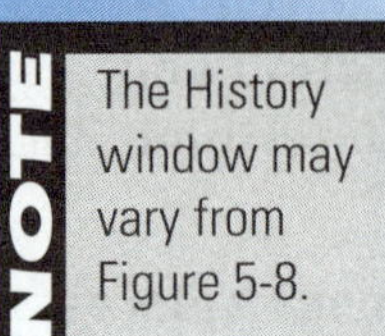

NOTE The History window may vary from Figure 5-8.

1. Open **Internet Explorer**.
2. Type **www.mainfunction.com** into the **Address Bar**. Press **Enter**. The MainFunction home page is open.
3. From the Links menu in the Favorites menu, click the **Best of the Web** link. The Microsoft Best of the Web page is on the screen.
4. Click the **History** button on the toolbar. The History window appears on the left side of Internet Explorer, as shown in Figure 5-8 with Today's links opened.

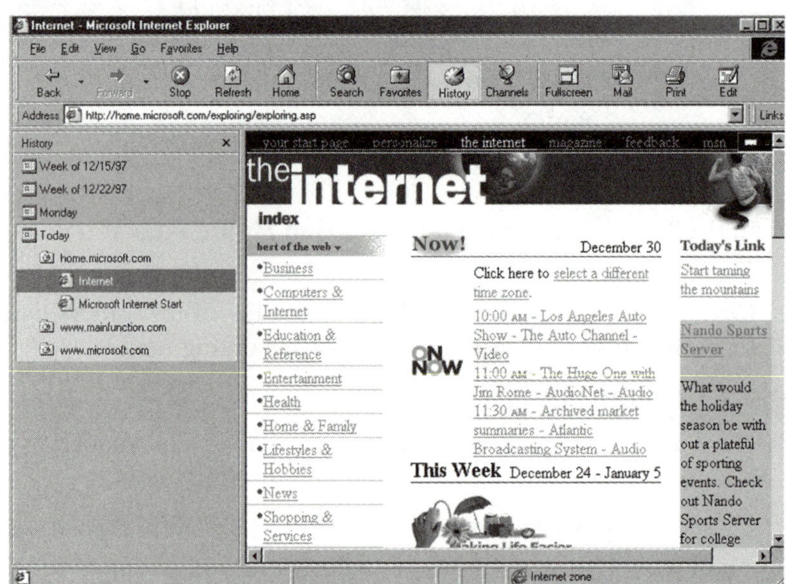

Figure 5-8 The History window

5. Under the topic of **Today**, click on the link back to MainFunction. The **MainFunction** page is back on the screen.

To Delete a History Item

6. Right click on the **Microsoft** link in the **History** window. A shortcut window appears.
7. Choose **Delete** from the menu. The Microsoft link is deleted from the History window.
8. Type **www.microsoft.com** in the address bar and press **Enter**. The Microsoft link returns to the History window.
9. Close **Internet Explorer**.

LESSON

54

ACTIVITY

1. Open **Internet Explorer**.
2. Open the web page at **www.swep.com**.
3. Click the **History** button.
4. Open the **MainFunction** site by clicking it in the **History** window.
5. Open the **Microsoft** web page.
6. Close **Internet Explorer**.

UNIT 5

LESSON 55

Browsing the Internet with My Computer

In this lesson, you will learn how to use My Computer as an Internet browser.

SKILL PRACTICE

To Browse the Internet with My Computer

1. Open **My Computer**.
2. Open the **C:** Drive.
3. Type **www.microsoft.com** into the address bar and press **Enter**. The Microsoft home page appears on the screen.
4. Click the **Maximize** button.
5. Click the **Back** button. Notice that My Computer is displaying the contents of the C drive.
6. Click the **Forward** button. The screen now displays the Microsoft home page.
7. Click the **Back** button again.
8. Close **My Computer**.

LESSON

55

ACTIVITY

1. Open **My Computer**.
2. Insert your work disk and double click on the drive it is in.
3. Open the Microsoft® Windows® 98 Simplified home page at **www.knowlton.net/win98**.
4. Go back and browse your work disk.
5. Close **My Computer**.

UNIT 5

Reinforcement Exercise

1. Start **Internet Explorer**.
2. Open the Microsoft® Windows® 98 Simplified Web page at **www.knowlton.net/win98**.
3. Go to MainFunction's Web page at **www.mainfunction.com**.
4. Type **www.microsoft.com** into the address bar and press **Enter**.
5. Return to the Microsoft® Windows® 98 Simplified Web page.
6. Using the Infoseek search engine, search for education on the Internet.
7. Open one of the search results.
8. Save the page as a favorite.
9. Close **Internet Explorer**.
10. Open the Windows directory with **My Computer**.
11. From the **Favorites** menu, open the link that you made in step 8.
12. Remove the link.
13. Use the **History** button to return to MainFunction's Web site.
14. Save this page to your work disk and print it.
15. Close all open windows

Challenge Exercise

1. Open **Internet Explorer**.
2. Use the search engine of your choice to find two articles relating to your favorite national park.
3. Add a folder to the favorites menu to save the links of both of the Web pages you found.
4. Switch between both Web sites and determine which is your favorite.
5. Print the Web page you have chosen as your favorite.
6. Delete the two links and the folder you added to the Favorites menu.
7. Close **Internet Explorer**.

UNIT 6

LESSON

56

Using Help Topics by Contents

In this lesson, you will learn to look up Windows Help topics by contents.

►SKILL PRACTICE

To Open a Book

1. Click the **Start** button.
2. Choose **Help** from the **Start** menu. Windows Help appears, as shown in Figure 6-1.

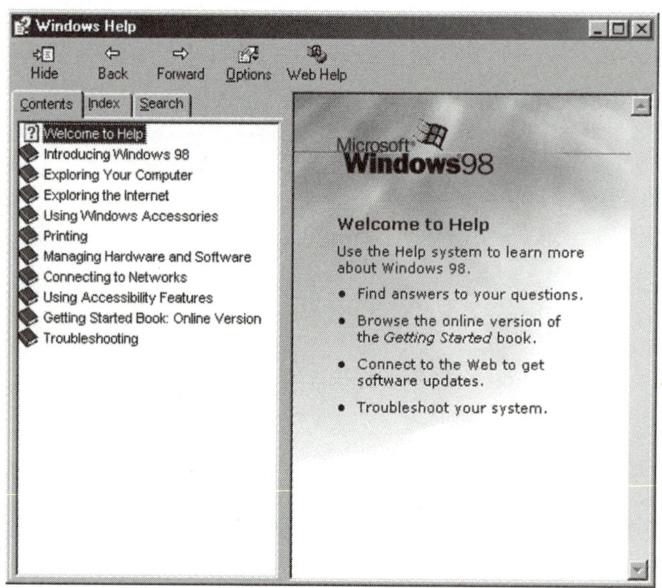

Figure 6-1 The Windows Help Window

NOTE If the books and topics specified here do not appear on your installation, simply make other selections.

3. Click the **Contents** tab of the Help Topics dialog box. The Contents section may already be displayed.
4. Click the **Introducing Windows 98** book. Other books are displayed indented below the Introduction book.
5. Click the **How to Use Help** book. Other books are displayed indented below the How to Use Help book.

NOTE Help topics are grouped into categories called *books*. Books are indicated by a small book icon. Topics are indicated by an icon with a question mark (?) on it.

(continued on next page)

GLOSSARY TERMS

BOOK • a category of Help topics

LESSON 56

ACTIVITY

1. Access the **Windows Help** window.
2. Open the **Printing** book.
3. Open the **Set up a printer** topic. The right side of the screen gives instructions on how to set up a printer.
4. Close the **Windows Help** window.

Skill Practice *(continued)*

To Open a Topic

6. Click the **Find a topic** topic. The right side of the Windows Help displays the information for the selected topic, as shown in Figure 6-2.

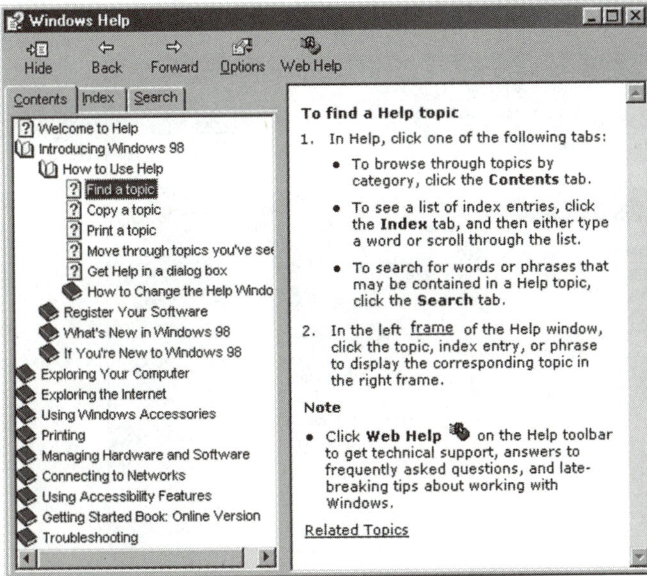

Figure 6-2 Windows Help Window

7. Click the **Copy a topic** subtopic in the How to Use Help book. The right side of the window changes and gives instructions on copying a help topic.
8. Close the **Windows Help** window.

UNIT 6

LESSON 57

Using Help Topics by Index

In this lesson, you will learn to use Windows Help topics by index.

►SKILL PRACTICE

To Access Help Topics by Index

1. Click the **Start** button.
2. Choose **Help** from the **Start** menu. The Windows Help window appears.
3. Click the **Index** tab of the Help dialog box.
4. Key **r**. The index moves to the first entry that begins with r.
5. Key **est** following the r. The index moves to the entry about restarting printing, as shown in Figure 6-3.
6. Click the entry for restarting your computer and click **Display**. A list of several topics appears.
7. Click the **To restart your computer** topic and click **Display** again. The right side of the Help window shows instructions on how to restart your computer.
8. Close the **Windows Help** window.

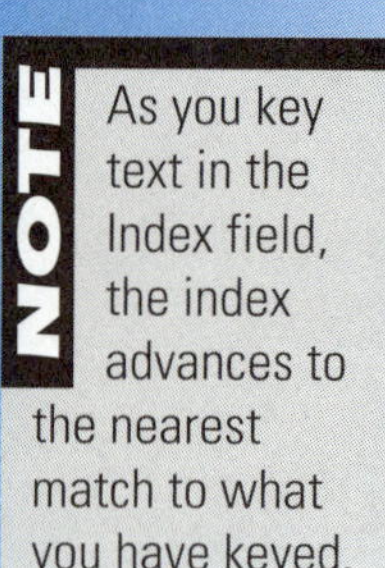

NOTE As you key text in the Index field, the index advances to the nearest match to what you have keyed.

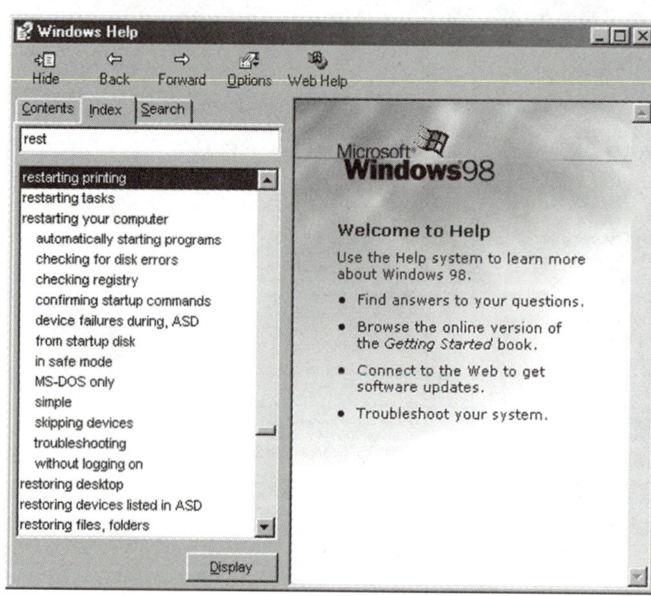

Figure 6-3 Help by Index

LESSON

57

ACTIVITY

1. Access the Help topics index.
2. Search for help on minimizing all open windows. Read the help information.
3. Search for help on using Send To to send a file or folder to a disk. The Windows Help window appears as shown in Figure 6-4.
4. Close the Windows Help window.

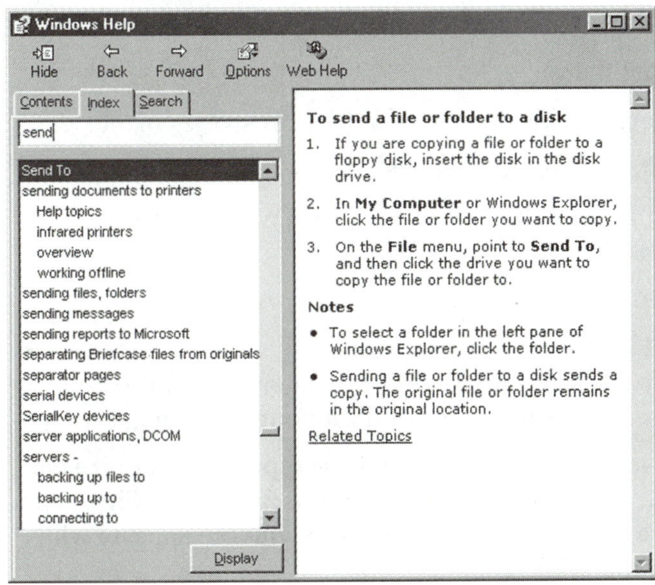

Figure 6-4 Help on using Send To

UNIT 6

LESSON 58

Using Search

In this lesson, you will learn to use Search with Windows Help topics.

SKILL PRACTICE

NOTE The Search feature is case sensitive meaning that keying the text for which you are searching in all caps will prevent the Find feature from finding the topic.

TIP You can also double-click a topic to display it without clicking the Display button.

To Access Help Topics Using Search

1. Click the **Start** button.
2. Open the **Programs** menu and then the Accessories menu.
3. Click **WordPad** in the **Accessories** menu. WordPad starts.
4. Click **Help Topics** in the **Help** menu. The WordPad Help window opens.
5. Click the **Search** tab.
6. Key **font** and click **List Topics**. Topics appear near the bottom of the dialog box. Your screen should appear similar to Figure 6-5. The number of topics found will vary among computers.
7. Click the topic named **To change a font type, style, or size** and click **Display**. If your screen includes more topics than Figure 6-5, you may have to scroll the list. The Help window appears with information on changing fonts.
8. Close the **WordPad Help** window and **WordPad**.

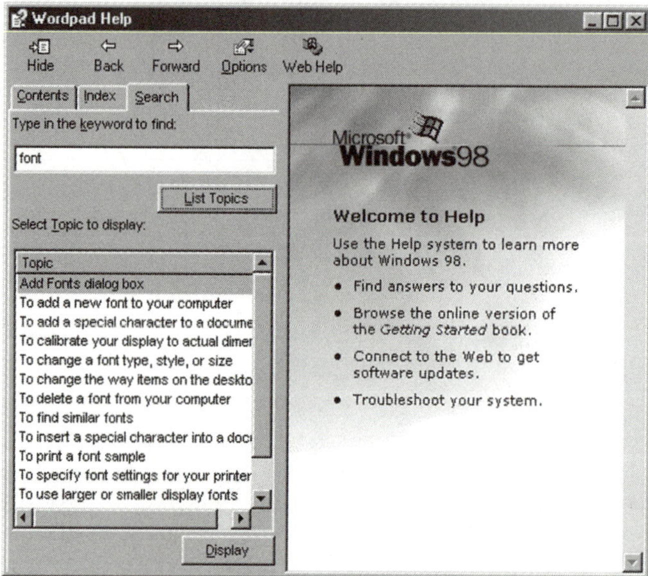

Figure 6-5 Using Find

LESSON

58

ACTIVITY

1. Open **WordPad**.
2. Use Search to find help on the **undo** command.
3. Choose the help topic on undoing the last action.
4. Display the help topic.
5. Close the **WordPad Help** window and **WordPad**.

UNIT 6

LESSON 59

Help Buttons

In this lesson, you will learn what the different help buttons do.

▶SKILL PRACTICE

To Hide the Contents Section of the Help Window

1. Start **Help** from the **Start** menu. The Windows Help window opens.
2. Click **Exploring the Internet** and open the **Explore the Internet** topic. The right side of the Windows Help window will display information on exploring the Internet.
3. Click the **Hide** button on the toolbar. The Contents section of the Windows Help window will close, as shown in Figure 6-6.

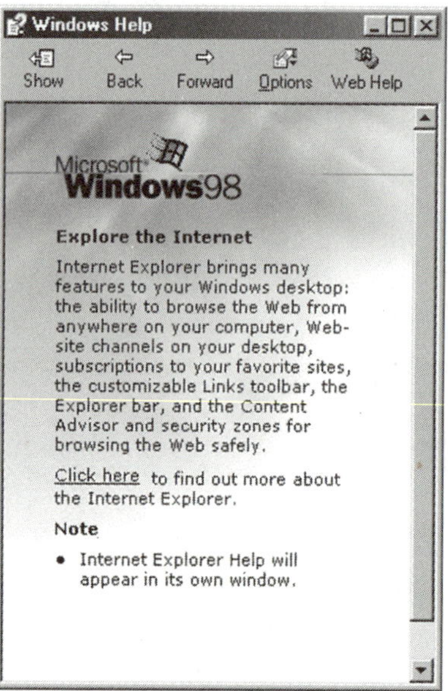

Figure 6-6 The Contents section of the Windows Help window is hidden.

4. Click the **Show** button on the toolbar. The Contents section of the Help window opens.

To View a Previously Opened Help Topic

5. Click the **Exploring Your Computer** book.
6. Click the **Work with Programs** book.
7. Open the **Start a program** topic. The right side of the Windows Help window will explain how to start a program.

(continued on next page)

LESSON

59

▶ACTIVITY

1. Open the **Windows Help** window.
2. Open the **Exploring Your Computer** book.
3. Open the **Keyboard Shortcuts** book.
4. Click the **For Windows** topic.
5. Hide the **Contents** side of the Window.
6. Click the **Back** button. You return to the Windows Help starting screen, as shown in Figure 6-7.
7. Click the **Forward** button.
8. Close the **Windows Help** window.

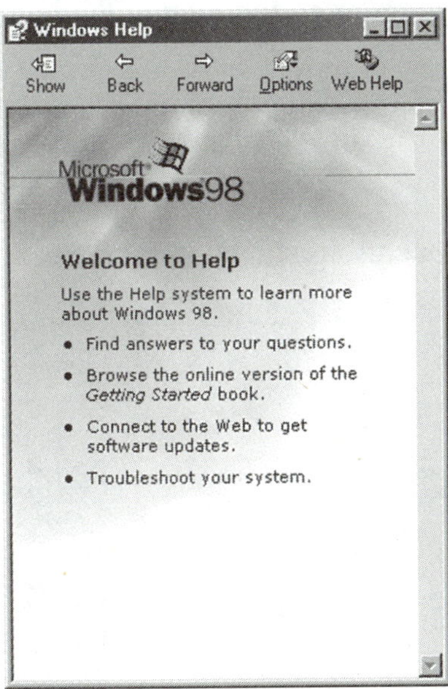

Figure 6-7 The Back button returns you to the previous content.

***Skill Practice** (continued)*

8. Click the **Back** button. The Windows Help window returns to the information about exploring the Internet.
9. Click the **Forward** button. The information on starting a program reappears.
10. Close the **Windows Help** window.

UNIT 6

LESSON 60

Printing Help Topics

In this lesson, you will print help topics.

►SKILL PRACTICE

To Print from the Windows Help Window

1. Choose **Help** from the **Start** menu.
2. Open the **Printing** book.
3. Open the **Set up a printer** topic.
4. Click the **Options** button. A menu appears, as shown in Figure 6-8.

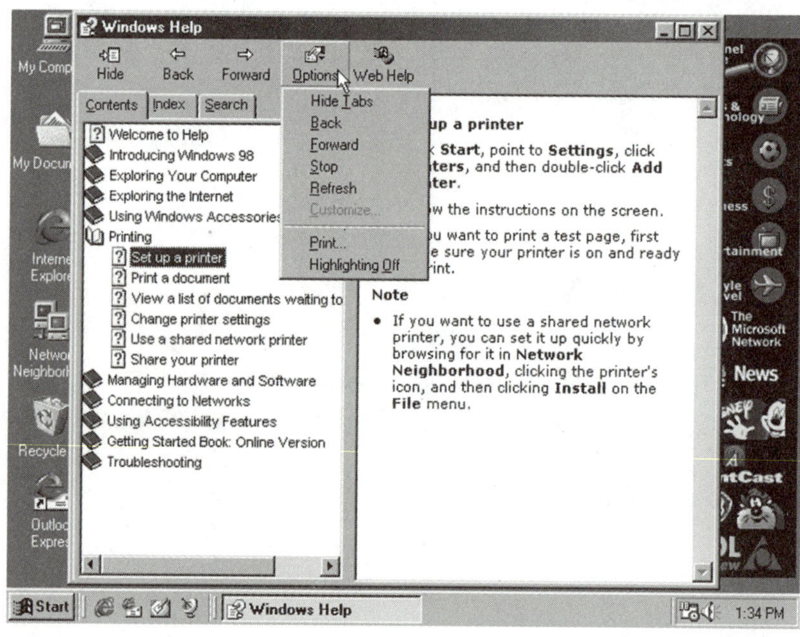

Figure 6-8 The Options Menu

5. Choose **Print** from the **Options** menu. A special Print dialog box appears, as shown in Figure 6-9. These print options allow you to choose how much of the Help information to print.

NOTE Regardless of the size of the Help window, the Help topic prints to the width of your printer.

(continued on next page)

LESSON

60

▶ACTIVITY

1. Use the index to find help on printing Help topics.
2. Print the topic.
3. Close the Windows Help window.

Skill Practice *(continued)*

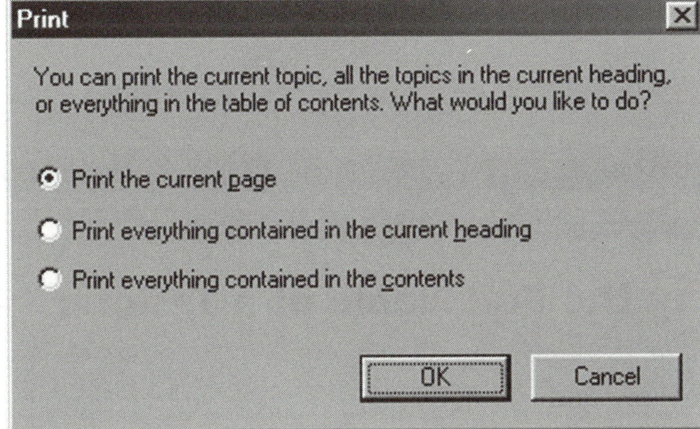

Figure 6-9 Print Options

6. Make sure the **Print the current page** option is selected and click **OK**. The standard Print dialog box appears.
7. Click **OK**. The topic prints.
8. Close the Help window.

UNIT 6

LESSON 61

Help with Button Names

In this lesson, you will learn how to get help identifying toolbar buttons.

►SKILL PRACTICE

To Identify the Name of a Button

1. Start **WordPad**.
2. Position the pointer over the first button on the left end of the toolbar (the New button). After a short pause, the name of the button appears.
3. Position the pointer on some of the other buttons on the toolbar.
4. Position the pointer on the Bold button on the Format bar, as shown in Figure 6-10.

TIP In order for the button name to appear, the pointer must rest on the button for about a second.

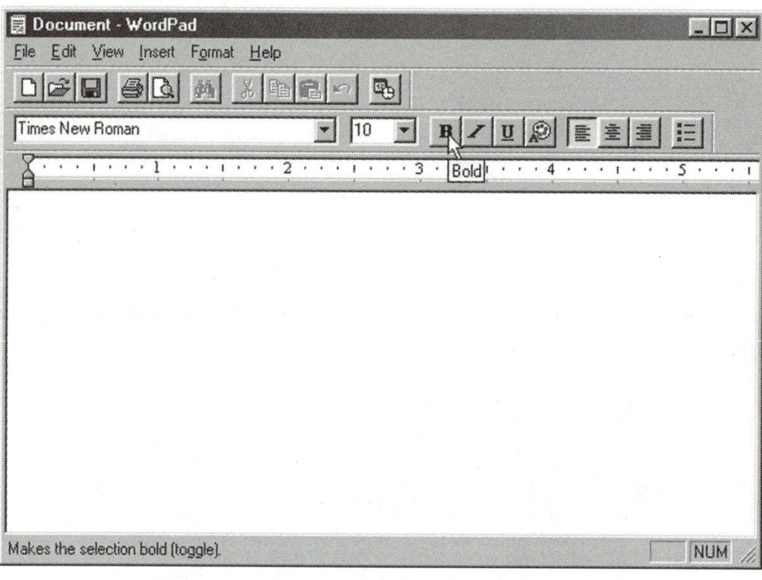

Figure 6-10 Resting the pointer on a button displays the button's name.

To Display the Full Name of a Taskbar Button

5. Minimize **WordPad**.
6. Open the **My Computer** window and the **Recycle Bin** window.
7. Position the pointer on the **WordPad** taskbar button. The full name of the task appears.
8. Exit **WordPad**.
9. Close the **My Computer** the **Recycle Bin** windows.

NOTE Displaying the full name of a taskbar button becomes important when so many windows are open that the taskbar buttons become too small to display the entire name. If the name of a taskbar button is fully displayed on the button, positioning the pointer on the button will have no effect.

LESSON

61

ACTIVITY

1. Start **WordPad**.
2. Rest the pointer on the buttons of the toolbar and Format bar one at a time. Write the name of the button next to its icon.

   ____

   ____

   ____

   ____

   ____

   B ______________________

   ____

   I ______________________

   ____

   U ______________________

3. Exit **WordPad**.

UNIT 6

LESSON

62

Help with Menu Commands

In this lesson, you will learn how to get help identifying menu commands.

►SKILL PRACTICE

Additional information about menu commands is provided in the status bar.

1. Start **WordPad**.
2. Pull down the **Insert** menu.
3. Move the pointer to the **Date and Time** command. A brief description of the command appears in the status bar, as shown in Figure 6-11.

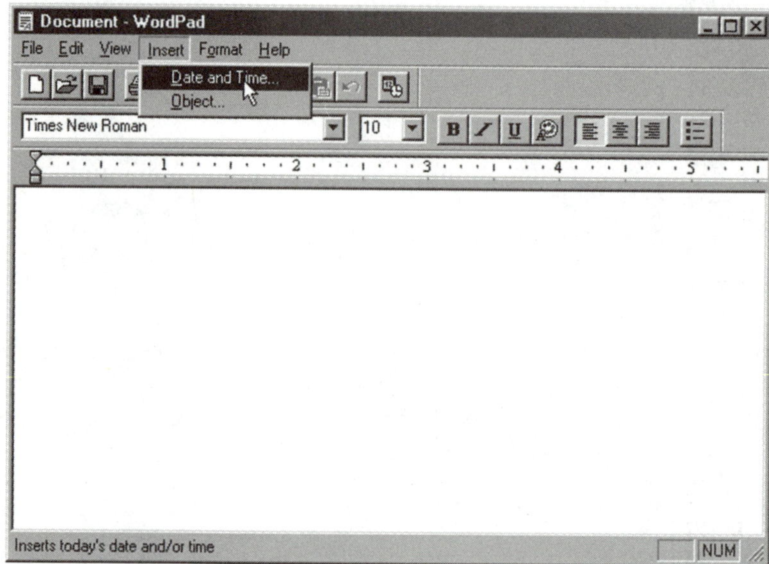

Figure 6-11 The status bar describes commands.

LESSON

62

▶ACTIVITY

1. With WordPad open, pull down the **File** menu.
2. Beside each of the command names, write the descriptive line which appears in the status bar when the pointer rests on the command.

New ______________________________

Open ______________________________

Save ______________________________

Save As ______________________________

Exit ______________________________

3. Exit **WordPad**.

UNIT 6

LESSON 63

Dialog Box Help

In this lesson, you will learn how to get help with dialog box controls.

SKILL PRACTICE

To Get Dialog Box Control Help

1. Start **WordPad**.
2. Choose **Print** from the **File** menu. The Print dialog box appears.
3. Click the **Help** button in the Print dialog box, as shown in Figure 6-12. A question mark (?) is added to the pointer.

Figure 6-12 The Help Button

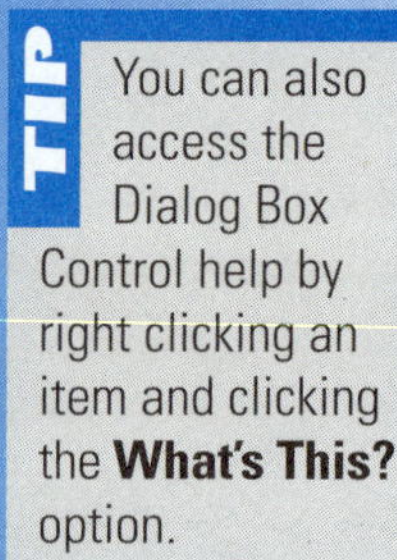

TIP You can also access the Dialog Box Control help by right clicking an item and clicking the **What's This?** option.

4. Click inside the **Number of copies** text box. A brief explanation of the use of the control appears in a pop-up window.
5. Click the pop-up window. The window closes.
6. Click the **Help** button again.
7. Click the **Cancel** button. A description of what the Cancel button does appears in a pop-up window.
8. Click the pop-up window.
9. Click **Cancel** to close the dialog box.

LESSON

63

ACTIVITY

1. Choose **Page Setup** the **File** menu.
2. In the blanks provided below, write the text provided in the Help button pop-up window for that area.
3. Close the **Page Setup** dialog box and exit **WordPad**.

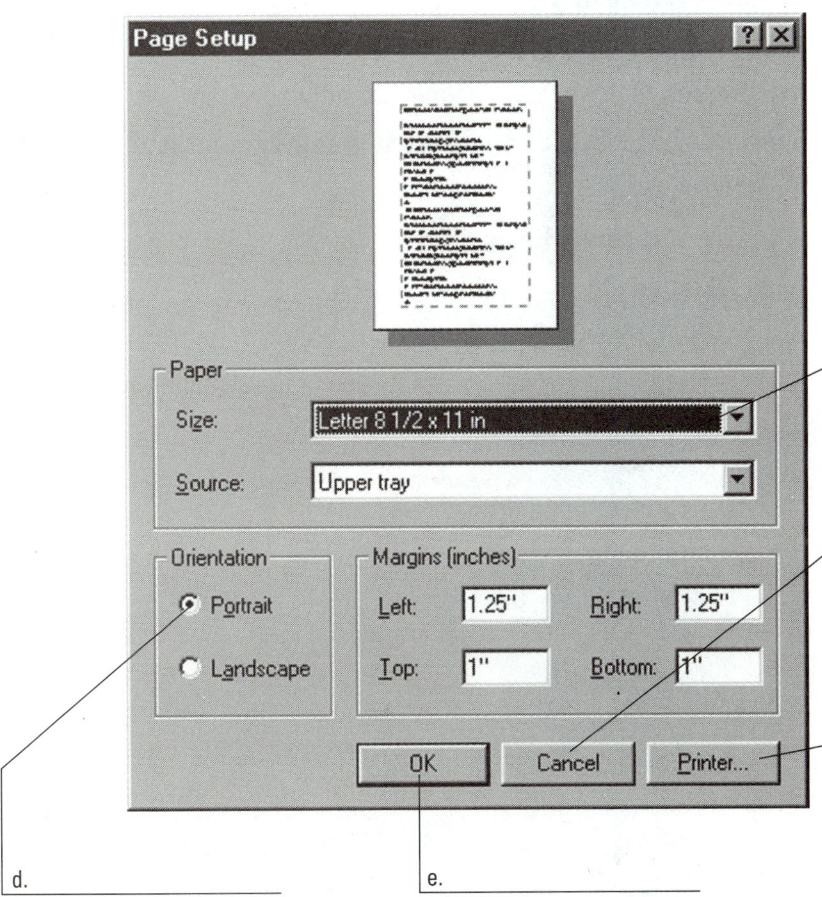

Figure 6-13

Reinforcement Exercise

1. Start **Help** and go to the **Contents** tab.
2. Open the **Introducing Windows 98** book.
3. Open the **How to Use Help** book.
4. Open a topic which interests you and read it.
5. Switch to the **Index** tab and look up **Help**.
6. Read the topic under Help named **To find a Help topic**.
7. Close the **Windows Help** window.
8. Start **Help** again.
9. Use **Search** to locate topics relating to software piracy.
10. Open the topic that begins with **What is software piracy?**
11. Print the topic.
12. Close the **Windows Help** window.
13. Start **Notepad**.
14. Choose **Find** from the **Search** menu.
15. Use the **Help** button to get an explanation of the Direction control.
16. Cancel the dialog box and exit **Notepad**.

Challenge Exercise

1. Open the **My Computer** window and the **Recycle Bin** window.
2. Start **WordPad**, the **Calculator**, and **Notepad**.
3. Start **Help** and use the Index to find and open the topic on the License Agreement.
4. Switch to **WordPad**.
5. Access the **Open** dialog box.
6. Use dialog box help to get an explanation of the File name text box.
7. Open the document called **Letter of Application** from your work disk.
8. Switch to the **Calculator**.
9. Switch back to **WordPad**.
10. Position the pointer over several toolbar buttons to display button names.
11. Position the pointer on each of the taskbar buttons long enough to display the entire button name.
12. Make the Windows Help window active.
13. Click the small button that appears in the Help topic next to **How is computer software protected by law**?
14. Print and read the topic which appears.
15. Close the **Windows Help** window.
16. Exit the programs which are running and close all windows.

UNIT 7

LESSON 64

Deleting a File or Folder

In this lesson, you will learn to delete a file or folder. Deleting moves a file or folder into the Recycle Bin, where it stays until the Recycle Bin is emptied.

SKILL PRACTICE

NOTE When deleting items from a floppy disk, the items are deleted immediately, rather than waiting in the Recycle Bin.

To Delete a File or Folder by Dragging

1. If your work disk is not in the floppy drive, insert it in the drive.
2. Open the work disk window.
3. Arrange the windows to make the Recycle Bin icon on the desktop visible.
4. Drag the folder named **Just for Practice** to the Recycle Bin. A message appears, asking if you are sure you want to remove the folder and all its contents.
5. Click **Yes**. The folder is removed from the floppy disk.

NOTE If a copy of the document named Amy is not in the Reports folder, copy the file from the Letters folder to the Reports folder.

To Delete a File or Folder by Right-Clicking

6. Open the **Reports** folder.
7. Select the document named **Amy**.
8. Right-click the document's icon. A shortcut menu appears.
9. Choose **Delete** from the shortcut menu. You will be prompted to verify your intention to delete.
10. Click **Yes**. The document is deleted.

TIP You can delete more than one file or folder at a time by selecting the items you wish to delete, right-clicking on one of the items, and choosing Delete.

To Delete a File or Folder Using the Delete Key

11. On your work disk, select the document named **Memo** that is outside the More Documents folder.
12. Press the **Delete** key. You are prompted to verify your intention to delete.
13. Click **Yes**. The document is deleted.
14. Close all open windows.

LESSON

64

ACTIVITY

1. Open the work disk window.
2. Open the **My Folder** folder.
3. Delete the folder named **Another Folder** by dragging it to the Recycle Bin.
4. Close the **My Folder** window.
5. Delete the **My Folder** folder using the shortcut menu.
6. Using the Delete key, delete the document named **Summer Convention** from the work disk window (not from the Reports folder).
7. Arrange the remaining icons in the work disk window.
8. Close all open windows.

UNIT 7

LESSON

65

Restoring Deleted Items and Emptying the Recycle Bin

In this lesson, you will learn to open the recycle bin, restore a deleted item, and empty the Recycle Bin.

►SKILL PRACTICE

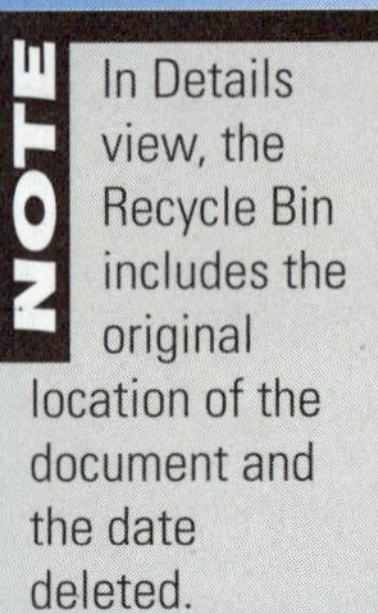

NOTE

In Details view, the Recycle Bin includes the original location of the document and the date deleted.

To Open the Recycle Bin

1. If your work disk is not in the floppy drive, insert it in the drive.
2. Open the work disk window.
3. Copy the document named **Poster** and the document named **The Internet** to the **C:** drive.
4. Open the **C:** drive window.
5. Delete the document named **Poster** and the document named **The Internet** from the **C:** drive.
6. Close all open windows.
7. Double-click the **Recycle Bin** icon on the desktop. The Recycle Bin window appears.
8. If necessary, change the view to Details view.
9. Maximize the **Recycle Bin** window. Your screen should look similar to Figure 7-1.

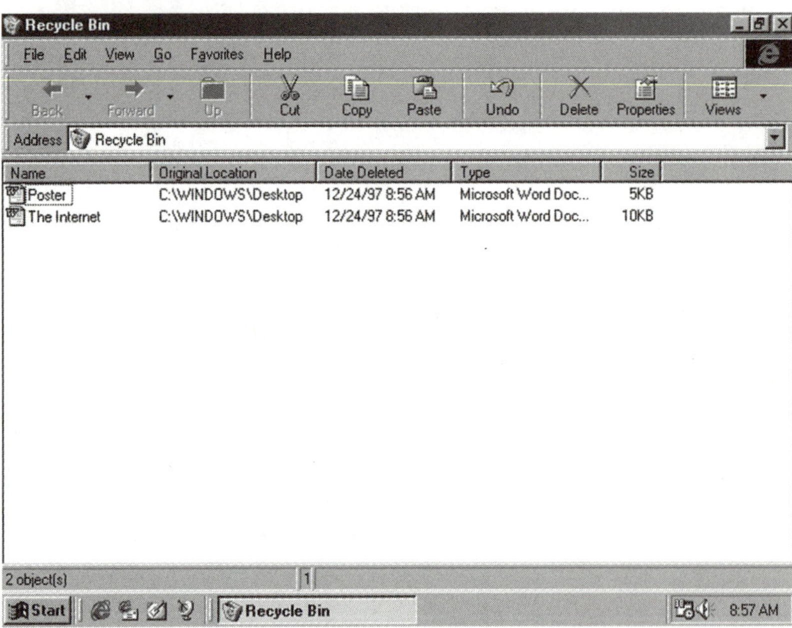

Figure 7-1 The Recycle Bin Window

(continued on next page)

LESSON

65

ACTIVITY

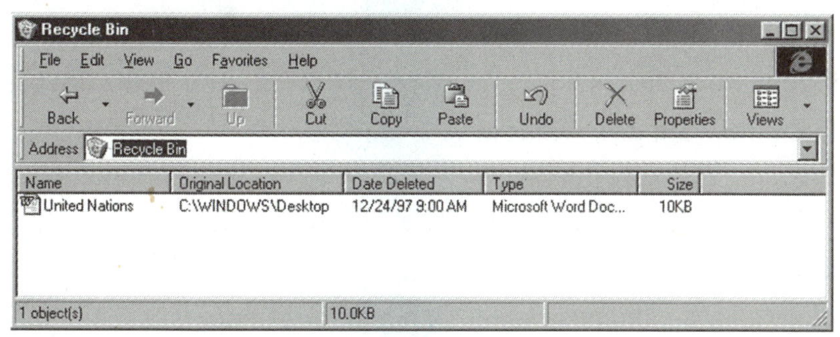

Figure 7-2 Deleted documents appear in the Recycle Bin.

1. Copy the document named **United Nations** from the work disk to the **C:** drive.
2. Drag the **United Nations** document from the **C:** drive to the **Recycle Bin**.
3. Open the **Recycle Bin**. The window should appear similar to Figure 7-2.
4. Restore the document to the **C:** drive.
5. Switch to the **C:** drive window and delete the file using the shortcut menu.
6. Close all open windows.
7. Empty the **Recycle Bin** by right-clicking the Recycle Bin icon and choosing Empty Recycle Bin from the shortcut menu.

Skill Practice (*continued*)

To Restore an Item in the Recycle Bin

10. In the **Recycle Bin** window, select the document named **The Internet**.
11. Choose **Restore** from the **File** menu. The document is returned to the **C:** drive.
12. Open the **C:** drive window and locate the document named **The Internet**.
13. Delete the document again to move it back to the **Recycle Bin**.

To Empty the Recycle Bin

To permanently delete the items in the Recycle Bin, you must empty the Recycle Bin.

14. Make the **Recycle Bin** window active and restore the window.
15. Choose **Empty Recycle Bin** from the **File** menu. A message will appear, asking you to verify your intention to delete the items.
16. Click **Yes**.
17. Close all open windows.

TIP You can empty the Recycle Bin without opening the Recycle Bin window by right-clicking the Recycle Bin icon and choosing Empty Recycle Bin from the shortcut menu that appears.

NOTE Remember, when deleting items from a floppy disk, the items are deleted immediately, rather than waiting in the Recycle Bin.

UNIT 7

LESSON 66

Copying and Saving to the Desktop

In this lesson, you will learn how to copy and save a document to the desktop. It is sometimes useful to have some commonly used documents appear on the desktop for quick access.

SKILL PRACTICE

NOTE When an item is copied to the desktop, it is saved in a folder named Desktop in the Windows folder of the drive from which Windows 98 booted.

NOTE Because the desktop is actually stored on the C: drive, you must hold down the Ctrl key when dragging an item from the C: drive to the desktop to prevent the file from being moved rather than copied. In some cases, however, you may want to move the item rather than copy it.

To Copy a Document to the Desktop

1. If your work disk is not in the floppy drive, insert it in the drive.
2. Open the work disk window.
3. Open the **Reports** folder.
4. Drag the document named **Notes for Fall Convention** to a blank area on the desktop.
5. Close all the windows.
6. Drag the document in line with the other desktop objects.

To Save a Document on the Desktop

7. Start **WordPad**.
8. Key the following sentence into a blank WordPad document.

   `Documents that are used frequently can be saved to the desktop.`

9. Choose **Save As** from the **File** menu. The Save As dialog box appears.
10. Choose **Desktop** from the **Save in** list box, as shown in Figure 7-3.

Figure 7-3 You can save on the desktop from the Save As dialog box.

(continued on next page)

LESSON 66

▶ACTIVITY

1. Copy the **Letters** folder from your work disk to the desktop.
2. Open the **Letters** folder on the desktop.
3. Close all windows.
4. Drag the **Letters** folder and the **Notes for Fall Convention** document to the right edge of the screen, as shown in Figure 7-4.
5. Drag the **Letters** folder to the **Recycle Bin**.
6. Drag the **Notes for Fall Convention** document to the **Recycle Bin** and empty the **Recycle Bin**.
7. Open the document named **Letter of Application** from your work disk.
8. Replace the address at the top of the document with your return address.
9. Use the **Save As** command to save the document on the desktop.
10. Exit **WordPad**.
11. Leave the document on the desktop for use in an upcoming lesson.
12. Close all open windows.

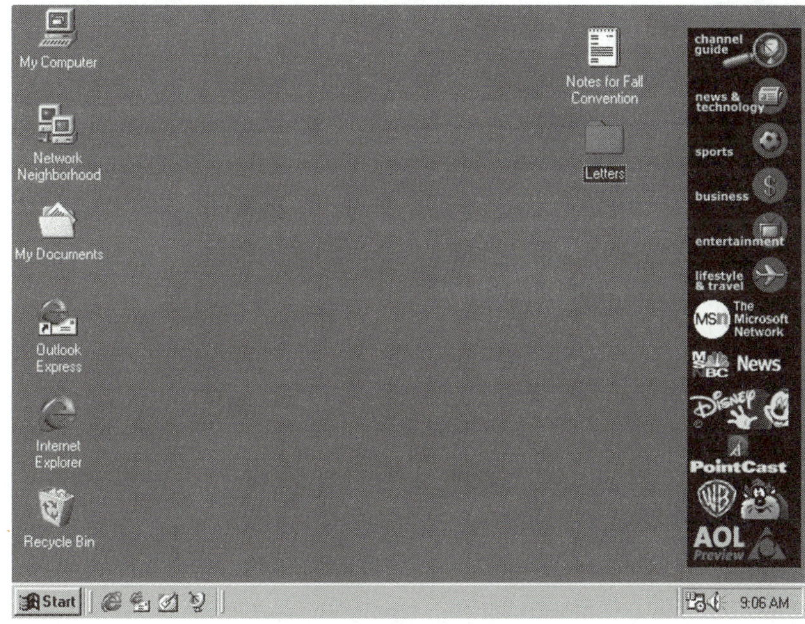

Figure 7-4 Desktop items can be arranged for the most convenience.

Skill Practice (continued)

11. Key **Desktop Document** as the filename.
12. Click **Save**.
13. Exit **WordPad**.
14. Locate the icon of the document you just saved on the desktop.
15. Drag the icon to the **Recycle Bin**.
16. Right-click the **Recycle Bin** icon. A shortcut menu appears.
17. Choose **Empty Recycle Bin** from the shortcut menu. A message appears, asking you to verify your intention to delete.
18. Click **Yes**.

UNIT 7

LESSON

67

The Documents Menu

In this lesson, you will learn how to use the Documents menu. You will also learn how to clear the Documents menu. This is useful when you want to clean up the Documents menu after the documents listed are no longer likely to be opened again.

SKILL PRACTICE

To Use the Documents Menu

1. Click the **Start** button. The Start menu appears.
2. Choose **Documents.** The Documents menu appears, showing as many as fifteen of the most recently opened documents.
3. Click outside the menu to close it without choosing a document.
4. If your work disk is not in the floppy drive, insert it in the drive.
5. Open the work disk window.
6. Double-click the document icon named **Printing from an Icon**. The document loads into the Notepad.
7. Exit **Notepad**.
8. Click the **Start** button and display the **Documents** menu. Notice that the **Printing from an Icon** document is listed.
9. Choose **Printing from an Icon**. The document loads into the Notepad.
10. Exit **Notepad**.

TIP: Use the Documents Menu to quickly access documents you have recently used.

To Clear the Documents Menu

11. Open the **Start** menu and access the **Documents** menu. Notice that documents are listed.
12. Click outside the menu to close it.
13. Right-click a blank area on the taskbar. A shortcut menu appears.
14. Choose **Properties** from the shortcut menu. The Taskbar Properties dialog box appears.
15. Click the **Start Menu Programs** tab, as shown in Figure 7-5.

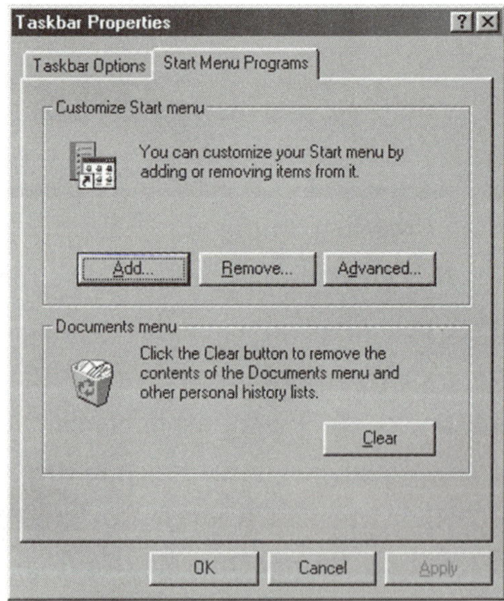

Figure 7-5 Taskbar Properties Dialog Box

LESSON

67

▶ACTIVITY

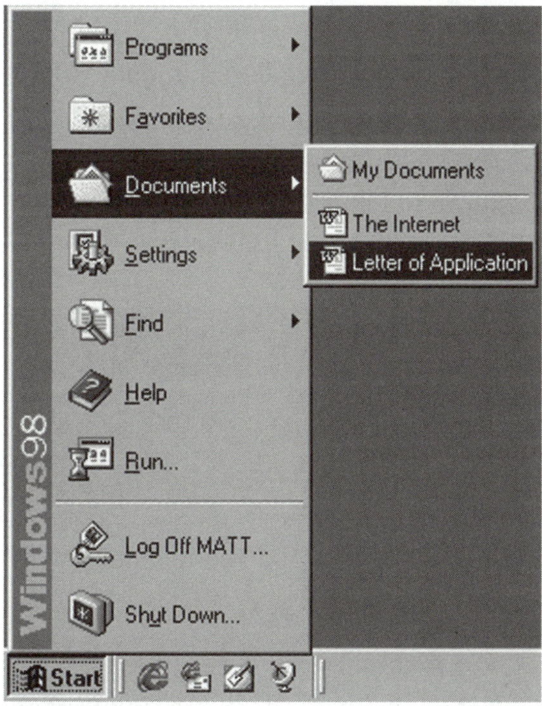

Figure 7-6 The Documents Menu

1. Double-click the document named **Poster** on your work disk. The document loads in WordPad.
2. Open the document named **Opening Documents** from your work disk.
3. Exit **WordPad**.
4. Use the **Documents** menu to open the document named **Poster**.
5. Exit **WordPad**.
6. Close all open windows.
7. Double-click the document on the desktop named **Letter of Application**. WordPad starts and loads the document. Note: If the document does not appear on the desktop, open it from your work disk.
8. Choose **Open** from the **File** menu. The Open dialog box appears.
9. Open the document named **The Internet** from your work disk.
10. Exit **WordPad**.
11. Open the **Start** menu and access the **Documents** menu. The documents you just opened appear in the Documents menu, as shown in Figure 7-6.
12. Close the menu without choosing a document.
13. Close all open windows.

***Skill Practice** (continued)*

16. Click the **Clear** button.
17. Click **OK**.
18. Open the **Start** menu and access the **Documents** menu. The Documents menu is empty.
19. Click outside the menu to close it.

UNIT 7

LESSON
68

Arranging the Desktop

In this lesson, you will learn how to arrange the desktop.

SKILL PRACTICE

To Arrange Items on the Desktop

1. If your work disk is not in the floppy drive, insert it in the drive.
2. Copy the **Letters** folder from your work disk to the desktop.
3. Drag some or all of the objects on the desktop to appear across the top of the screen, as shown in Figure 7-7. The objects on your screen may vary from the ones in the figure. Do not attempt to align the icons perfectly.

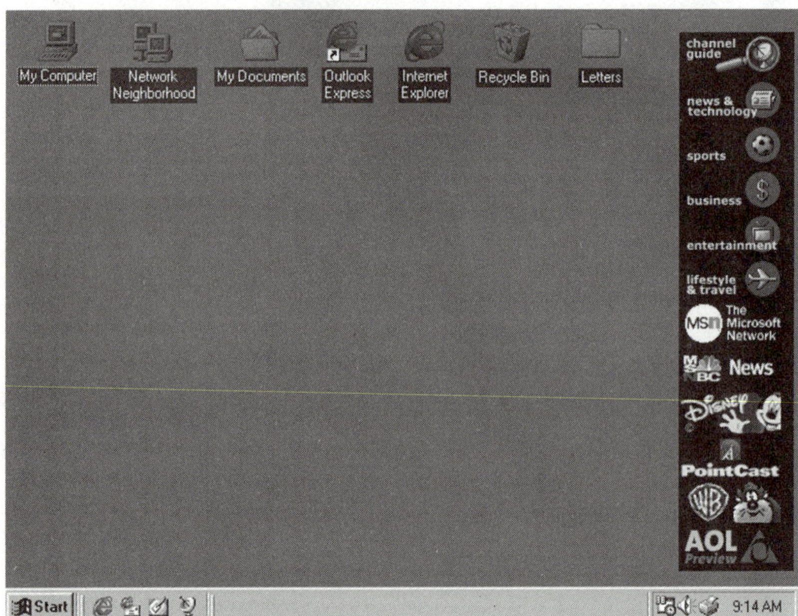

Figure 7-7 Items on the desktop can be moved to any location on the screen.

4. Right-click in a blank area of the desktop. A shortcut menu appears.
5. Choose **Line Up Icons** from the shortcut menu. The objects align.
6. Right-click in a blank area of the desktop. The shortcut menu appears again.
7. Choose **Arrange Icons** and choose **by Name** from the submenu. The objects return to the left edge of the screen.

(continued on next page)

LESSON

68

ACTIVITY

1. Arrange some or all of the items on the desktop in a circle, as shown in Figure 7-8.
2. Right-click a blank area of the desktop. A shortcut menu appears.
3. Choose **Line up Icons** from the shortcut menu. The items align into a rectangular shape.
4. Right-click a blank area of the desktop. A shortcut menu appears.
5. Choose to arrange icons by name. The items return to the left edge of the screen.

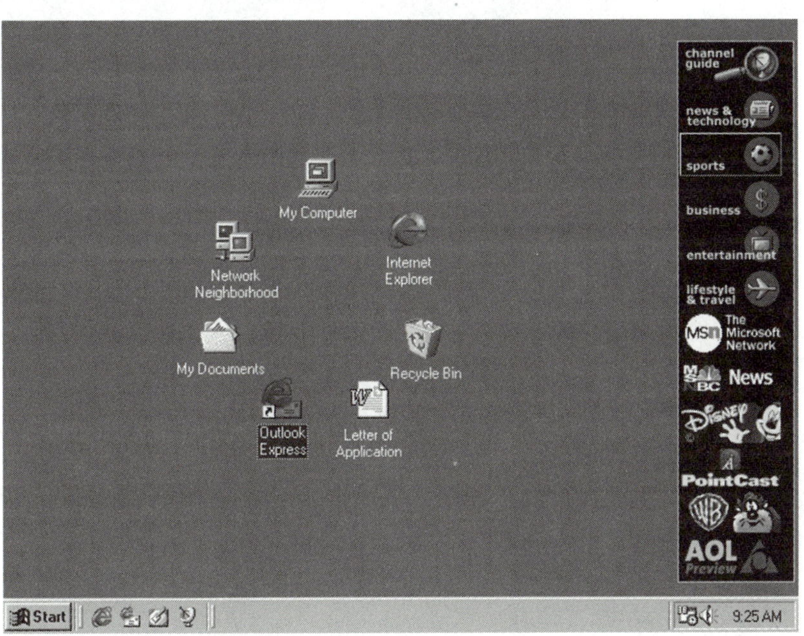

Figure 7-8 A Creative Way to Arrange Desktop Items

Skill Practice (continued)

To Auto Arrange Items

The Auto Arrange feature arranges desktop items each time an object is moved, deleted, or added.

8. Right-click the desktop to access the shortcut menu.
9. Choose **Arrange Icons** and choose **Auto Arrange** from the submenu.
10. Drag the **Letters** folder to the center of the screen. As soon as you release the mouse button, the Letters folder is moved back into alignment.
11. Copy the document named **United Nations** from your work disk to the desktop. The icon is automatically aligned. (You may need to move some windows to see this.)
12. Drag the **Letters** folder and the **United Nations** document to the **Recycle Bin**.
13. Empty the **Recycle Bin**.
14. Right-click the desktop to access the shortcut menu.
15. Choose **Arrange Icons** and choose **Auto Arrange** to deselect the feature.
16. Close any windows that may be opened.

UNIT 7

LESSON 69

Creating a Shortcut

In this lesson, you will learn how to create an icon that provides a shortcut to another object. Shortcuts allow you to quickly open documents and programs that you use regularly.

SKILL PRACTICE

TIP Shortcuts can be placed in any folder. They are most useful, however, on the desktop or in the Start menu.

NOTE A shortcut is not a copy of the original file or folder. Whether a file is opened from the original icon or the shortcut icon, the same file on the disk is accessed.

NOTE Shortcuts do not have to be named using the word *shortcut*. To make shortcuts easy to identify, an arrow in a small box is added to the icon.

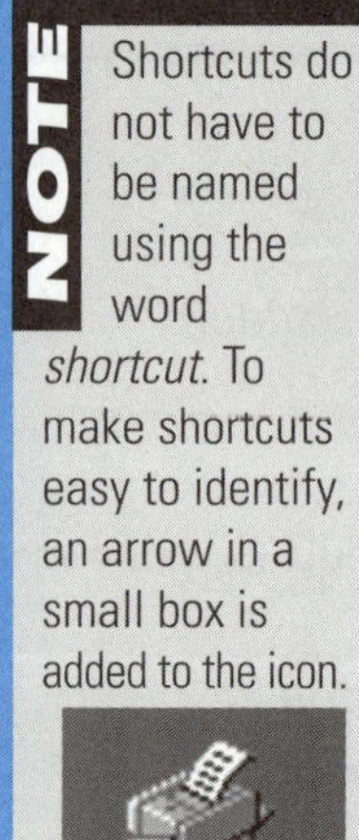

To Create a Shortcut

1. Open the **My Computer** window.
2. Open the **C:** drive and then the **Windows** folder.
3. Select the file named **Calc** (the Calculator accessory).
4. Choose **Create Shortcut** from the **File** menu.

   Or

   Right-click the **Calc** icon and choose **Create Shortcut** from the shortcut menu.

   A file named Shortcut to Calc appears in the Windows folder.
5. Move the **Shortcut to Calc** file to the desktop.
6. Change the name of the shortcut to **Calculator**. (You may need to close or minimize open windows to see the shortcut on the desktop.)
7. Close all open windows.
8. Double-click the **Calculator** shortcut. The Calculator accessory loads.
9. Close the **Calculator**.
10. Arrange the items on the desktop by name.

LESSON

69

ACTIVITY

1. Open the **My Computer** window.
2. Right-click the icon that represents the floppy disk drive that contains your work disk. A shortcut menu appears.
3. Choose **Create Shortcut** from the shortcut menu. A message appears saying that Windows cannot create a shortcut in the My Computer window. The message asks if you want the shortcut created on the desktop.
4. Click **Yes**.
5. Close the **My Computer** window.
6. Double-click the shortcut for your floppy drive. The contents of the work disk appear.
7. Close the work disk window.

UNIT 7

LESSON

70

Creating a Printer Shortcut

In this lesson, you will learn to create a shortcut to your computer's printer. Dragging a document to a printer shortcut will cause the document to print to that printer.

SKILL PRACTICE

To Create a Printer Shortcut

1. Open the **My Computer** window.
2. Open the **Printers** folder. The printer to which your computer prints has an icon in the Printers folder. You may have more than one printer icon in the Printers folder.
3. Right-click the icon that represents your printer. If you have more that one printer available to you, right-click the one you print to most often. A shortcut menu appears.
4. Choose **Create Shortcut** from the shortcut menu. Because a printer shortcut cannot appear in the Printers folder, you are asked if you would like to create the shortcut on the desktop.
5. Click **Yes**. The printer shortcut is created on the desktop.
6. Close the **Printers** folder and the **My Computer** window.

To Use the Printer Shortcut to Print a Document

7. If your work disk is not in the floppy drive, insert it in the drive.
8. Open the work disk window using the shortcut on the desktop.
9. Open the **More Documents** folder on the work disk.
10. Drag the document named **Fax Numbers** to the printer shortcut on the desktop. The document prints.
11. Close all open windows.

NOTE The process of dragging an item from one location to another to perform an operation is called *drag and drop.*

GLOSSARY TERMS

DRAG AND DROP • dragging an item from one location to another to perform an operation

LESSON 70

ACTIVITY

Figure 7-9 Printer Shortcut

1. Drag the existing printer shortcut to the **Recycle Bin**.
2. Empty the **Recycle Bin**.
3. Create a new shortcut to your printer and place it on the desktop.
4. Change the name of the printer shortcut to **My Printer** (see Figure 7-9).
5. Drag the document named **Letter of Application** from the desktop to the **My Printer** shortcut. The document prints.

UNIT 7

LESSON 71

Shortcut Properties

In this lesson, you will learn how to view the properties of a shortcut. A shortcut's properties provide information about the file or folder to which the shortcut points.

SKILL PRACTICE

To View the Properties of a Shortcut

1. Right-click the **Calculator** shortcut on the desktop. A shortcut menu appears.
2. Choose **Properties** from the shortcut menu. The Calculator Properties dialog box appears, as shown in Figure 7-10.

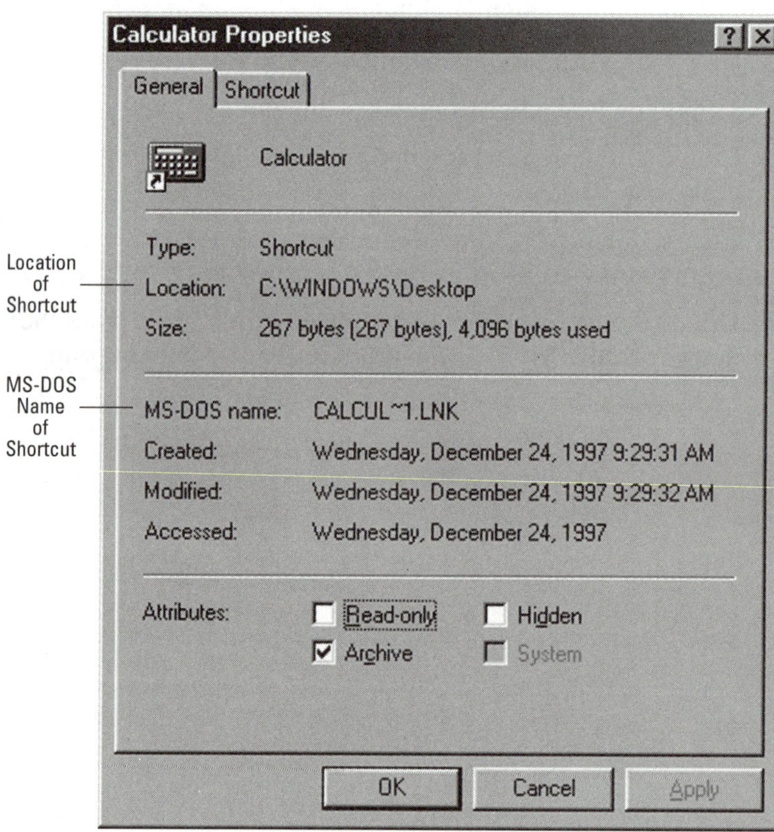

Figure 7-10 General Properties of the Calculator Shortcut

3. Click the **Shortcut** tab in the dialog box if it is not already selected. The Shortcut section of the dialog box appears, as shown in Figure 7-11.

(continued on next page)

LESSON 71

ACTIVITY

1. View the properties of the shortcut to your floppy disk drive.
2. View the properties of the shortcut to your printer. The dialog box should appear similar to Figure 7-12.
3. Close the dialog box.

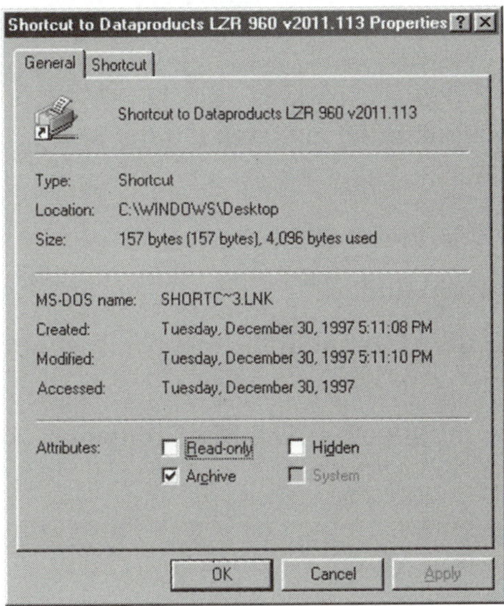

Figure 7-12 Printer Shortcut Properties

Skill Practice (continued)

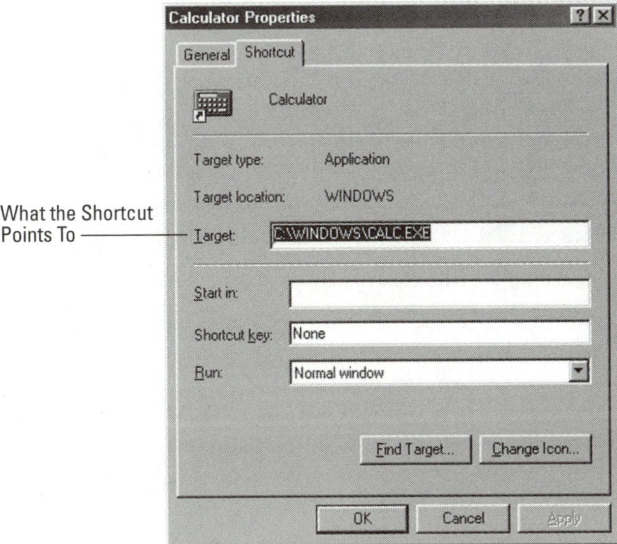

Figure 7-11 Shortcut Properties of the Calculator Shortcut

4. Click **Cancel**.

UNIT 7

LESSON

72

Closing a Minimized Program or Window

In this lesson, you will learn how to close a minimized program or window.

SKILL PRACTICE

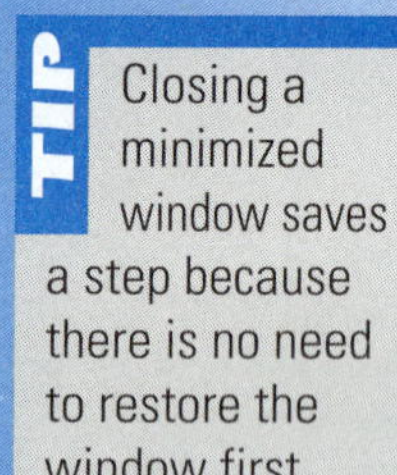

TIP Closing a minimized window saves a step because there is no need to restore the window first.

To Close a Minimized Program or Window

1. Start **WordPad**.
2. Key your name in the document that appears. Do not save.
3. Minimize **WordPad**.
4. Open the **My Computer** window.
5. Minimize the **My Computer** window.
6. Right-click the **My Computer** button on the taskbar. A shortcut menu appears.
7. Choose **Close** from the shortcut menu. The My Computer window closes.
8. Right-click the **WordPad** button on the taskbar. A shortcut menu appears.
9. Choose **Close** from the shortcut menu. You are given an opportunity to save before closing, as shown in Figure 7-13.
10. Click **No**. WordPad exits.

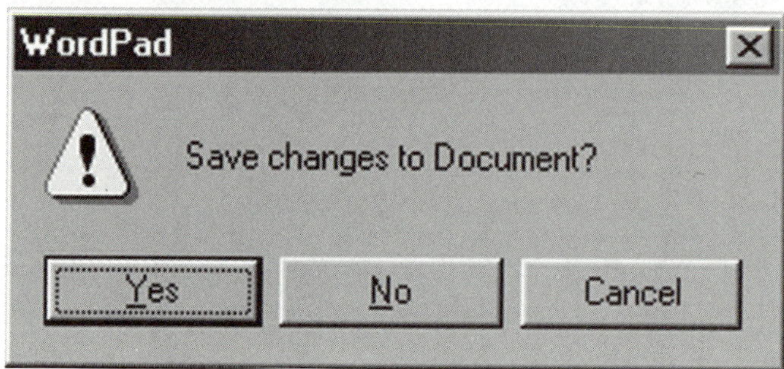

Figure 7-13 Closing a program with unsaved changes generates a message.

LESSON

72

ACTIVITY

1. Start the **Calculator** from the desktop shortcut.
2. Minimize the **Calculator**.
3. Close the **Calculator** from the taskbar.

UNIT 7

LESSON

73

Positioning the Taskbar

In this lesson, you will learn how to customize the taskbar.

SKILL PRACTICE

TIP Most of the time, you will find that the taskbar does not need to be larger than the default size. When working with many windows, however, you may wish to enlarge it.

To Move the Taskbar

Move the taskbar to another edge of the screen by dragging it.

1. Position the mouse pointer over a blank area of the taskbar.
2. Drag the **taskbar** to the left edge of the screen. The taskbar attaches to the left edge of the screen with the Start button on top.
3. Drag the **taskbar** to the top of the screen.
4. Drag the **taskbar** to the right edge of the screen.
5. Drag the **taskbar** to its original position at the bottom of the screen.

To Resize the Taskbar

Resize the taskbar by dragging its top edge (innermost edge when moved from bottom of screen).

6. Position the mouse pointer on the top edge of the **taskbar**. The pointer changes to a double-headed arrow.
7. Drag the top border of the **taskbar** up about $\frac{1}{2}$ inch. Release the mouse button.

To Manually Hide the Taskbar

8. Drag the top border of the **taskbar** to the bottom of the screen and release the mouse button. The taskbar cannot be seen, except for a thin line at the bottom of the screen.
9. Position the pointer on the line at the bottom of the screen and drag the **taskbar** back to its default size.

(continued on next page)

LESSON
73

1. Move the **taskbar** to the right edge of the screen.
2. Select the **My Computer** icon.
3. Move the pointer back to the right edge to make the taskbar appear.
4. Right-click a blank area of the taskbar and choose **Properties** from the shortcut menu.
5. Turn off the **Auto hide** option.
6. Click **OK**.
7. Move the **taskbar** back to the bottom of the screen.
8. Enlarge the **taskbar** to the largest allowable size.
9. Drag the edge of the **taskbar** to the bottom of the screen to hide it.
10. Return the **taskbar** to its default size.

Skill Practice (*continued*)

To Automatically Hide the Taskbar

10. Right-click a blank area of the **taskbar**. A shortcut menu appears.
11. Choose **Properties** from the shortcut menu. The Taskbar Properties dialog box appears, as shown in Figure 7-14.

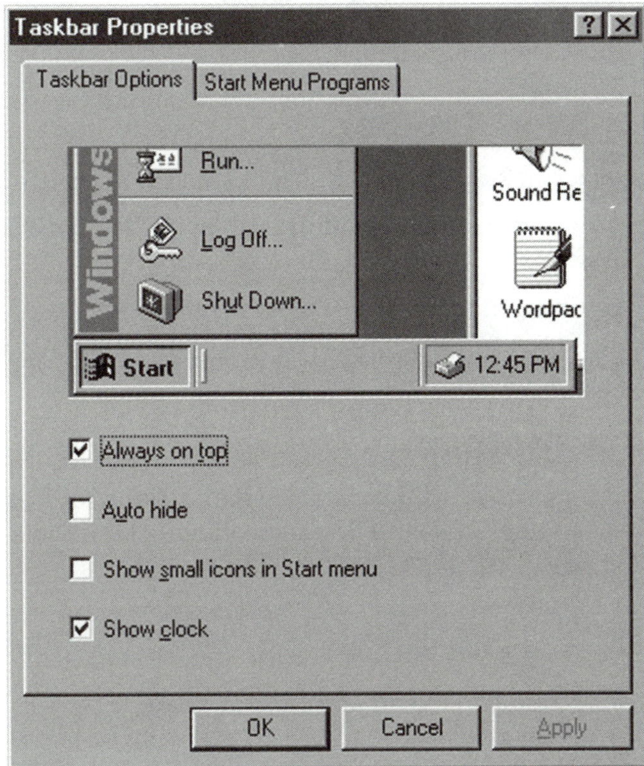

Figure 7-14 Taskbar Properties Dialog Box

12. Turn on the **Auto hide** option and click **OK**. The taskbar is hidden.
13. Move the mouse pointer to the bottom of the screen. The taskbar automatically appears.
14. Move the mouse pointer up (away from the taskbar). The taskbar is again hidden.

NOTE Other taskbar properties include an option to remove the clock from the taskbar and an option to allow windows to overlap the taskbar.

UNIT 7

LESSON 74

Adding Toolbars to the Taskbar

In this lesson, you will learn how to add different toolbars to the taskbar.

SKILL PRACTICE

To Add a Toolbar to the Taskbar

1. Right click on a blank area of the taskbar. A shortcut menu appears.
2. Choose **Desktop** from the **Toolbars** submenu. The Desktop toolbar appears to the right of the other toolbars.
3. Enlarge the taskbar about $\frac{1}{2}$ inch. The Desktop toolbar moves below the other toolbars as shown in Figure 7-15.

Figure 7-15 Desktop Toolbar on the Taskbar

TIP You can also drag a folder from the desktop to the taskbar to add a new toolbar.

NOTE If a toolbar has more icons than what will fit on the screen, arrows appear which allow you to scroll through the selections.

To Make a New Toolbar

4. Right click on a blank area of the taskbar. A shortcut menu appears.
5. Select **New Toolbar** from the **Toolbars** submenu. The New Toolbar Dialog box will appear.
6. Click the **My Computer** icon from the scrolling list.
7. Click **OK**. The My Computer toolbar now appears on the bottom row of the taskbar.

To Resize a Toolbar

8. Position your mouse on the line between the Desktop toolbar and the My Computer toolbar. The cursor should change to a double-sided arrow, similar to Figure 7-16.

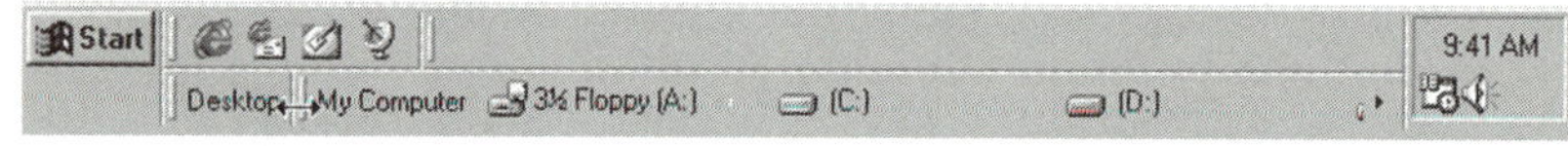

Figure 7-16 A double-sided arrow appears when resizing a toolbar.

TIP To remove the descriptions of the icons on the toolbars, right click the name of the toolbar and remove the check mark from the Show Text option.

9. Click and drag the line to the center the taskbar.

(continued on next page)

LESSON

74

ACTIVITY

1. Add the **Desktop** toolbar to the taskbar.
2. Make the **My Documents** folder a new toolbar and add it to the taskbar.
3. Click the **My Computer** button on the Desktop toolbar.
4. Resize the toolbars and the taskbar.
5. Remove the **Desktop** and **My Documents** toolbars from the taskbar.
6. Close **My Computer**.

Skill Practice *(continued)*

To Remove a Toolbar

10. Right click on a blank area of the taskbar.
11. Open the **Toolbars** menu.
12. Remove the check mark from the **My Computer** toolbar. The My Computer toolbar is removed from the taskbar.
13. Access the Toolbars menu again and remove the check mark from the Desktop toolbar. The Desktop toolbar is removed from the taskbar.

UNIT 7

LESSON

75

Address Toolbar

In this lesson, you will learn how to use the Address toolbar on the taskbar.

SKILL PRACTICE

To Browse with the Address Toolbar

1. Right click a blank area of the taskbar. A shortcut menu appears.
2. From the **Toolbars** submenu select **Address**. The Address toolbar appears on the screen.
3. Enlarge the taskbar so the Address toolbar appears on the bottom of the taskbar, as shown in Figure 7-17.

Figure 7-17 The Address toolbar appears on the bottom of the Taskbar.

4. Highlight the contents in the Address toolbar.
5. Type **www.mainfunction.com** in the Address toolbar and press **Enter**. Internet Explorer opens and the MainFunction Web page appears on the screen.
6. Type **www.knowlton.net/win98** in the Address toolbar and press **Enter**.
7. Click the arrow on the right side of the Address toolbar. A list of the most recent addresses appears.
8. Click the link to MainFunction. The home page for MainFunction reappears on the screen.
9. Type **c:\windows** in the Address toolbar and press **Enter**. The Windows folder appears on the screen.
10. Close all open windows.

LESSON

75

ACTIVITY

1. View the contents on the c: drive using the Address toolbar.
2. Open Microsoft's Web page at **www.microsoft.com**.
3. Browse the contents of **c:\windows**.
4. Open the link to MainFunction at **www.mainfunction.com**.
5. Close **Internet Explorer**.
6. Remove the Address toolbar from the taskbar.

UNIT 7

LESSON

76

Active Desktop

In this lesson, you will learn how to use the active desktop feature.

►SKILL PRACTICE

To Start an Active Desktop Item

1. Open the **Settings** menu from the **Start** menu.
2. Open the **Control Panel**.
3. Double click the **Display** icon.
4. Click the **Web** tab. The Web Display Properties window appears, as in Figure 7-18.

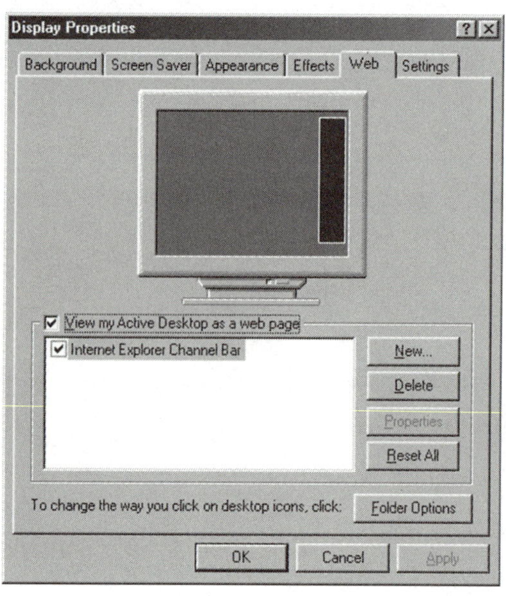

Figure 7-18 The Web Display Properties window shows the different Active Desktop items.

NOTE The number of selections in the Items of the Active Desktop window will vary.

5. Make sure the **View my Active Desktop as a web page** option is checked.
6. Check the **Internet Explorer Channel Bar** option. A rectangular box will appear in the picture of the monitor above the selection window showing where the Internet Explorer Channel Bar will appear on the desktop.
7. Click **OK**. The Internet Explorer Channel Bar appears on your desktop. You may have to move a window to see the Channel Bar.

(continued on next page)

LESSON

76

ACTIVITY

1. Add the **Internet Explorer Channel Bar** to the Desktop.
2. Click one of the **Internet Explorer Channel Bar** buttons.
3. Browse the page and then close **Internet Explorer**.
4. Resize the **Internet Explorer Channel Bar** to form a square.
5. Move the **Internet Explorer Channel Bar** to the bottom right corner of the screen.
6. Remove the **Internet Explorer Channel Bar** from the Desktop.

Skill Practice *(continued)*

8. Click on one of the buttons. Internet Explorer opens and displays the Web page of the button that was clicked.
9. Close **Internet Explorer**.

To Move an Active Desktop Item on the Desktop

10. Move the mouse to the top of the **Internet Explorer Channel Bar** and a title bar appears.
11. Click and drag the title bar to the center of the screen. The Internet Explorer Channel Bar is repositioned.

To Resize an Active Desktop Item

12. Position the mouse on the bottom left corner of the Internet Explorer Channel Bar.
13. Click and drag the corner of the Internet Explorer Channel Bar to widen the box to accommodate two columns.

To Remove an Active Desktop Item from the Desktop

14. Right click on the **Desktop**. A shortcut menu appears.
15. Choose **Customize my Desktop** from the **Active Desktop** submenu.
16. Click the **Web** tab. Notice how the picture of the monitor reflects the changes made to the Internet Explorer Channel Bar.
17. Remove the checkmark from the **Internet Explorer Channel Bar**.
18. Click **OK**. The Internet Explorer Channel Bar is removed from the screen.

UNIT 7

LESSON 77

Customizing Active Desktop

In this lesson, you will learn how to customize the Active Desktop. This lesson assumes that your computer is connected to the Internet.

SKILL PRACTICE

NOTE The Active Desktop gallery contains links to Web pages that have Active Desktop items to download.

NOTE The Customize Subscription button allows you to set an automatic update to an Active Desktop Web page. If necessary, a user name and password option is available for protected Web pages.

TIP The Reset All button deletes all Active Desktop items except for the Internet Explorer Channel Bar and also changes the background back to default wallpaper.

To Add a New Active Desktop Item

1. Right click on the **Desktop** and select **Customize my Desktop** from the **Active Desktop** submenu. The Display Properties window appears.
2. Click the **Web** tab.
3. Click the **New** button. A dialog box may appear asking if you want to visit the Active Desktop gallery. Choose **No**.
4. In the **Location** box of the New Active Desktop Item dialog box, type **www.mainfunction.com**.
5. Click **OK**.
6. The Add Item to Active Desktop dialog box will appear to verify downloading the page. Click **OK**. The Mainfunction page begins to download to your computer and is soon highlighted in the Display Properties dialog box.
7. Click **OK**. The Mainfunction page appears on the active desktop.

To Delete an Active Desktop Item

8. Open the **Display Properties** dialog box and click the Web tab.
9. Click the **Mainfunction** address to highlight it.
10. Click the **Delete** button in the **View my Active Desktop as a web page** area.
11. Choose **Yes** to verify deleting the Active Desktop item. The Mainfunction address is removed from the screen.
12. Click **OK** to return to the Desktop.

LESSON

77

ACTIVITY

1. Open the **Display Properties** dialog box.
2. Make **www.knowlton.net/win98** a new Active Desktop item.
3. Center the Web page in the middle of the screen.
4. Delete **www.knowlton.net/win98** from the Active Desktop list.

Reinforcement Exercise

1. Change the name of the **Letter of Application** document on the desktop to **Letter of Application 2**.
2. If necessary, insert your work disk in the floppy disk drive.
3. Drag **Letter of Application 2** to the shortcut to your floppy disk drive.
4. Double-click the shortcut to your floppy disk drive.
5. Delete the **Letter of Application 2** document from your work disk.
6. Close the work disk window.
7. Drag the document named **Letter of Application 2** from the desktop to the Recycle Bin.
8. Restore **Letter of Application 2** to the desktop.
9. Delete the **Calculator** shortcut. Empty the Recycle Bin.
11. Add the **Address Bar** to the taskbar.
12. Open the document named **Poster** from your work disk using the Address Bar.
13. Change the last line of the document to read **60%-80% OFF**.
14. Save the document to the desktop as **Poster 60-80**.
15. Exit **WordPad**.
16. Load **Poster 60-80** from the **Documents** menu.
17. Exit **WordPad**.
18. Make **www.knowlton.net/win98** an Active Desktop item.
19. Resize the Active Desktop window into a square and move it to the upper right corner of the screen.
20. Remove **www.knowlton.net/win98** from the Desktop.
21. Arrange the icons on the desktop by namc.
22. Capture the screen, paste it into **Paint**, and print.
23. Minimize **Paint**.
24. Close **Paint** from the taskbar.
25. Print **Poster 60-80** by dragging its icon to the printer shortcut.
26. Drag **Poster 60-80** to the shortcut that points to your work disk.
27. Delete **Poster 60-80** from the desktop.
28. Remove the **Address Bar** from the taskbar.
29. Empty the **Recycle Bin**.

Challenge Exercise

1. Select the **Letter of Application 2** document, the **My Printer** shortcut, and the shortcut to your floppy disk drive.
2. Drag all three items to the **Recycle Bin**.
3. Empty the **Recycle Bin**.
4. Delete **www.knowlton.net/win98** from the Active Desktop items list.
5. Create a desktop shortcut for each of the storage devices on your computer system. Note: If your system has several, just create shortcuts for three or four of them.
6. Create a desktop shortcut for your printer.
7. View the properties of any one of the storage device shortcuts.
8. Move the **taskbar** to the left edge of the screen.
9. Add the **Desktop** toolbar to the taskbar.
10. Resize the **taskbar** to about twice the default width.
11. Hide the **taskbar** without using the Auto hide feature.
12. Resize the **taskbar** to approximately the original size.
13. Remove the **Desktop** toolbar.
14. Turn on the **Auto hide** feature.
15. Drag all of the desktop items to the right edge of the screen. Note: If your desktop has a large number of desktop items, just drag about five or six of them.
16. Turn off the **Auto hide** feature.
17. Drag the **taskbar** back to the bottom of the screen and return it to the default size.
18. Clear the **Documents** menu.
19. Delete the desktop shortcuts created in this lesson.
20. Empty the **Recycle Bin**.
21. Arrange the icons on the desktop by name.

UNIT 8

LESSON

78

Starting the Windows Explorer

In this lesson, you will learn about the Explorer and how to start it.

SKILL PRACTICE

NOTE If you have ever used the File Manager in previous versions of Windows, some features of the Explorer will be familiar to you.

The Explorer is a program that provides an alternative to the My Computer icon. You can use the Explorer to browse a disk, move and copy files, delete files and folders, format and copy disks, and more. You can even run other applications from Explorer.

To Start the Explorer

1. Click the **Start** button.
2. Choose **Windows Explorer** from the **Programs** menu. The Explorer starts. The Explorer displays two panes (see Figure 8-1). The left pane displays a directory structure of all drives and folders of your computer. The right pane displays the contents of the folder or drive selected in the left pane.
3. Resize the Explorer window, if necessary, to approximate the size of Figure 8-1.
4. Choose **Close** from the **File** menu. The Explorer closes.

NOTE The Explorer on your screen may vary from Figure 8-1.

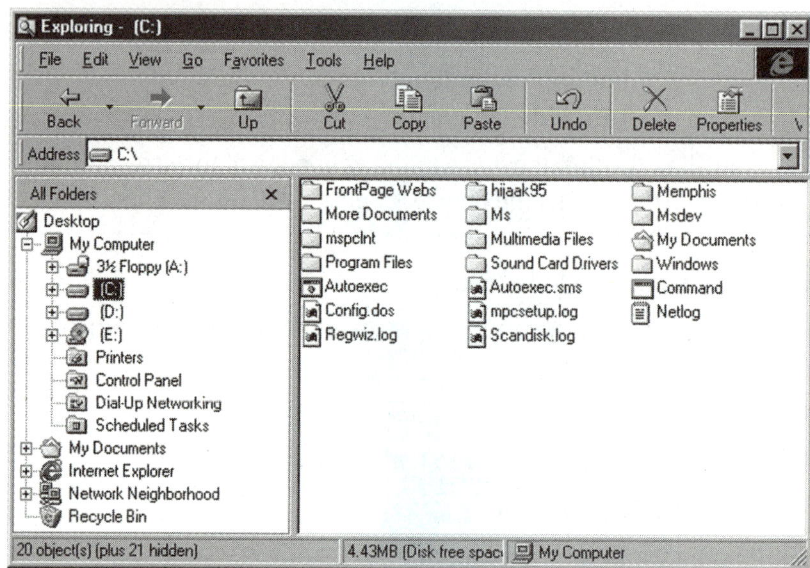

Figure 8-1 The Explorer

(continued on next page)

LESSON
78

ACTIVITY

1. Using the **My Computer** window, open the **C:** drive, and then the **Windows** folder.
2. Right-click the **System** folder and start the **Explorer**. The Explorer starts and displays the contents of the System folder. The Explorer appears similar to Figure 8-2.
3. Close the **Explorer**.
4. Close all open windows.

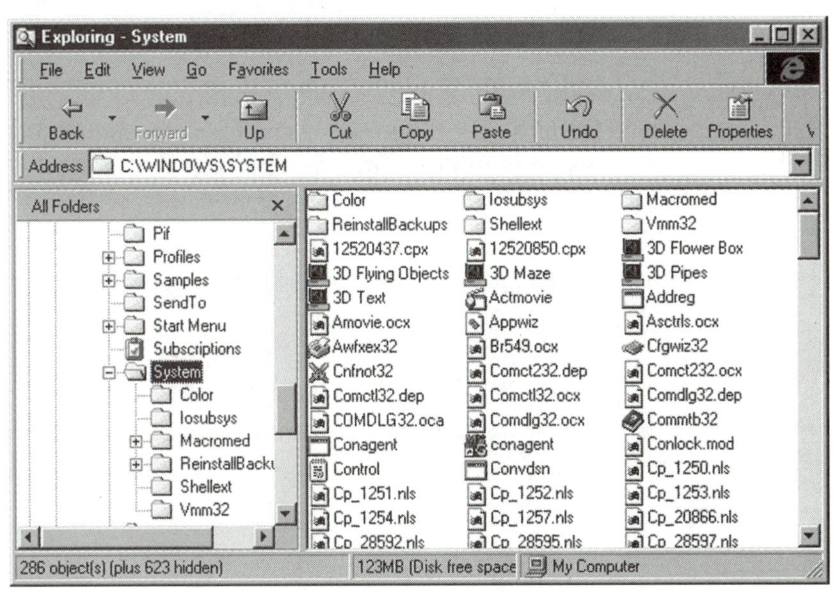

Figure 8-2 The System Folder Displayed in the Explorer

__Skill Practice__ (continued)

To Start the Explorer Displaying a Specific Drive or Folder

5. Open the **My Computer** window.
6. If not already in the floppy drive, insert your work disk.
7. Open the window that shows the contents of your work disk.
8. Right-click the **More Documents** folder and choose **Explore** from the shortcut menu that appears. Explorer starts and the right pane displays the contents of the More Documents folder.
9. Close the **Explorer**.
10. Close the window displaying the contents of your work disk.

UNIT 8

LESSON 79

Expanding and Collapsing Folders

In this lesson, you will learn how to expand and collapse folders in the Explorer.

SKILL PRACTICE

To Expand and Collapse Folders

1. Right-click the **My Computer** icon. A shortcut menu appears.
2. Choose **Explore** from the shortcut menu. The Explorer starts and displays the devices on your computer. Your screen will be similar to Figure 8-3. The devices listed on your screen will probably differ.

NOTE The hierarchical display in the left pane is sometimes called a *tree*.

NOTE You can adjust the amount of space given to each pane by dragging the bar that separates the panes.

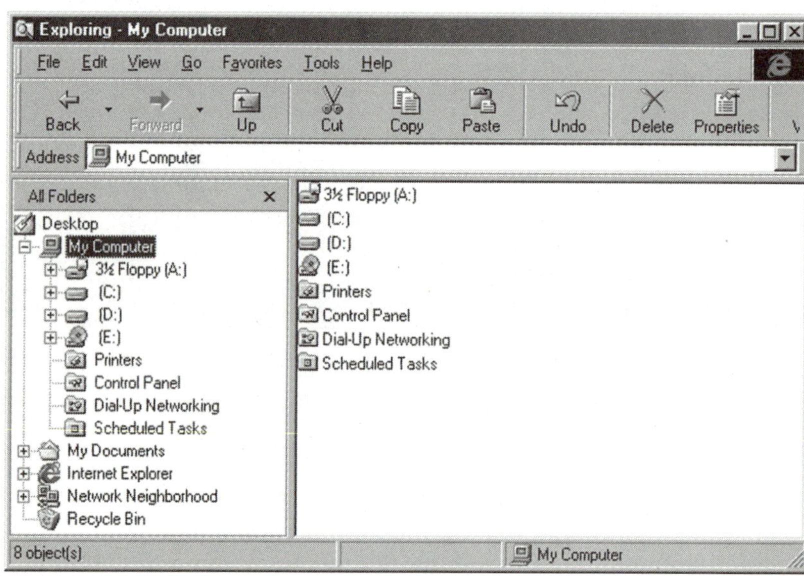

Figure 8-3 The Explorer as Started from the My Computer Icon

Notice in Figure 8-3 that the left pane displays the devices and objects of the desktop. The objects, devices, and folders are displayed in a hierarchical (or outline) form. Also notice that a minus sign (-) appears next to My Computer in the left pane. The minus sign indicates that all the folders (or devices) under that item are visible. Notice that the devices (such as the hard disk drives) have plus signs (+), which indicate that more folders are to be displayed within that folder or device. A plus sign appears only if the folder contains one or more folders. If the folder has only files in it, no plus sign will appear.

(continued on next page)

GLOSSARY TERMS

TREE • a hierarchical display of the directory structure of a storage device

LESSON 79

▶ACTIVITY

1. If not already in the floppy disk drive, insert your work disk.
2. In the left pane, click the plus sign next to the icon that represents your work disk.
3. Click on each folder displayed to see the contents of each. The listing will appear in the right pane.
4. Click the minus sign next to the floppy disk drive icon to collapse it.
5. In the left pane, expand the **C:** drive icon.
6. Maximize the **Explorer**.
7. Expand at least three folders on the **C:** drive.
8. Restore and close the **Explorer**.

Skill Practice *(continued)*

3. Click the minus sign next to the **My Computer** icon in the left pane. The devices listed under My Computer are no longer listed. The item has been *collapsed*. The box next to the My Computer icon now displays a plus sign to indicate that the item is collapsed (see Figure 8-4).
4. Click the plus sign next to the **My Computer** icon in the left pane. The item is *expanded* to show all the items under it.
5. Click the plus sign next to the icon that represents the **C:** drive. The item is expanded.
6. Click the minus sign that now appears next to the icon that represents the **C:** drive. The item is collapsed.

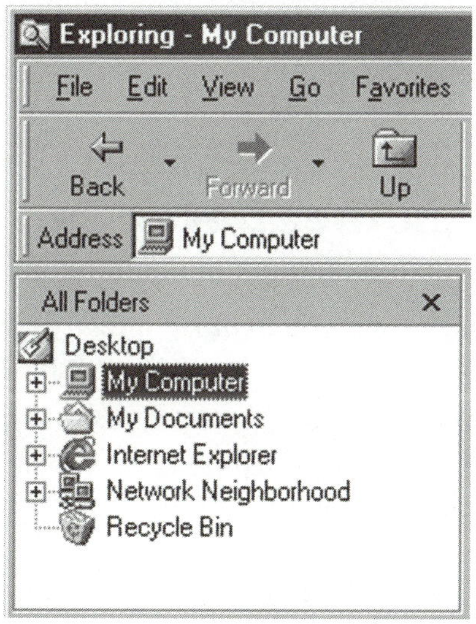

Figure 8-4 A plus sign indicates a collapsed folder or device.

UNIT 8

LESSON 80

Browsing a Disk

In this lesson, you will browse disks and view the contents of folders.

SKILL PRACTICE

To Browse a Disk

1. Right-click the **My Computer** icon. A shortcut menu appears.
2. Choose **Explore** from the shortcut menu. The Explorer starts and displays the devices on your computer.
3. In the left pane, click the icon that represents the **C:** drive. The contents of the C: drive appear in the right pane.

   The right pane is nearly identical to the windows you see when browsing with the My Computer icon. You can display the same toolbar and choose among the views that you used when browsing with the My Computer icon. When using the Explorer, however, browsing always occurs in a single window. Also, the left pane provides information not available when browsing with the My Computer icon.

NOTE When viewing the contents of a folder, the icon of the folder in the left pane changes to that of an open folder.

To Display the Toolbar

4. If the Standard Buttons toolbar is not already visible, choose **Toolbars** from the **View** menu and select **Standard Buttons** from the submenu.
5. Double-click the **Windows** folder in the right pane. The contents of the Windows folder appear in the right pane. Also notice that the left pane is updated to show the contents of the C: drive.

To Start a Program or Open a Document from the Explorer

6. Double-click the **Calc** icon in the **Windows** folder. The Calculator starts.
7. Close the **Calculator**.

TIP If you cannot immediately locate the Calc icon, sort the contents of the right pane by name.

To Quickly Move to Another Device or Folder

The Explorer has the advantage of allowing you to move directly to the contents of any device or folder that you can locate in the left pane.

8. If not already in the floppy disk drive, insert your work disk.
9. In the left pane, click the icon that represents the floppy disk drive that holds your work disk. The contents of your work disk appear in the right pane.
10. Leave the contents of your work disk visible for the Activity that follows.

LESSON

80

▶ACTIVITY

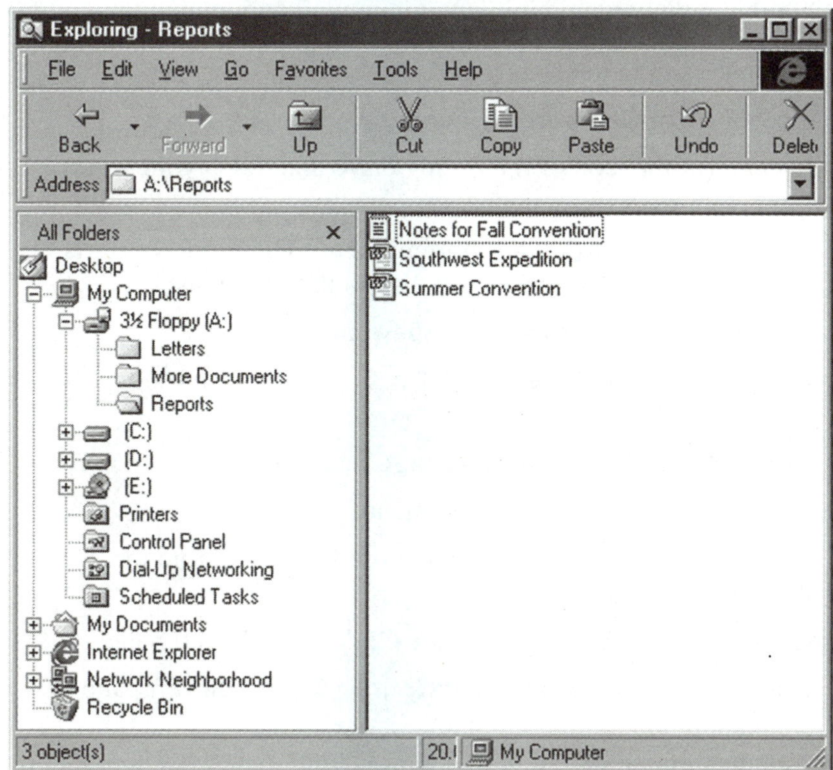

Figure 8-5 The Contents of the Reports Folder

The Explorer should be running, with the contents of your work disk displayed in the right pane.

1. Double-click the **Letters** folder in the right pane.
2. Click the **Reports** folder in the left pane. The contents of the Reports folder appear, as shown in Figure 8-5.
3. Click the **C:** drive icon in the left pane.
4. Click the **Windows** folder (not the plus sign) in the left pane.
5. Expand the **Windows** folder in the left pane.
6. Expand the **System** folder.
7. Click the **System** folder to display its contents.
8. Close the **Explorer**.

UNIT 8

LESSON

81

Arranging Icons and Sorting Files

In this lesson, you will learn to arrange icons and sort files in the Explorer.

►SKILL PRACTICE

To Arrange Icons

1. If not already in the floppy disk drive, insert your work disk.
2. Open the **My Computer** window.
3. Right click the icon of the floppy drive that holds your work disk. A shortcut menu appears.
4. Choose **Explore** from the shortcut menu. The Explorer starts, with the contents of your work disk in the right pane.
5. Choose **Large Icons** from the **View** menu.
6. Pull down the **View** menu and access the **Arrange Icons** submenu.
7. Choose **by Type** from the **Arrange Icons** submenu.
8. Choose **Details** from the **View** menu.
9. Pull down the **View** menu and choose **by Name** from the **Arrange Icons** submenu.
10. Click the icon that represents the **C:** drive in the left pane.
11. Click the plus sign next to the **C:** drive icon in the left pane to expand the device.
12. Click the plus sign next to the **Windows** folder in the left pane to expand the folder.
13. Click the **System** folder to display its contents in the right pane. The contents of the System folder should appear in Details view.
14. Click the **Name** header twice to sort the contents in descending order by name, as shown in Figure 8-6.
15. Close the **Explorer** and all other open windows.

LESSON

81

▶ACTIVITY

1. Open the **My Computer** window.
2. Right-click the icon of the floppy drive that holds your work disk and start the **Explorer**.
3. View the contents of the right pane by large icon.
4. Arrange the icons by date.
5. Switch to **Details** view.
6. Using the Name header, sort the contents by name in descending order.
7. Close the **Explorer** and all other open windows.

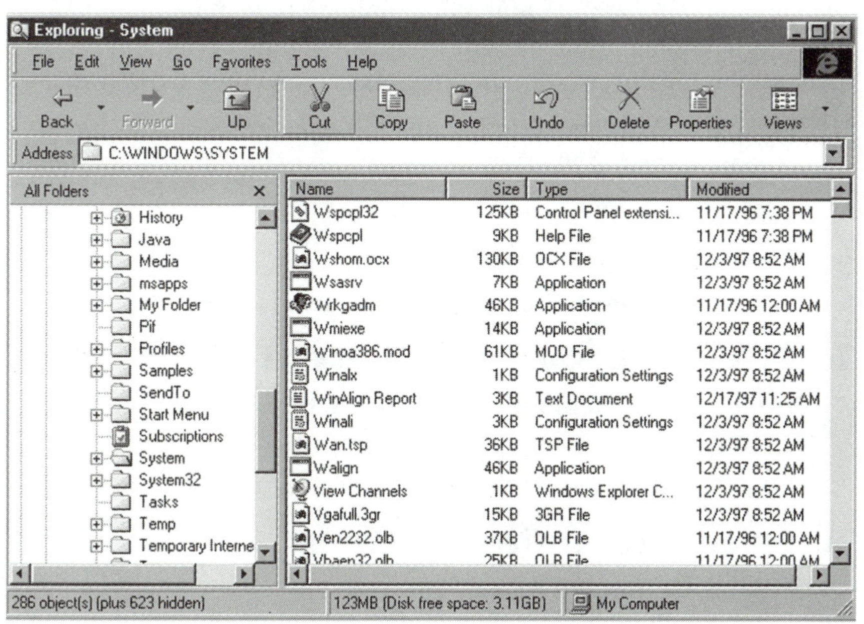

Figure 8-6 You can arrange and sort icons using the same methods you used in the My Computer window.

UNIT 8

LESSON

82

Selecting Objects

In this lesson, you will review the techniques for selecting objects and learn to select all objects and invert a selection.

SKILL PRACTICE

To Select an Item

1. Start the **Explorer** from the **Programs** menu on the **Start** menu.
2. Locate the **Windows** folder in the left pane and select it. Its contents appear in the right pane.
3. Choose **List** from the **View** menu.
4. Arrange the icons by name.
5. Click the **Command** folder icon. The item is selected.

To Select a Group of Adjacent Items

6. Position the pointer to the left of the first icon in the second column.
7. Drag a selection box around the entire second column of items.

To Select Nonadjacent Items

8. Click the **Command** folder icon.
9. Hold down the **Ctrl** key and click the **System** folder.

To Invert a Selection

Inverting a selection selects all items that are not currently selected and deselects all selected items. This is useful when you need to select all but a few items. Select the items you do not want selected and then invert the selection.

10. Click the **Calc** icon.
11. Hold down the **Ctrl** key and click the **System** folder. The Calc icon and System folder are selected.
12. Choose **Invert Selection** from the **Edit** menu. All items except the Calc icon and System folder are selected.

To Select All Items

13. Click the **My Computer** icon in the left pane. The devices of your computer are shown in the right pane.
14. Choose **Select All** from the **Edit** menu. All the items in the right pane are selected.
15. Leave the Explorer open for the Activity that follows.

LESSON

82

ACTIVITY

The Explorer should be running.

1. Display the contents of the **Windows** folder in the right pane.
2. Select the **Start Menu** folder.
3. View by large icon.
4. Select the four folders in the upper left corner of the right pane.
5. Select the **Command** folder and the **Help** folder.
6. Invert the selection.
7. Select all items using the **Select All** command. You will be asked if you also want to select hidden files. You will learn about hidden files later in this unit.
8. Click **OK**.
9. Close the **Explorer**.

NOTE If your settings are such that hidden files are displayed, you will not be prompted as indicated in Step 7.

LESSON 83

Creating Folders

In this lesson, you will learn to create folders in the Explorer.

SKILL PRACTICE

To Create a New Folder

1. If not already in the floppy disk drive, insert your work disk.
2. Start the **Explorer** from the **Programs** menu on the **Start** menu.
3. In the left pane, locate the icon of the floppy disk drive that holds your work disk.
4. Click the floppy disk drive icon to display the contents of your work disk in the right pane.
5. Choose **New** from the **File** menu and choose **Folder** from the New submenu.
6. Key **Explorer Folder** as the name for the new folder and press **Enter**.
7. Leave the **Explorer** open for the Activity that follows.

LESSON

83

▶ACTIVITY

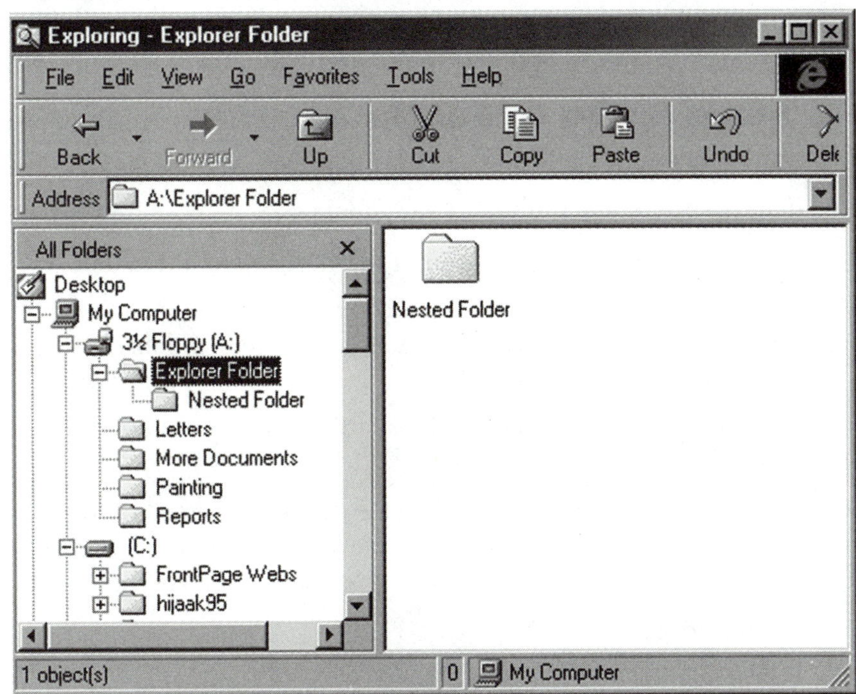

Figure 8-7 The folder named *Explorer Folder* is expanded.

The Explorer should be open, with the contents of your work disk displayed in the right pane.

1. Double-click the folder named **Explorer Folder** in the right pane.
2. Create a folder in **Explorer Folder** named **Nested Folder**.
3. Click the plus sign next to the folder named **Explorer Folder** in the left pane. The new folder appears under the folder named Explorer Folder. Your Explorer should appear similar to Figure 8-7.
4. Close the **Explorer**.

LESSON 84

Moving and Copying Files and Folders

In this lesson, you will learn to move and copy files and folders.

SKILL PRACTICE

The Explorer can make moving and copying files easier. You can drag a file or folder from the right pane to the destination in the left pane.

To Move a File or Folder

1. If not already in the floppy disk drive, insert your work disk.
2. Start the **Explorer** from the **Programs** menu on the **Start** menu.
3. In the left pane, locate the icon of the floppy disk drive that holds your work disk.
4. Click the floppy disk drive icon to display the contents of your work disk in the right pane.
5. In the left pane, expand or collapse folders as necessary to make the C: drive icon visible.
6. Using the right mouse button, drag the document named **Letter of Application** to the **C:** drive icon in the left pane. When you release the mouse button, a shortcut menu appears, as shown in Figure 8-8.

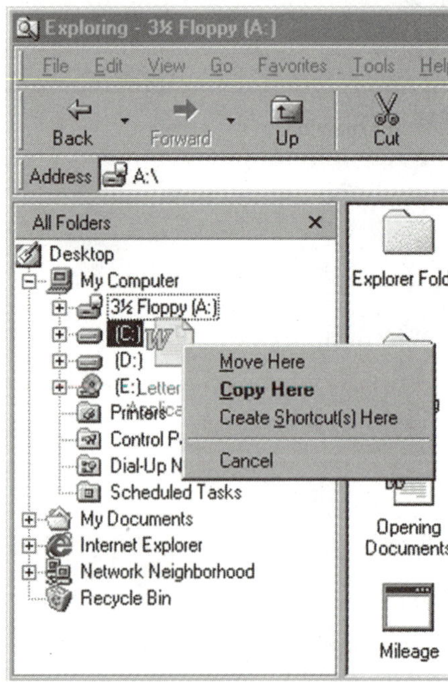

Figure 8-8 Dragging with the right mouse button allows you to choose whether to copy or move the item.

NOTE
You can also use Cut, Copy, and Paste to move and copy files in the Explorer.

(continued on next page)

LESSON

84

ACTIVITY

1. Copy the document named **Poster** from the top level of your work disk to the folder named **Explorer Folder**.
2. Open **Explorer Folder**.
3. Move the **Poster** document into the folder named **Nested Folder**.
4. Copy the folder named **Explorer Folder** to the **C:** drive and close the **Explorer**.

Skill Practice *(continued)*

To Copy a File or Folder

7. Choose **Move Here** from the shortcut menu. The file is moved to the C: drive.
8. Click the **C:** drive icon in the left pane. The contents of the C: drive appear.
9. In the right pane, locate the document named **Letter of Application** that you just copied to the C: drive.
10. Verify that the icon of the floppy disk drive that contains your work disk is visible in the left pane.
11. Using the right mouse button, drag the document named **Letter of Application** from the right pane to the floppy disk drive icon in the left pane. Release the mouse button. A shortcut menu appears.
12. Choose **Copy Here** from the shortcut menu. The file is copied to the floppy disk drive.
13. Display the contents of your work disk.
14. Leave the Explorer open for the Activity that follows.

UNIT 8

LESSON

85

Deleting a File or Folder

In this lesson, you will learn to delete files and folders.

SKILL PRACTICE

TIP
You can also delete a file or folder by right-clicking it in either pane and choosing Delete from the shortcut menu.

TIP
You can also empty the Recycle Bin by right-clicking the Recycle Bin in the left pane and choosing Empty Recycle Bin from the shortcut menu.

To Delete a File or Folder

1. Start **Explorer** and display the contents of the **C:** drive in the right pane.
2. Locate the document named **Letter of Application** in the right pane and select it.
3. Choose **Delete** from the **File** menu. You are asked if you are sure you want to send the document to the Recycle Bin.
4. Click **Yes**. The document is put into the Recycle Bin.

To Empty the Recycle Bin from the Explorer

5. Click the **Recycle Bin** icon in the left pane. The contents of the Recycle Bin appear in the right pane.
6. Choose **Empty Recycle Bin** from the **File** menu. You are asked to verify your intention to delete.
7. Click **Yes**. The Recycle Bin empties.
8. Leave the Explorer open for the Activity that follows.

LESSON

85

▶ACTIVITY

1. Delete the folder named **Explorer Folder** from your work disk.
2. Delete the folder named **Explorer Folder** from the **C:** drive.
3. Empty the **Recycle Bin** from the Explorer.
4. Close the **Explorer**.

UNIT 8

LESSON

86 Formatting a Floppy Disk

In this lesson, you will learn to format a disk from the Explorer.

SKILL PRACTICE

For this lesson, you will need an unformatted diskette or a diskette that can be reformatted without losing any important data. Do not use your work disk for this lesson.

To Format a Floppy Disk

1. Start **Explorer**.
2. Insert a diskette to be formatted into the floppy disk drive.
3. In the left pane, click the **My Computer** icon.
4. In the right pane, click the icon of the floppy drive that contains the disk to be formatted.
5. Choose **Format** from the **File** menu. The Format dialog box appears, as shown in Figure 8-9.

NOTE The Quick format type simply removes files from a disk that is already formatted. The Full format type reformats the disk and checks for bad spots on the disk. The Copy system files only format type creates a startup disk from an already formatted disk.

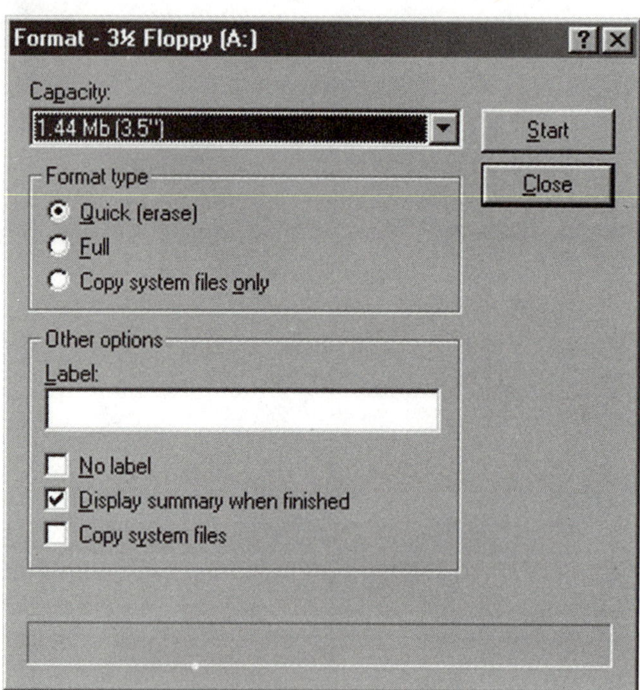

Figure 8-9 Format Dialog Box

(continued on next page)

LESSON

86

ACTIVITY

Use the Explorer to reformat the floppy disk you formatted in the Skill Practice. Label the disk with your first name.

Skill Practice *(continued)*

6. Choose the appropriate capacity from the **Capacity** list box. If you are unsure of the capacity, ask your instructor.
7. Select **Full** from the **Format type** options.
8. Click in the **Label** text box and key **New Disk** as the disk label.
9. Click **Start**. Formatting begins. The process of formatting a disk may take a minute or more. When the format is complete, the results of the format are displayed.
10. Click **Close**. The Format dialog box is active.
11. Click **Close**. The Format dialog box closes.
12. Close **Explorer**.

UNIT 8

LESSON 87

Copying a Floppy Disk

In this lesson, you will learn to copy a disk from the Explorer.

SKILL PRACTICE

For this lesson, you will need your work disk and the disk you formatted in the previous lesson.

To Write-Protect a Disk

Before copying a disk, it is a good idea to write-protect the disk you are copying to prevent the original disk from being overwritten accidentally.

1. If your work disk is in the floppy disk drive, eject it.
2. Slide the small tab in the corner of the disk to expose the hole. The disk is now write-protected.

NOTE If your work disk is a 5 1/4-inch disk, write-protect it by placing a write-protect tab over the notch in the disk.

To Copy a Floppy Disk

3. Start **Explorer**.
4. Insert your work disk into the floppy disk drive.
5. In the left pane, click the **My Computer** icon.
6. In the right pane, click the icon of the floppy drive that contains your work disk.
7. Choose **Copy Disk** from the **File** menu. The Copy Disk dialog box appears, as shown in Figure 8-10. Your Copy Disk dialog box may vary from the one in the figure.

TIP You can also access the Copy Disk dialog box by right-clicking the floppy drive icon in either pane and choosing Copy Disk from the shortcut menu.

Figure 8-10 Copy Disk Dialog Box

(continued on next page)

GLOSSARY TERMS

WRITE-PROTECT • to protect the contents of a disk by preventing the computer from making changes to the disk

LESSON 87

►ACTIVITY

1. Use the Explorer to copy your work disk again. You may use the same destination floppy disk or another one.
2. Remove the write-protection from your work disk.
3. Close the **Explorer**.

Skill Practice (continued)

8. In both the **Copy from** and **Copy to** boxes, select the drive that holds your work disk. The selection may already be made for you.
9. Click **Start**. The source disk is read. After the disk has been read, you will be prompted to insert the disk you are copying to.
10. When prompted, eject your work disk and insert the disk you formatted in the previous lesson.
11. Click **OK**. The data are written to the destination disk. When the copy is complete, a message will appear in the Copy Disk dialog box, as shown in Figure 8-11.
12. Click **Close**.
13. Leave the Explorer open for the Activity that follows.

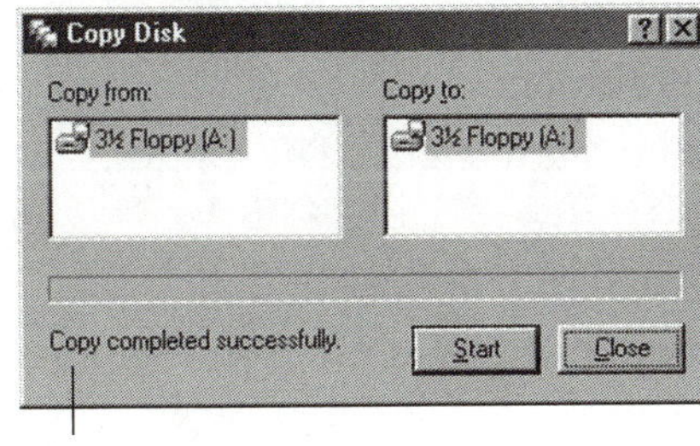

Figure 8-11 The copy is complete.

You can copy another disk by clicking Start again or return to the Explorer by clicking Close.

UNIT 8

LESSON 88

Viewing MS-DOS Filename Extensions and Paths

In this lesson, you will learn to view MS-DOS filename extensions and paths in the Explorer.

SKILL PRACTICE

To View Extensions

On your disks, files are stored using names that are compatible with MS-DOS. MS-DOS filenames include a three-character filename extension that is used to identify the various types of files. Windows 95 also uses these extensions but usually hides them from your view. You can choose to have the extensions displayed.

1. Start **Explorer**.
2. Choose **Folder Options** from the **View** menu. The Options dialog box appears.
3. If necessary, click the **View** tab. The option called **Hide file extensions** is selected by default.
4. Click the **Hide file extensions** for known file types option to deselect it.
5. Click **OK**. The dialog box closes.
6. View the contents of the **Windows** folder on the **C:** drive.
7. View the contents by small icon. Notice that the filenames include extensions. For example, **Calc** is now **Calc.exe**.

TIP Setting the option that displays filename extensions also causes extensions to be displayed when using the My Computer icon to browse a disk. You can also set the filename extension option by choosing Options from the View menu in the My Computer window.

To View the Full MS-DOS Path

In MS-DOS, the *path* is the drive letter and the directories that lead you to a particular file. By default, only the current folder is displayed in the title bar of the Explorer. You can, however, have the full MS-DOS path displayed.

8. Choose Folder **Options** from the **View** menu. The Options dialog box appears. Click the **View** tab.
9. Select the **Display the full path in title bar** option.
10. Click **OK**. Notice that the MS-DOS path name appears in the title bar.
11. Double-click the **System** folder in the right pane. The path is extended to include the System folder.
12. Choose Folder **Options** from the **View** menu. The Options dialog box appears.
13. Turn off the **Display the full path in title bar** option.
14. Turn on the **Hide file extensions** for known file types option.
15. Click **OK**.
16. Close the **Explorer**.

GLOSSARY TERMS

PATH • the drive letter and directories that lead to a particular file

LESSON 88

ACTIVITY

1. Start the **Explorer**.
2. Set the option that causes filename extensions to be viewed.
3. Set the option that causes full MS-DOS paths to be viewed.
4. Close the **Explorer**.
5. Double-click the **My Computer** icon.
6. Open the **C:** drive window.
7. Open the **Windows** folder. Notice the path in the title bar and the filename extensions in the window.
8. Choose Folder **Options** from the **View** menu.
9. Click the **View** tab.
10. Deselect the option to display the path.
11. Select the option that hides extensions.
12. Click **OK**.
13. Close all windows.

UNIT 8

LESSON 89

Viewing Hidden Files and Folders

In this lesson, you will learn to view hidden files and folders.

SKILL PRACTICE

To View Hidden Files and Folders

Disks contain files that are not automatically visible. These files are usually files used by the operating system, but other files and folders may also be hidden.

1. Start **Explorer**.
2. View the contents of the **Windows** folder. Notice that the bottom left corner of the Explorer window tells you how many objects are displayed and how many are hidden.
3. Choose Folder **Options** from the **View** menu. The Options dialog box appears.
4. Click the **View** tab to display the View section of the dialog box. Notice that there are three options under Hidden Files (see Figure 8-12).

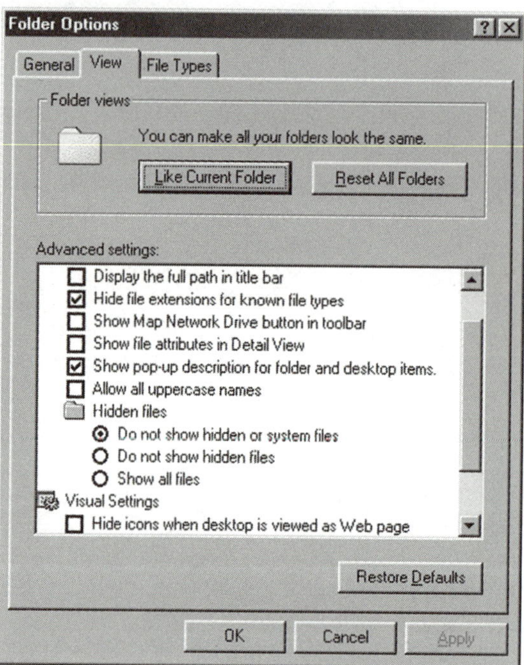

Figure 8-12 There are three settings in the Hidden Files folder.

5. Select the **Show all files** option and click **OK**. Hidden files and folders are now visible.

(continued on next page)

GLOSSARY TERMS

HIDDEN FILES AND FOLDERS • files and folders that are usually hidden from view

LESSON

89

ACTIVITY

1. Start the **Explorer**.
2. Display the contents of the **Windows** folder.
3. Open the **System** folder.
4. Open the **Iosubsys** folder. Notice how many items are visible.
5. Set the option that makes all files visible. Notice how many items are now visible.
6. Set the option that hides files that are usually hidden.
7. Close the **Explorer**.

Skill Practice *(continued)*

6. Choose Folder **Options** from the **View** menu. The Folder Options dialog box appears. Click the **View** tab.
7. Select the **Do not show hidden or system files** option and click **OK**.
8. Close the **Explorer**.

UNIT 8

LESSON 90

Customizing Folders

In this lesson, you will learn how to customize folders.

SKILL PRACTICE

To Add a Background to a Folder

1. Start **Windows Explorer**.
2. Insert your work disk into the computer and select the drive that your disk is in.
3. Create a folder called **My Customized Folder**, and open it.
4. Choose **Customize this Folder** from the **View** menu. The Customize this Folder dialog box appears, as shown in Figure 8-13.

NOTE: The **Create or edit an HTML document** option allows you to use HTML code when customizing a folder.

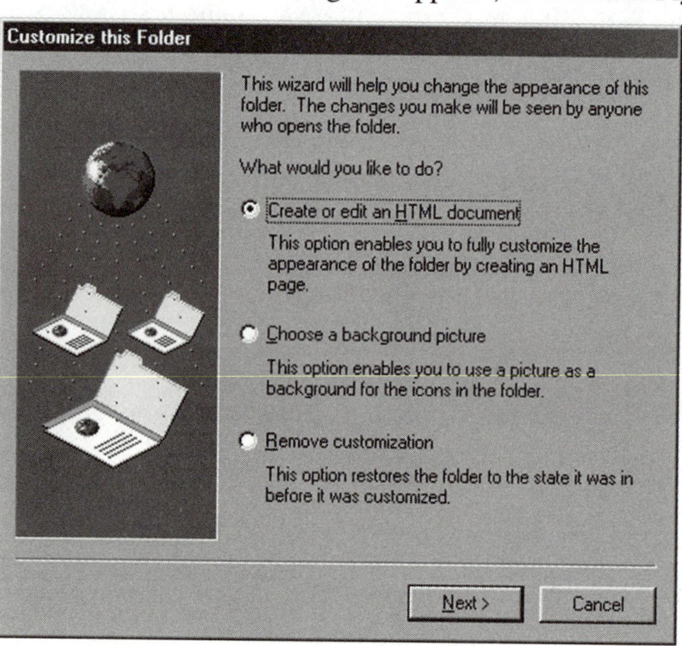

Figure 8-13 Customize this Folder dialog box.

5. Select the **Choose a background picture** option.
6. Click **Next**. A dialog box appears with several different backgrounds that are available.
7. Scroll through the list of backgrounds and select the one you like the best. A picture of the background will appear on the left side of the dialog box.
8. In the **Icon caption colors** part of the dialog box, click the **Text** box. The Color dialog box appears.

(continued on next page)

LESSON

90

ACTIVITY

1. Select the **My Customized Folder** on your work disk.
2. Add a background and a different font color to the folder.
3. Remove the Customization from the folder.
4. Delete **My Customized Folder** and all of its contents from your work disk.
5. Close **Windows Explorer**.

Skill Practice *(continued)*

9. Select a color for the words in the folder, and click **OK**.
10. Click **Next**. A dialog box appears verifying that changes were made to the folder.
11. Click **Finish**. The changes are made to the folder.
12. Create another folder in the My Customized Folder and name it **My Other Folder**. Notice the name of the folder is the color that you selected earlier.

To Remove a Background from a Folder

13. Right click an empty space in the **My Customized Folder**.
14. Click the **Customize this Folder** option.
15. Select **Remove Customization** from the **Customize this folder** dialog box and Click **Next**. A dialog box appear warning you that the background is about to be removed.
16. Click **Next**. Another Dialog box appears verifying the changes that were made.
17. Click **Finish**. The Background is removed from the folder.
18. Leave **Windows Explorer** open for the next activity.

Reinforcement Exercise

1. Start the **Explorer** and display the contents of your work disk.
2. Display the contents of the **C:** drive.
3. Expand the **Windows** folder and all folders within the Windows folder.
4. Collapse all folders and devices.
5. Use the Explorer to locate the accessory named **Calc** in the **Windows** folder and start it from the icon.
6. Close the **Calculator**.
7. View the contents of the **Windows** folder by small icon.
8. Arrange the icons by type.
9. Using the **Invert Selection** command, select all items in the **Windows** folder except the **Help** folder.
10. Create a folder on your work disk named **Temporary Folder**.
11. Copy the **Letters** folder into the folder named **Temporary Folder**.
12. Customize the Temporary Folder with a background picture.
13. Move the folder named **Temporary Folder** to the **C:** drive.
14. Delete **Temporary Folder** from the C: drive.
15. Empty the **Recycle Bin**.
16. Close the **Explorer**.

Challenge Exercise

To complete this exercise, you will need two blank or erasable disks in addition to your work disk.

1. Start the **Explorer**.
2. Set the option that allows filename extensions to be viewed.
3. Set the option that allows the full MS-DOS path to be displayed.
4. Set the option that allows hidden files and folders to be viewed.
5. In the left pane, expand the **Program Files** folder on the **C:** drive.
6. Expand every folder within the **Program Files** folder.
7. Locate **WordPad** in the **Accessories** folder in the **Program Files** folder.
8. Start **WordPad** from the Explorer.
9. Exit **WordPad**.
10. Create a folder named **Challenge Folder** on the **C:** drive.
11. Customize the Challenge Folder with the background picture named specks.bmp on your work disk.
12. Copy the **Reports** folder from your work disk to the **Challenge Folder** on the **C:** drive.
13. Eject your work disk and insert a blank disk or a disk that can be reformatted without losing important data.
14. Format the disk.
15. Move the **Challenge Folder** to the floppy disk you just formatted.
16. Remove the customization from the folder.
17. Copy the disk that is now in the floppy disk drive to a blank disk or to a disk that can be reformatted without losing important data.
18. Set the option that hides hidden files and folders.
19. Set the option that hides MS-DOS filename extensions.
20. Set the option that prevents the MS-DOS path from appearing.
21. Close the **Explorer**.

UNIT 9

LESSON 91

Starting Find

In this lesson, you will learn to start Find from the Start menu, the Explorer, and My Computer.

SKILL PRACTICE

NOTE The Find menu includes utilities for finding computers, Web sites, and people. This unit covers only finding files and folders.

TIP You can right-click the My Computer icon, any device in the My Computer window, or any folder to start Find. Find will then search within that device or folder.

Find allows you to quickly locate a file or folder. You can search by name and location, date modified, size, or type. You can even search for files that contain specified text.

To Start Find from the Start Menu

1. Click the **Start** button.
2. Choose **Find** from the **Start** menu. The Find menu appears.
3. Choose **Files or Folders** from the **Find** menu. The Find dialog box appears, as shown in Figure 9-1.
4. Choose **Close** from the **File** menu. Find closes.

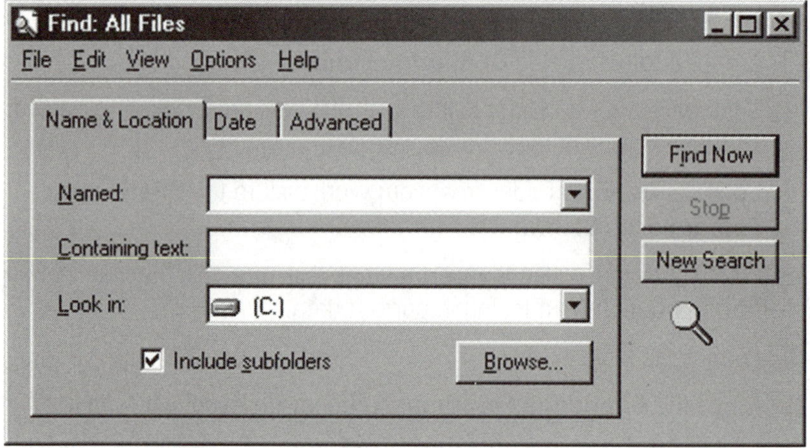

Figure 9-1 Find Dialog Box

To Start Find from the Explorer

5. Start the **Explorer**.
6. Choose **Find** from the **Tools** menu. The Find menu appears.
7. Choose **Files or Folders** from the **Find** menu. The Find dialog box appears.
8. Choose **Close** from the **File** menu. Find closes.
9. Close the **Explorer**.

(continued on next page)

LESSON

91

ACTIVITY

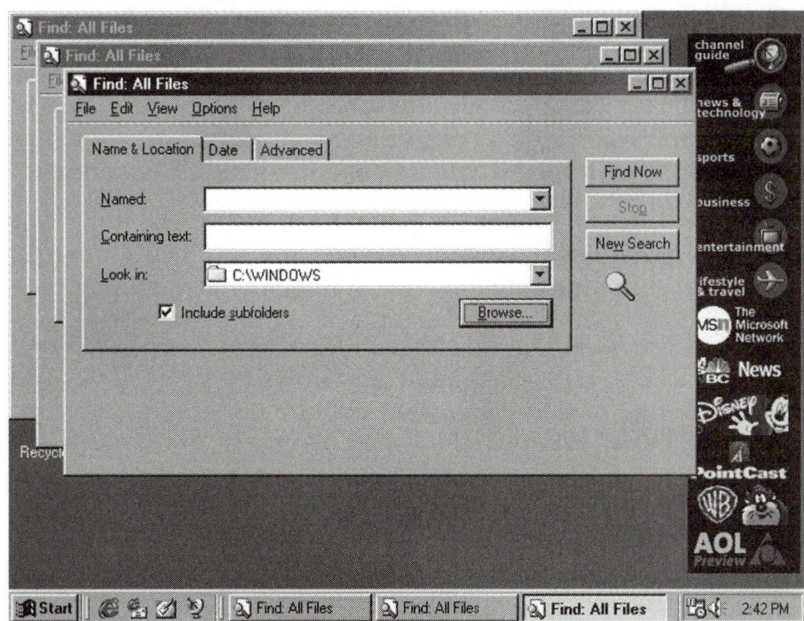

Figure 9-2 You can run Find multiple times.

Skill Practice (continued)

To Start Find from the My Computer Window

10. Open the **My Computer** window.
11. Click the **C:** drive icon.
12. Choose **Find** from the **File** menu. The Find dialog box appears.
13. Click the Close button on the Find dialog box. Find closes.
14. Close the **My Computer** window.

To Start Find by Right-Clicking

15. Right-click the **My Computer** icon. A shortcut menu appears.
16. Choose **Find** from the shortcut menu. The Find dialog box appears.
17. Close **Find**.

1. Start **Find** from the Start menu.
2. Start the **Explorer** while leaving **Find** open.
3. Start **Find** again from the **Explorer**. Two Find windows are now open.
4. Click the **Exploring** button on the taskbar.
5. Close the **Explorer** but leave the Find windows open.
6. Minimize both **Find** windows.
7. Open the **My Computer** window.
8. Open the **C:** drive window.
9. Right-click the **Windows** folder and choose **Find** from the shortcut menu. Notice that the Find dialog box that appears is set to search in the Windows folder.
10. Close the **C:** drive window and the **My Computer** window.
11. Redisplay the minimized **Find** windows. Note: In the Challenge Exercise at the end of this Unit, you will run two searches at the same time by opening two Find dialog boxes.
12. Right-click a blank area on the taskbar and choose to **Cascade** the windows. Your screen should appear similar to Figure 9-2.
13. Close all **Find** dialog boxes.

UNIT 9

LESSON 92

Finding Files and Folders by Name and Location

In this lesson, you will learn to find files and folders by name and location.

SKILL PRACTICE

To Find a File or Folder by Name and Location

1. Click the **Start** button.
2. Choose **Find** from the **Start** menu. The Find menu appears.
3. Choose **Files or Folders** from the **Find** menu. The Find dialog box appears. If necessary, click the **Name & Location** tab to make that section active.
4. If not already in the floppy disk drive, insert your work disk.
5. If necessary, click the **Named** text box.
6. Key **Logo**.
7. Click the arrow in the **Look in** text box and choose the floppy disk drive that holds your work disk, as shown in Figure 9-3.

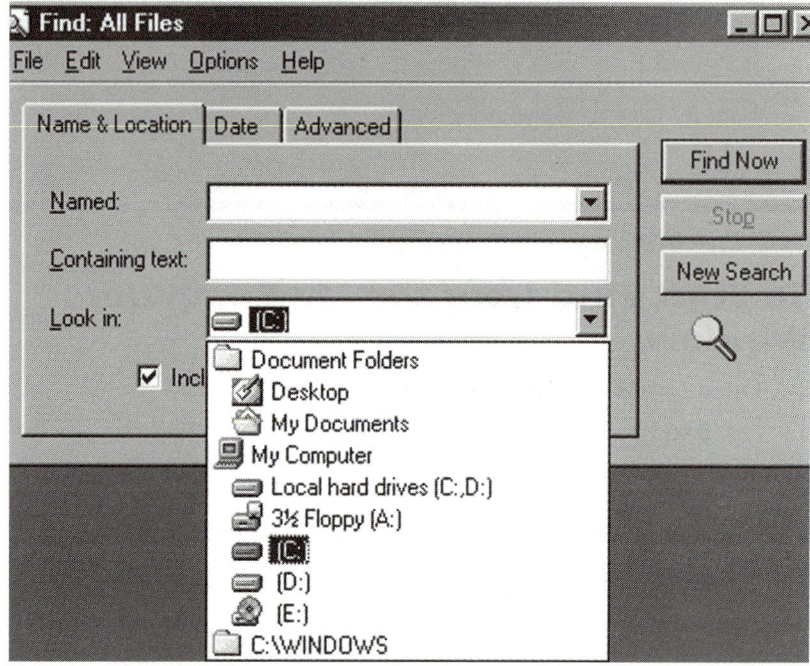

Figure 9-3 The Look in box allows you to narrow the search.

TIP Clicking the Browse button allows you to specify a folder in which to search.

8. Click **Find Now**. A file is found and is displayed in the bottom of the dialog box.

(continued on next page)

LESSON

92

ACTIVITY

1. Use **Find** to locate the document named **Southwest Expedition** on your work disk.
2. Open the folder that contains the document.
3. Close the open window.
4. Close **Find**.

Skill Practice (*continued*)

To Open the Folder That Contains the Located File

9. If necessary, select the **Logo** file at the bottom of the dialog box.
10. Choose **Open Containing Folder** from the **File** menu. The More Documents folder opens.
11. Close the **More Documents** folder.
12. Choose **Close** from the **File** menu. Find closes.

UNIT 9

LESSON 93

Finding Files and Folders by Date Modified

In this lesson, you will learn to find files and folders by date modified.

SKILL PRACTICE

To Find a File or Folder by Date Modified

1. Start **Explorer**.
2. Choose **Find** from the **Tools** menu. The Find menu appears.
3. Choose **Files or Folders** from the **Find** menu. The Find dialog box appears.
4. Choose **My Computer** from the **Look in** list.
5. Click the **Date** tab. The dialog box appears as shown in Figure 9-4.

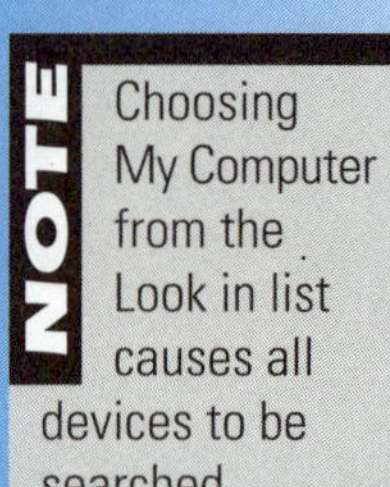

NOTE Choosing My Computer from the Look in list causes all devices to be searched.

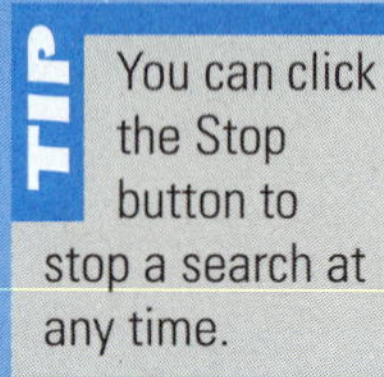

TIP You can click the Stop button to stop a search at any time.

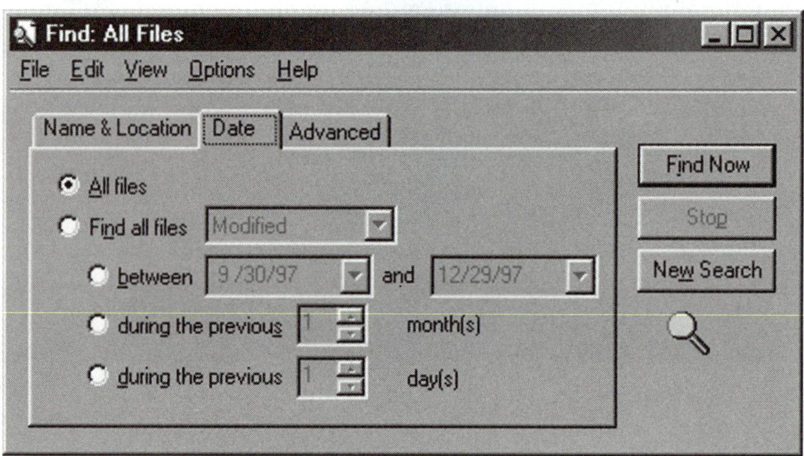

Figure 9-4 Date Modified Section of the Find Dialog Box

6. Click the **Find all files** option.
7. Click the **during the previous 1 days** option. Leave the number of days set to 1.
8. Click **Find Now**. Find begins searching all storage devices for files modified within the last day. The files appear in a list at the bottom of the dialog box. Many of the files listed will be temporary files or operating system files.
9. Close **Find**.
10. Close the **Explorer**.

LESSON

93

ACTIVITY

1. Start **WordPad**.
2. In the blank document that appears, key **My name is** and key your full name.
3. Save the document on your work disk as **Name Document** and exit **WordPad**.
4. Right-click the **My Computer** icon and choose **Find** from the shortcut menu.
5. Look in **My Computer** for files created or modified during the previous 1 day. The document you just saved in WordPad should appear in the list at the bottom of the dialog box.
6. When you see **Name Document** appear in the list, click **Stop** to stop the search.
7. Click the **New Search** button. A message appears, warning you that your current search will be cleared.
8. Click **OK**.
9. Click the **Name & Location** tab.
10. Choose your work disk from the **Look in** box.
11. Click the **Date** tab.
12. Specify that you want to search for files created or modified during the previous 2 months. (Hint: Click the up arrow in the months box to increment the number of months to 2. The files on your work disk that were created or modified in the last 2 months appear in the list at the bottom of the dialog box.)
13. Click **Find Now**.
14. Close **Find**.

UNIT 9

LESSON

94

Finding Files by File Type and Size

In this lesson, you will learn to find files using two advanced find features. You will search for files by type and by size.

SKILL PRACTICE

To Find a File by Type

1. Open the **My Computer** window.
2. Right-click the icon of the floppy disk that contains your work disk.
3. Start **Find** from the shortcut menu.
4. Click the **Advanced** tab.
5. Click the arrow in the **Of type** box. An extensive list of every file type registered with your system appears.
6. Choose **Text Document** from the list.
7. Click **Find Now**. Find searches your work disk for text documents. The text documents appear in the list at the bottom of the dialog box.
8. After the search is complete, click **New Search** and click **OK**.

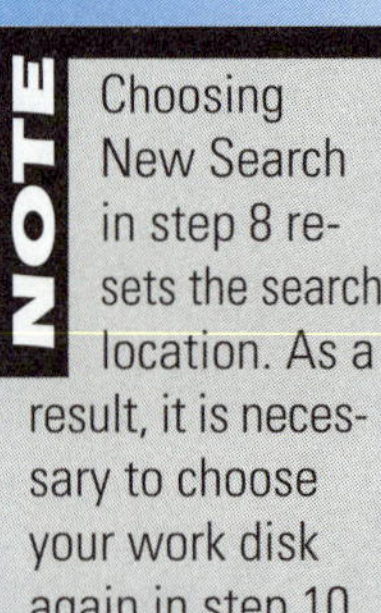

Choosing New Search in step 8 resets the search location. As a result, it is necessary to choose your work disk again in step 10.

To Find a File by Size

9. Click the **Name & Location** tab.
10. Choose your work disk from the **Look in** box.
11. Click the **Advanced** tab.
12. Choose **At most** from the **Size is** box.
13. Click in the **KB** box and key **6** (see Figure 9-5).
14. Click **Find Now**. The files that are 6 kilobytes or less in size are listed.
15. Close **Find** and the **My Computer** window.

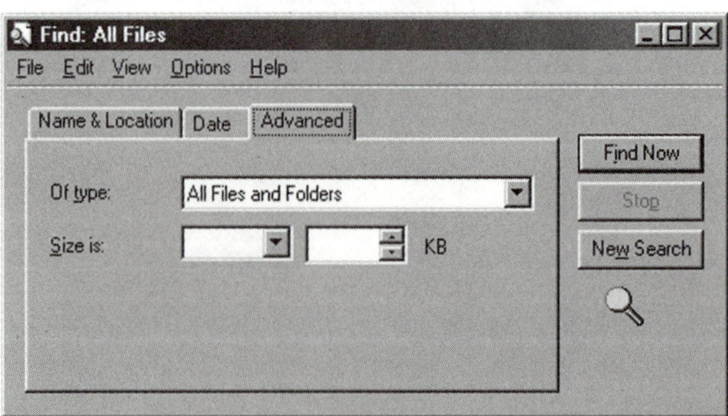

Figure 9-5 Files can be searched by size.

LESSON

94

ACTIVITY

1. Start **Find**.
2. Search all the devices on your system for bitmap images.
3. Search all the devices on your system for files of at least 1 megabyte (1000 KB).
4. Search your **C:** drive for files of at least 500KB.
5. Close **Find**.

UNIT 9

LESSON

95

Finding Files by the Text Contained in the Files

In this lesson, you will learn how to find files by searching the text within the files.

SKILL PRACTICE

To Find a File by the Text It Contains

1. If necessary, open the **My Computer** window.
2. Right-click the icon of the floppy disk that contains your work disk.
3. Start **Find** from the shortcut menu.
4. Key **China** in the **Containing text** box.
5. Click **Find Now**. Find begins searching your work disk for documents that contain the word *China*. One document is found, as shown in Figure 9-6.
6. Close **Find**.

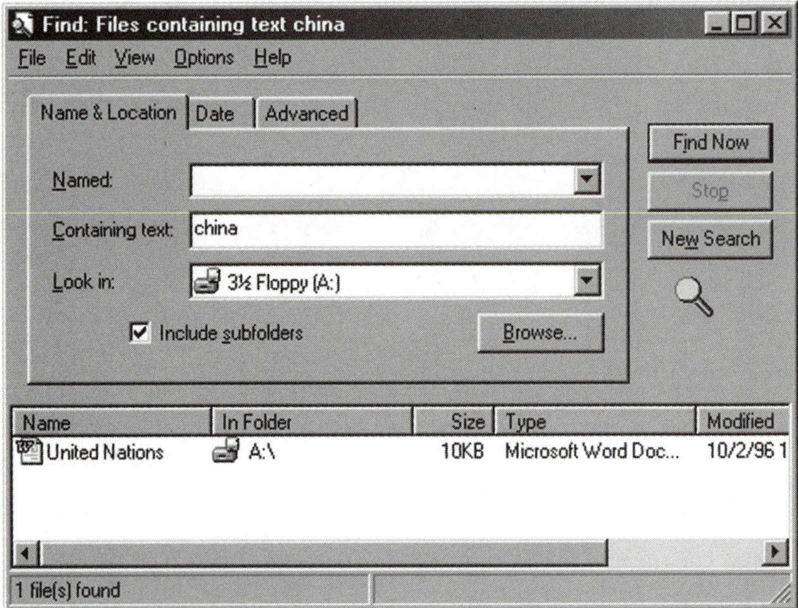

Figure 9-6 Find can locate files that contain specified text.

LESSON

95

ACTIVITY

1. Start **Find**.
2. Search your work disk for the document that contains your name. (The document you created in the previous lesson.)
3. Double-click **Name Document** in the list to open the document. You do not have to wait for the entire disk to be searched before opening the document.
4. Exit **WordPad**.
5. Close **Find**.
6. Close the **My Computer** window.

UNIT 9

LESSON

96

Saving Search Criteria and Results

In this lesson, you will learn to save search criteria and search results.

►SKILL PRACTICE

To Save Search Criteria

1. Open the **My Computer** window.
2. Right-click the icon of the floppy disk that contains your work disk.
3. Start **Find** from the shortcut menu.
4. Key **government** in the **Containing text** box.
5. Click **Find Now**. Find begins searching your work disk for documents that contain the word *government*. Two documents are found.
6. Pull down the **Options** menu. The Save Results option should not have a check mark by it. If the option is selected, choose it from the menu to turn off the option.
7. Choose **Save Search** from the **File** menu. The search criteria are saved to the desktop.
8. Close **Find** and the **My Computer** window.
9. The search icon appears on the desktop, as shown in Figure 9-7.

Figure 9-7 Searches are saved to the desktop.

(continued on next page)

LESSON

96

►ACTIVITY

1. Use **Find** to search for any documents on the **C:** drive larger than 300 kilobytes.
2. Save the search criteria without the results.
3. Close **Find**.
4. On the desktop, change the name of the Search icon you just saved to **More than 300K**.
5. Double-click **More than 300K** to start Find with the search criteria.
6. Perform the search.
7. Save the search criteria with the results.
8. Close **Find**.
9. Double-click the Search icon you just saved to start Find and display the results of the last search.
10. Turn off the option that causes results to be saved.
11. Close **Find**.
12. Drag all Search icons to the **Recycle Bin** and empty the Recycle Bin.

Skill Practice *(continued)*

To Use a Saved Search

10. Double-click the Search icon on the desktop. Find starts, and the criteria for the saved search are set.
11. Click **Find Now**. The search begins. The two files that meet the criteria are found again.

To Save Search Results

You can save the search results along with the criteria. The list of files found by the search will appear when you double-click the Search icon.

12. Choose **Save Results** from the **Options** menu. The Save Results option is turned on.
13. Choose **Save Search** from the **File** menu.
14. Close **Find**.
15. Another Search icon appears on the desktop. The new Search icon has the same name as the first but has a (2) added to the end of the name.
16. Double-click the new Search icon. Find starts and displays the results of the saved search.
17. Choose **Save Results** from the **Options** menu. The Save Results option is turned off.
18. Close **Find**.

NOTE When you save the results with a search, the results that appear when you reload the previous search will not reflect any changes to your computer since the results were saved. You must perform the search again to have an up-to-date list.

Reinforcement Exercise

1. Start **Find** by right-clicking the **Windows** folder on the **C:** drive.
2. Find the files in the **Windows** folder that were created or modified in the previous month.
3. Start a new search.
4. Key **pad** in the **Named** box and click **Find Now**. Find locates all files with *pad* in the name.
5. Scroll through the list of files found and locate the file named **WordPad** with a file type of Application.
6. Double-click the file to start **WordPad**.
7. Key the following sentence into **WordPad**:

   Find is a useful and flexible feature of Windows 98.
8. Save the document on your work disk as **About Find**.
9. Exit **WordPad**.
10. Close **Find**.
11. Start **Find** from the **Start** menu.
12. Search your work disk for documents that contain the text **Windows 98**.
13. Search the **Program Files** folder on the **C:** drive for files that are at least 100 kilobytes in size.
14. Search the same folder for files of type **Application** that are at least 100 kilobytes in size.
15. Save the search criteria but not the results.
16. Close **Find**.
17. Use the search icon on the desktop to repeat the last search.
18. Close **Find**.
19. Delete the Search icon on the desktop.
20. Empty the **Recycle Bin**.

Challenge Exercise

1. Use **Find** to search for documents on your work disk that contain the text **print**.
2. Save the search and the results.
3. Close **Find**.
4. On your work disk, copy the document named **Printing from an Icon** to the **More Documents** folder.
5. From the desktop, open the saved search. The results of the previous search are visible in the dialog box.
6. Perform the search again. The copy of the file is found in the **More Documents** folder.
7. Close **Find**.
8. Delete the Search icon and empty the **Recycle Bin**.
9. Start **Find** from the **Explorer**.
10. Start **Find** again from the **Start** menu.
11. Close all windows (including the **Explorer**) except for the Find dialog boxes.
12. Tile the **Find** dialog boxes horizontally.
13. Make the top dialog box active.
14. Prepare a search of all devices for files created or modified in the last 3 days. Do not begin the search.
15. Switch to the bottom **Find** dialog box.
16. Begin a search of the **C:** drive for files that are at least 50 kilobytes in size. As soon as the search begins, switch to the top Find dialog box and start the search. Both Find dialog boxes will search simultaneously.
17. Allow both searches to end and close both windows.

UNIT 10

LESSON 97

Introducing Paint

In this lesson, you will learn how to start Paint and open and close an existing painting. You will also learn about the Paint window and its parts.

►SKILL PRACTICE

Paint is a program that allows you to create pictures, designs, or other graphics. Images you create in Paint can be used in other applications.

To Start Paint

1. Click the **Start** button.
2. Open the **Programs** menu and then the **Accessories** menu.
3. Click **Paint** in the Accessories menu. Paint starts, as shown in Figure 10-1.
4. If necessary, maximize the **Paint** window.

Figure 10-1 The Paint Window

5. Familiarize yourself with the parts of the Paint screen as identified in Figure 10-1.

(continued on next page)

LESSON

97

ACTIVITY

1. Briefly describe the steps required to start Paint.

2. What is the purpose of the work area in the Paint window?

3. What appears in the tool box?

4. What part of the screen allows you to choose colors while painting?

5. Where does the name of your painting appear?

***Skill Practice** (continued)*

The Paint window includes the parts you have worked with in other applications: a title bar, a menu bar, and a status bar. The name of your painting appears in the title bar. Paint also includes a work area where you will do your painting. Special parts of the window include the tool box, which is where the drawing tools are located; and the color box, which is a palette of colors from which to choose while painting.

6. Exit **Paint**.

UNIT 10

LESSON 98

Opening a Drawing

In this lesson, you will learn how to open a drawing.

SKILL PRACTICE

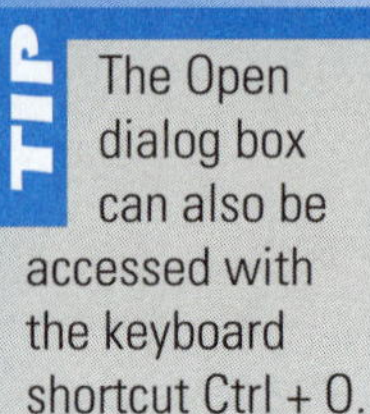

TIP The Open dialog box can also be accessed with the keyboard shortcut Ctrl + O.

NOTE Paint allows only one painting to be open at a time. Opening a painting automatically closes any document that may have been open.

To Open a Drawing

1. Start **Paint**.
2. Insert your work disk in the floppy disk drive.
3. Choose **Open** from the **File** menu. The Open dialog box appears.
4. Choose the floppy disk drive that contains your work disk from the **Look in** box.
5. Double-click the **Painting** folder on the work disk.
6. Click on the painting named **River**.
7. Click the **Open** button. The River drawing opens.
8. Leave **Paint** open for the Activity that follows.

LESSON

98

ACTIVITY

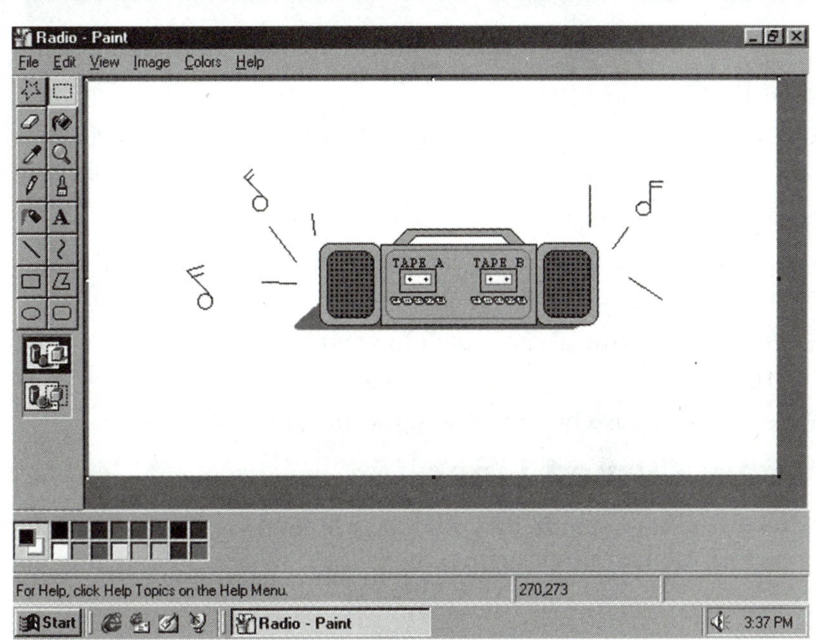

Figure 10-2 An Open Painting

1. Open the document named **Radio** from the **Painting** folder on your work disk. The River painting closes, and a graphic of a radio appears, as shown in Figure 10-2.
2. Open the **River** painting again.
3. Exit **Paint**.

UNIT 10

LESSON 99

Drawing Lines

In this lesson, you will learn how to draw straight and curved lines.

SKILL PRACTICE

TIP To draw a horizontal, vertical, or 45-degree line, hold down the Shift key while dragging the mouse. Release the mouse button before you release the Shift key.

To Draw Straight Lines

1. Start **Paint**.
2. Click the **Line** tool from the tool box. When the Line tool is selected, a choice of line widths is displayed below the tool box.
3. Choose the third of the five available line widths.
4. Position the mouse pointer near the top left corner of the work area.
5. Drag to draw a line about 1 inch long and sloping down and to the right.
6. Release the mouse button. A straight line appears.

To Draw Curved Lines

7. Click the **Curve** tool in the tool box. The line width options appear at the bottom of the tool box.
8. Choose the fourth of the five available line widths.
9. Position the mouse pointer about 1 inch below the straight line you drew in the steps above.
10. Drag a line down the screen about 2 inches and release the mouse button. A straight line appears.
11. Position the pointer on the right side of the line, as shown in Figure 10-3.

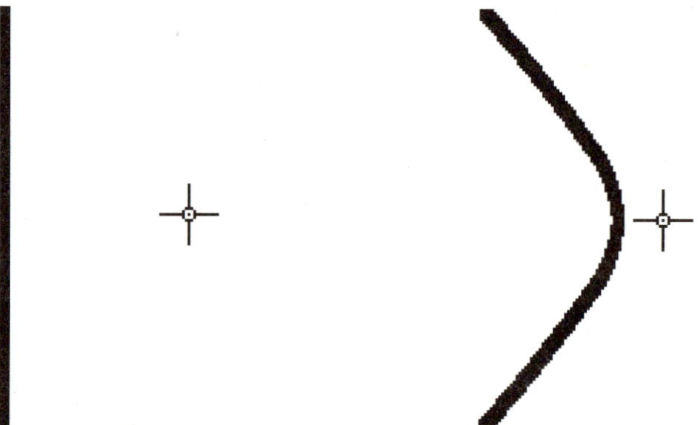

Figure 10-3 Preparing to Curve the Line

Figure 10-4 Drag to adjust the curve.

(continued on next page)

LESSON

99

ACTIVITY

1. Choose **New** from the **File** menu. Do not save changes to the current painting.
2. Practice using the **Curve** tool. Create lines that curve twice.
3. Choose **New** from the **File** menu. There is no need to save.
4. Using the **Line** tool and the **Curve** tool, attempt to duplicate the painting shown in Figure 10-5. (Hint: Use the Shift key when painting to draw the horizontal lines.)
5. Exit **Paint** without saving.

Figure 10-5 These lines were drawn with the Line and Curve tools.

***Skill Practice** (continued)*

12. Click and hold down the left mouse button. The line curves toward the pointer.
13. Continue holding down the mouse button and drag to adjust the curve.
14. When your curve looks similar to Figure 10-4, release the mouse button.
15. Without moving the pointer, click again to deactivate the tool.
16. Leave **Paint** open for the Activity that follows.

TIP You can curve a line in two directions. After making your first click to adjust the curve in one direction, click the mouse again to curve the line toward a second point. If you curve a line in two directions, the final click in step 15 is not necessary.

UNIT 10

LESSON 100

Saving and Printing a Painting

In this lesson, you will learn how to save and print your paintings.

SKILL PRACTICE

To Save a Painting

1. Start **Paint**.
2. Use the **Line** tool to draw a frame for playing tick-tack-toe.
3. Choose **Save As** from the **File** menu. The Save dialog box appears. If necessary, choose your work disk from the **Save in** box.
4. Choose **Monochrome Bitmap** from the **Save as type** box at the bottom of the dialog box, as shown in Figure 10-6.

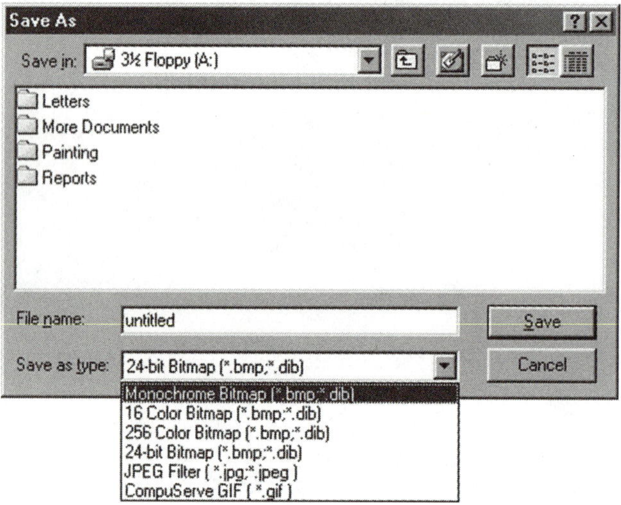

Figure 10-6 The Save Dialog Box

5. If necessary, double-click the **Painting** folder to open it.
6. Key **Tick-Tack-Toe** in the File name box.
7. Click **Save**. You may be warned that some color will be lost. If so, click Yes to continue.

To Print a Painting

Printing a painting is no different from printing any other document.

8. Choose **Print** from the **File** menu.
9. Click **OK**. The document prints.

NOTE The file types that allow for the most colors (such as the 256 color bitmap) require more disk space than those of fewer colors. When a painting is only black and white, saving as a monochrome bitmap will save a considerable amount of space.

LESSON

100

ACTIVITY

Figure 10-7 A Star Created with the Line Tool

1. Choose **New** from the **File** menu.
2. Use the **Line** tool to draw a star. (See Figure 10-7.)
3. Save the painting in the **Painting** folder on your work disk as a **monochrome bitmap** and name it **Star**.
4. Print the painting.
5. Exit **Paint**.

UNIT 10

LESSON 101

Drawing Shapes

In this lesson, you will learn how to draw shapes.

►SKILL PRACTICE

TIP To choose the width of a shape's border, click the Line tool and choose a width. The width most recently selected from the Line tool is used when drawing shapes.

To Draw a Rectangle

1. Start **Paint**.
2. Click the **Rectangle** tool.
3. Position the mouse pointer near the top left corner of the work area.
4. Drag down and to the right to draw a rectangle approximately 2 inches tall and 3 inches wide.
5. Release the button.

To Draw an Ellipse

6. Click the **Ellipse** tool.
7. Position the pointer below the rectangle.
8. Drag an ellipse about the size of an egg.
9. Release the button.

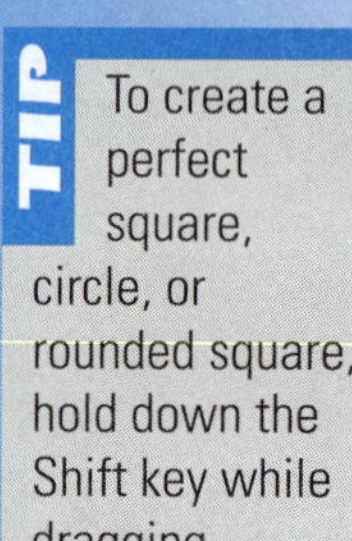

TIP To create a perfect square, circle, or rounded square, hold down the Shift key while dragging.

To Draw a Rounded Rectangle

10. Click the **Rounded Rectangle** tool.
11. Position the mouse pointer in a blank portion of the work area.
12. While holding down the **Shift** key, drag a rounded square about 1 inch in width.
13. Release the button.
14. Save the painting in the **Painting** folder on your work disk as a **monochrome bitmap** named **Shapes**.
15. Print the painting.
16. Leave **Paint** open for the Activity which follows.

LESSON

101

ACTIVITY

1. Choose **New** from the **File** menu.
2. Draw a face using only the **Ellipse** tool.
3. Draw a rectangle around the face.
4. Print the painting.
5. Exit **Paint** without saving.

UNIT 10

LESSON

102

Using Colors

In this lesson, you will learn how to use the color box when drawing.

SKILL PRACTICE

TIP

If your screen does not show the Color Box, choose Color Box from the View menu.

NOTE

There are three Rectangle Fill options. The first option is the default rectangle with no fill color. The second option creates a rectangle with a border and a fill color. The third option creates a rectangle with a fill color but no border. These same fill options are available for ellipses and rounded rectangles.

Figure 10-9 Rectangle Fill Options

The Color Box allows you to choose a foreground and background color. The foreground color is used for lines and borders of shapes. The background color is used to fill shapes.

To Choose Colors

To choose the foreground or outline color, left-click the desired color in the Color Box. The foreground color appears in the top color choice box (see Figure 10-8). To choose the background or fill color, right-click on the desired color. The background color appears in the bottom color choice box.

Figure 10-8 The Color Box

1. Start **Paint**.
2. With the left mouse button, click a **red** color in the Color Box. The foreground color is set to red.
3. With the right mouse button, click a **blue** color in the Color Box. The background color is set to blue.

To Paint with the Selected Colors

4. Select the **Line** tool.
5. Choose the widest line width.
6. Draw a line anywhere in the work area. A red line is drawn.
7. Select the **Rectangle** tool. Three Rectangle Fill options appear under the toolbox, as shown in Figure 10-9.
8. Choose the filled rectangle with border from the Rectangle Fill options.
9. Draw a rectangle anywhere in the work area. The rectangle has a red border and is filled with blue.

(continued on next page)

LESSON 102

ACTIVITY

1. Start **Paint**.
2. Draw a yellow circle with a black border.
3. Draw a green square with no border.
4. Draw a blue-bordered rounded rectangle with no fill.
5. Select a blue foreground and a red background.
6. Connect the yellow circle and the green square with a blue line.
7. Connect the green square and the blue rectangle with a red line.
8. Exit **Paint** without saving.

***Skill Practice** (continued)*

To Paint with the Colors Reversed

You can drag with the right mouse button to reverse the colors.

10. Using the right mouse button, drag another rectangle in the work area. The border and fill colors are reversed.
11. Select the **Line** tool.
12. Using the right mouse button, drag another line in the work area. The line appears in the blue background color.
13. Exit **Paint** without saving.

UNIT 10

LESSON 103

Erasing and Using Undo

In this lesson, you will learn how to erase and undo in paint.

►SKILL PRACTICE

To Erase

1. Start **Paint**.
2. Select the **Line** tool.
3. Draw a line anywhere in the work area.

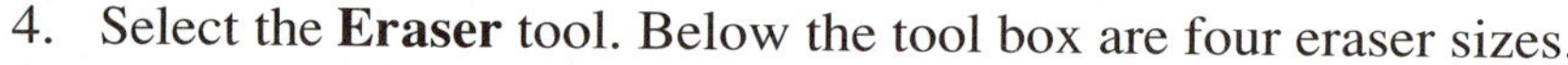

4. Select the **Eraser** tool. Below the tool box are four eraser sizes.
5. Choose the largest eraser size.
6. Drag the eraser over the line until it is completely erased.

To Undo

You can undo the three most previous operations.

7. Draw a rectangle anywhere in the work area.
8. Draw an ellipse anywhere in the work area.
9. Draw a rounded rectangle anywhere in the work area.
10. Draw a line anywhere in the work area.
11. Choose **Undo** from the **Edit** menu.
12. The line is erased.
13. Choose **Undo** from the **Edit** menu.
14. The rounded rectangle is erased.
15. Choose **Undo** from the **Edit** menu.
16. The ellipse is erased.
17. Pull down the **Edit** menu. Notice that Undo is no longer available.
18. Leave Paint open for the Activity which follows.

LESSON

103

ACTIVITY

1. Choose **New** from the **File** menu. Do not save.
2. Draw a circle.
3. Erase the circle completely. If possible, erase the entire circle by dragging the eraser only once or twice.
4. Undo the erase.
5. Exit **Paint**.

UNIT 10

LESSON 104

Using the Selection Tools

In this lesson, you will learn how to use the selection tools. These tools allow you to select rectangular areas or irregularly shaped areas.

SKILL PRACTICE

To Select an Irregularly Shaped Area

1. Start **Paint**.
2. Draw a rectangle with a light fill color about 2 inches tall and 3 inches wide.
3. Below the rectangle, draw a circle with no fill color about 1 inch in diameter.

4. Select the **Free-Form Select** tool.
5. Drag the pointer all the way around the circle, as shown in Figure 10-10. When you release the mouse button, a rectangular frame appears around the circle.
6. Position the pointer over the circle and drag it up to the rectangle. Place the circle in front of the rectangle. Notice how only the circle was selected.
7. Release the mouse button, leaving the circle in front of the rectangle.

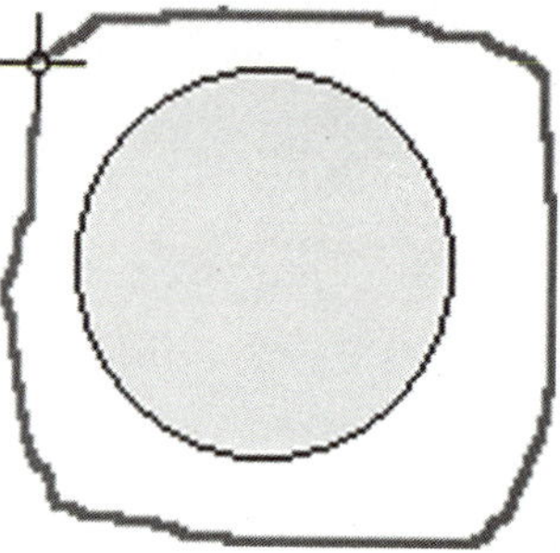

Figure 10-10 The Free-Form Select tool selects irregularly shaped areas.

(continued on next page)

LESSON

104

►ACTIVITY

1. Open the painting named **Star** from the **Painting** folder on your work disk.
2. In an area near the star, draw a rounded rectangle larger than the star with no fill.
3. Use the **Free-Form Select** tool to select the star.
4. Move the selected star over the rounded rectangle.
5. Use the **Select** tool to select the rounded rectangle and the star which appears over it.
6. Center the selected image in the work area.
7. Save the painting as **Star 2**.
8. Print the painting.
9. Exit **Paint**.

Skill Practice *(continued)*

To Select a Rectangular Area

8. Select the **Select** tool.
9. Drag a rectangle around the circle, as shown in Figure 10-11. Release the mouse button.
10. Position the pointer over the selected rectangle and drag it down about an inch. All of the painting in the rectangle moves with the selection rectangle.
11. Leave Paint open for the Activity which follows.

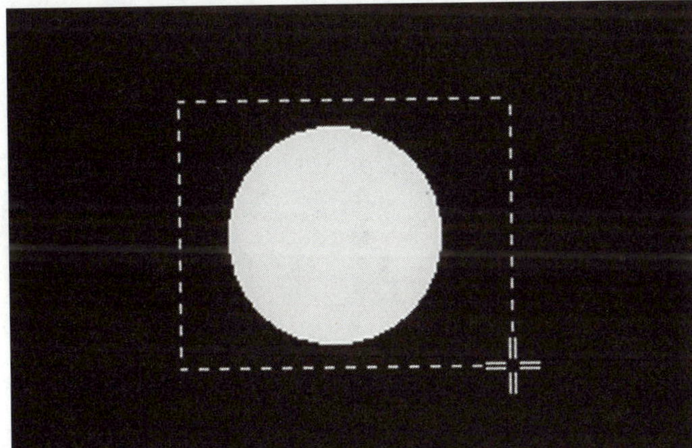

Figure 10-11 The Select tool selects rectangular areas.

UNIT 10

LESSON 105

Adding Text

In this lesson, you will learn how to add text to your paintings.

►SKILL PRACTICE

TIP You can edit the text in the text box, change font, style, and size, and resize the text box until the text box is no longer selected. At that point, the text becomes part of the painting and cannot be edited. The only way changes can be made after that point is to erase the text and use the Text tool again.

To Add Text to a Painting

1. Start **Paint**.
2. From the Color Box, choose a foreground color that appeals to you.

3. Click the **Text** button.
4. Drag a text box in the work area about $\frac{1}{2}$ inch tall and 4 inches wide. A box appears in the work area.
5. Key your name in the text box.
6. If the text toolbar, shown in Figure 10-12, does not appear, choose **Text Toolbar** from the **View** menu.

Figure 10-12 Text Toolbar

7. From the Text toolbar, choose a font that appeals to you.
8. Choose the largest font size that allows your name to fit within the bounds of the box.
9. Leave Paint open for the Activity that follows.

LESSON

105

▶ACTIVITY

1. Choose **New** from the **File** menu. Do not save changes to the current painting.
2. Draw a large red rectangle in the work area.
3. Add the text *Windows 98* over the red rectangle in a dark color or black. Make the text large and bold but keep it within the bounds of the red rectangle.
4. Print the painting.
5. Exit **Paint** without saving.

UNIT 10

LESSON 106

Using Paintings in Other Applications

In this lesson, you will learn how to use paintings in other applications.

SKILL PRACTICE

To Copy a Painting

1. Open the painting named **Radio** from the **Painting** folder on your work disk.
2. Use the **Select** tool to select the radio and the sounds that surround it.
3. Choose **Copy** from the **Edit** menu.

To Paste the Painting into Another Application

4. Start **WordPad**.
5. Choose **Paste** from the **Edit** menu. The painting appears in the document, as shown in Figure 10-13.
6. Exit **WordPad** without saving.
7. Leave Paint open for the Activity that follows.

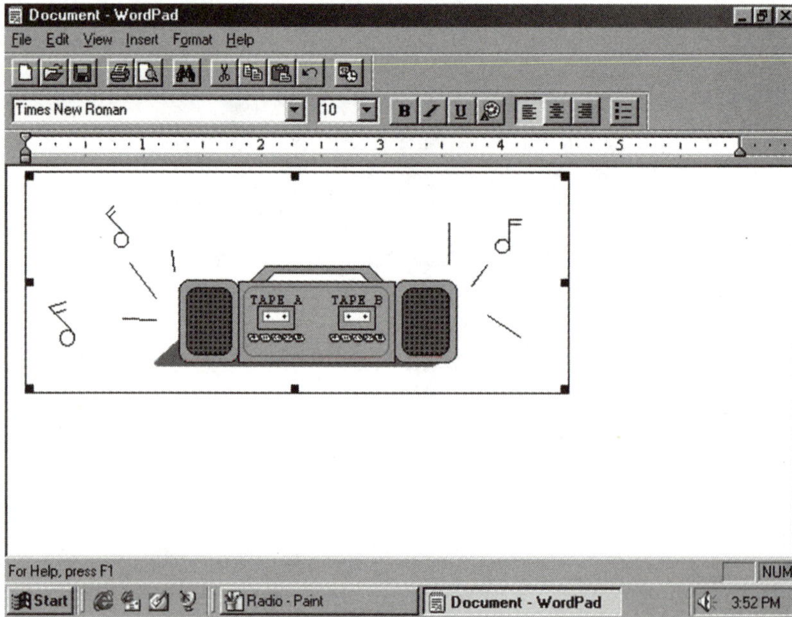

Figure 10-13 Paintings can be copied to other applications.

LESSON

106

ACTIVITY

Figure 10-14 This logo can be copied to WordPad or another application.

1. Choose **New** from the **File** menu. Do not save changes.
2. Create a logo similar to the one in Figure 10-14.
3. Select and copy the logo.
4. Start **WordPad**.
5. Press **Enter** several times to create at least four blank lines.
6. Place the cursor at the top of the document.
7. Paste the logo.
8. Click the **Center** button to center the logo on the line.
9. Save the document on your work disk as **Logo Header**.
10. Print the document.
11. Exit **WordPad**.
12. Exit **Paint**.

UNIT 10

LESSON 107

Capturing Screens and Windows

In this lesson, you will learn how to capture the contents of the screen or a window for use in a document.

SKILL PRACTICE

To Capture the Screen

1. Open the **My Computer** window and move it near the center of the screen. Size it to appear similar to Figure 10-15. Close any other open windows.

Figure 10-15 The Print Screen key will capture the entire screen image.

2. Press the **Print Screen** key. A graphic of the current screen is copied to the Clipboard.
3. Start **Paint** from the **Accessories** menu.
4. Choose **Paste** from the **Edit** menu. The picture of the screen appears in the Paint document.
5. Choose **Print** from the **File** menu. The Print dialog box appears.
6. Click **OK**. The captured screen prints.
7. **Minimize** Paint.

(continued on next page)

LESSON
107

►ACTIVITY

1. Start **WordPad** and maximize it.
2. Capture the screen to the clipboard.
3. Start **Paint**.
4. Paste the captured screen into a Paint document.
5. Print the Paint document.
6. Minimize **Paint**.
7. In WordPad, choose **Paragraph** from the **Format** menu.
8. Capture the window.
9. Click **Cancel** to close the dialog box.
10. Position the cursor at the end of the document and press **Enter**.
11. Choose **Paste** from the **Edit** menu. The image of the Paragraph dialog box appears.
12. Choose **Exit** from the **File** menu. You will be asked if you want to save changes.
13. Click **Yes**. The document saves.
14. Click the **Paint** button on the taskbar.
15. Choose **New** from the **File** menu. Do not save the current document.
16. Choose **Paste** from the **Edit** menu. The image of the Paragraph dialog box appears in the new document.
17. Print the document and exit **Paint** without saving.

***Skill Practice** (continued)*

To Capture a Window

8. Make the **My Computer** window active.
9. Press **Alt + Print Screen**. A graphic of the My Computer window is copied to the Clipboard.
10. Click the **Paint** button on the taskbar.
11. Choose **New** from the **File** menu. You will be asked if you want to save the current document.
12. Click **No**.
13. Choose **Paste** from the **Edit** menu. The picture of the My Computer window appears in the Paint document.
14. Choose **Print** from the **File** menu. The Print dialog box appears.
15. Click **OK**. The captured window prints.
16. Exit **Paint** without saving and close the My Computer window.

UNIT 10

Reinforcement Exercise

1. Start **Paint**.
2. Open the painting named **Star 2** from the **Painting** folder on your work disk.
3. Create a new painting.
4. Use the **Line** tool and **Ellipse** tool to draw a stick figure.
5. Use the **Curve** tool to draw a small mound for the stick figure to stand on.
6. Save the painting as a **16 Color Bitmap**. Name the painting **Stick Person**.
7. Draw a square about 1 inch across below the mound.
8. Draw a rounded rectangle next to the stick figure. Make the shape as tall as the stick figure.
9. Use the **Eraser** tool to erase the square.
10. Use **Undo** to bring back the square.
11. Use the **Eraser** tool to erase the square again.
12. Use the **Text** tool to add your name to the painting.
13. Save the painting again.
14. Print the painting.
15. Exit **Paint**.

Challenge Exercise

1. Use **Paint** to design a letterhead. Use the **Text** tool to put your name, address, and telephone number on the letterhead. Use any graphics you want to use in the design.
2. Copy the letterhead to a **WordPad** document.
3. Capture the screen showing the letterhead in the WordPad document.
4. Paste the captured screen into Paint and print it.
5. Save the **WordPad** document as **My Letterhead**.
6. Print the document.
7. Close **WordPad** and **Paint**.

UNIT 11

LESSON 108

Using the Calculator

In this lesson, you will learn to use the Calculator.

SKILL PRACTICE

TIP You may have to press the Num Lock key to allow numbers to be entered from the keypad.

NOTE You can also enter numbers and choose keys on the calculator by clicking the buttons with the mouse.

NOTE You may choose between a standard calculator or a scientific calculator using the View menu.

To Use the Calculator

1. Start the **Calculator** from the **Accessories** menu. The Calculator appears, as shown in Figure 11-1.
2. Using the numeric keypad, key **725**.
3. Press the + key on the numeric key pad.
4. Now key **423**.
5. Press **Enter**. The answer is displayed.

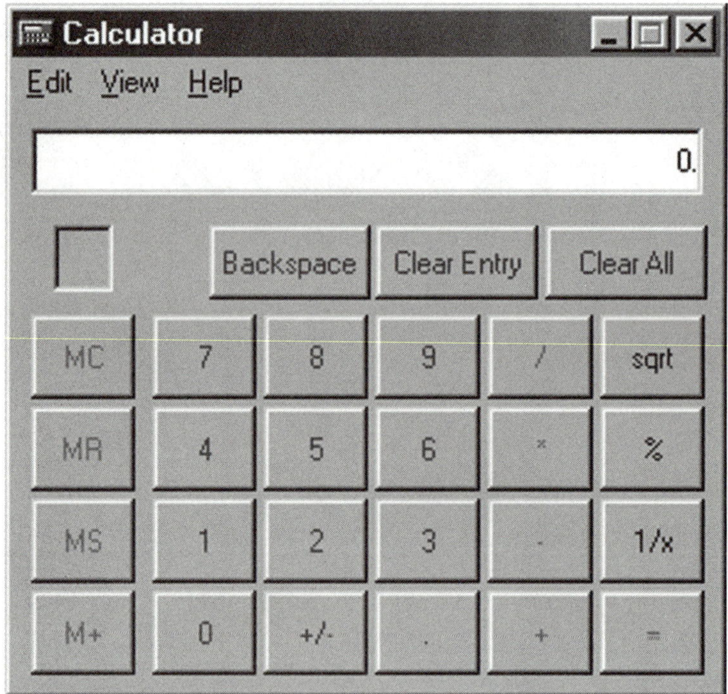

Figure 11-1 The Calculator

(continued on next page)

LESSON

108

ACTIVITY

1. Start the **Calculator**.
2. Use the **Calculator** to solve the following problems:

   693 + 354 =

   5629 * 437 =

   6108 / 16 + 1.25 =

   56309 * 6 =

   4195835 / 3145727 * 3145727 - 4195835 =
3. Close the **Calculator**.

Skill Practice *(continued)*

The table below presents a summary of the functions of the standard calculator.

Function	Keyboard Equivalent	Description
MS	Ctrl+M	Save current value in memory
MR	Ctrl+R	Recall value from memory
M+	Ctrl+P	Add current value to the value in memory
MC	Ctrl+L	Clear memory
sqrt	@	Calculates the square root of the current value
%	%	Displays the result of multiplication as a percentage
1/X	R	Calculates the reciprocal of the current value
BACKSPACE	Backspace	Clear the last keystroke when entering values
CLEAR ENTRY	Delete	Clear the last entry
CLEAR ALL	Esc	Clear all

Table 11-1

6. Close the **Calculator**.

UNIT 11

LESSON

109

Using the Notepad

In this lesson, you will learn to use the Notepad. The Notepad is a simple text editor that has almost none of the features of a word processor.

SKILL PRACTICE

NOTE The Notepad works with files that contain text only. No special formatting or fonts are available in Notepad. WordPad should be used for documents that require these features.

To Start the Notepad

1. Start **Notepad** from the **Accessories** menu.

To Open a Text File

2. Choose **Open** from the **File** menu.
3. Open the document named **Printing from an Icon** from your work disk. The text document appears.

To Create a New File

4. Choose **New** from the **File** menu. The Notepad is cleared.
5. Make sure the Word Wrap option is checked in the Edit menu. If not, choose **Word Wrap** from the **Edit** menu. The Word Wrap feature causes text to wrap within the boundaries of the window.
6. Enter the following text into the Notepad:

   Notepad is ideal for making lists or quick notes. Because Notepad starts quickly and uses less memory than a word processor, it works well for simple text that you access often, such as a "things to do" list. Notepad is also good for editing existing text files.

To Save and Exit Notepad

7. Choose **Save As** from the **File** menu. Save the file on your work disk as **About Notepad**.
8. Choose **Exit** from the **File** menu. Notepad closes.

LESSON

109

►ACTIVITY

1. Start **Notepad**.
2. Open the file you saved in the Skill Practice (**About Notepad**).
3. Add the following paragraph to the file:

   Notepad can also be used to prepare text to be e-mailed or distributed to others. Because Notepad saves files as simple text files, the files can be read by others no matter what word processor or text editor they use.
4. Save and print the file.
5. Exit **Notepad**.

LESSON 110

Playing a Music CD

In this lesson, you will learn to play a music CD using the Windows 98 CD Player. If your computer system does not have a CD-ROM capable of playing music CDs, you will not be able to complete this lesson.

SKILL PRACTICE

NOTE: This lesson requires that you have a CD-ROM and an audio or music CD.

To Start the CD Player

1. Click the **Start** button and access the **Accessories** menu.
2. Click **Entertainment** in the **Accessories** menu. The Entertainment menu appears.
3. Choose **CD Player** from the **Entertainment** menu. The CD Player appears, as shown in Figure 11-2.

Figure 11-2 CD Player

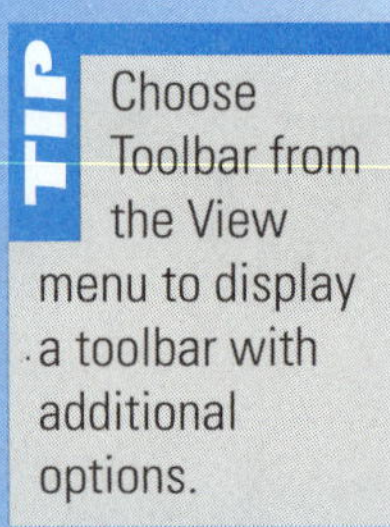
TIP: Choose Toolbar from the View menu to display a toolbar with additional options.

To Play a Music CD

4. Insert the music CD into the CD-ROM drive.
5. Click the **Play** button. The CD begins to play.
6. Click the **Pause** button. The music pauses.
7. Click the **Pause** button again. The music resumes.
8. Click the **Stop** button. The music stops.
9. Choose **Exit** from the **Disc** menu. The CD Player closes.

LESSON

110

ACTIVITY

Button	Description
	Allows you to enter the artist and title of the CD and choose which tracks to play
	Causes the time elapsed in the current song to be displayed
	Causes the time remaining in the current song to be displayed
	Causes the time remaining on the entire CD to be displayed
	Causes songs to be played in random order
	Causes the first song to repeat when end of CD is reached
	Causes only the first few seconds of each song to be played
	Moves to the previous song. If a song is playing, the button causes the song to begin at the beginning
	Moves backward in the current song
	Moves forward in the current song
	Moves to the next song
	Ejects the CD

Table 11-2 describes the purpose of the other buttons on the CD Player.

1. Start the **CD Player**.
2. If necessary, insert a music CD.
3. Start playing with the third song.
4. Stop the CD from playing.
5. Exit the **CD Player**.

Using the Media Player

In this lesson, you will learn how to use the Media Player.

SKILL PRACTICE

To Start the Media Player

1. Click the **Start** button and access the **Accessories** menu.
2. Click **Entertainment** in the **Accessories** menu. The Entertainment menu appears.
3. Choose **Media Player** from the **Entertainment** menu. The Media Player appears (see Figure 11-3).

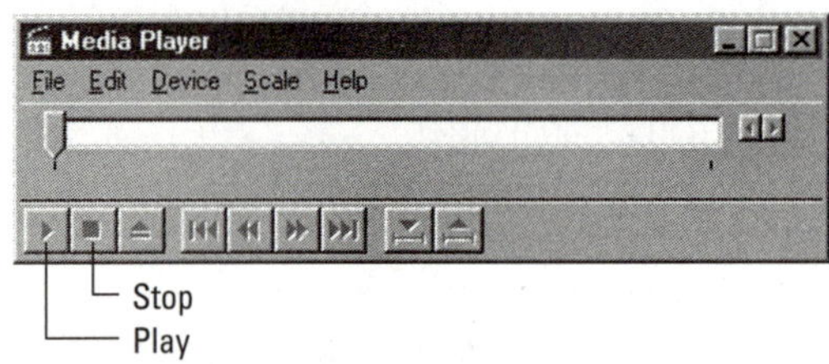

Figure 11-3 The Media Player

To Play a Sound

4. Choose **Open** from the **File** menu. The Open dialog box appears.
5. If necessary, change to the **Media** folder in the **Windows** folder of the **C:** drive.
6. Select **The Microsoft Sound** and click **Open**.
7. Click the **Play** button (see Figure 11-3). The sound plays.
8. Exit the Media Player.

To Play a Video Clip

9. Copy the file named **Win98** from your work disk to the desktop.
10. Start the Media Player.
11. Choose **Open** from the **File** menu. The Open dialog box appears.
12. Choose **Desktop** from the **Look in** box.
13. Choose **Video for Windows (*.avi)** from the **File of type:** box.

(continued on next page)

NOTE This lesson asks you to copy the video clip to the desktop because playing a video clip from floppy disk can result in delays in the presentation.

LESSON
111

►ACTIVITY

1. Start the **Media Player**.
2. Open **The Microsoft Sound** and play it.
3. Open the **Win98** video clip and play it.
4. Close the **Media Player**.
5. Leave the **Win98** file on the desktop for Lesson 114.

Skill Practice *(continued)*

14. Select the file named **Win98** and click **Open**. A window appears, displaying the first frame of the video clip (see Figure 11-4).

Figure 11-4 Video Clip

15. Choose **Options** from the **Edit** menu.
16. If not already selected, select the **Auto Repeat** option.
17. Click **OK**.
18. Click the **Play** button. The video clip plays. Because you set the option to auto repeat, the clip plays continuously.
19. Click the **Stop** button. The video clip stops.
20. Choose **Exit** from the **File** menu. The Media Player closes.

UNIT 11

LESSON 112

Recording Sounds

In this lesson, you will learn how to record sounds using the Sound Recorder. If your computer does not have a sound card that supports sound recording and a microphone, you will not be able to complete this lesson.

SKILL PRACTICE

To Start the Sound Recorder

1. Click the **Start** button and access the **Accessories** menu.
2. Click **Entertainment** in the **Accessories** menu. The Entertainment menu appears.
3. Choose **Sound Recorder** from the **Entertainment** menu. The Sound Recorder appears (see Figure 11-5).

Figure 11-5 The Sound Recorder

To Record a Sound

4. Click the **Record** button.
5. Speak into the microphone for about 3 seconds.
6. When you are finished speaking, click the **Stop** button.

To Play a Sound

7. Click the **Play** button. The sound you just recorded plays.
8. Choose **Exit** from the **File** menu. There is no need to save. The Sound Recorder closes.

LESSON

112

ACTIVITY

1. Start the **Sound Recorder**.
2. Record your name.
3. Choose **Save As** from the **File** menu.
4. Save the sound on your work disk as **My Sound**. If you do not have room on your work disk, save to your hard disk.
5. Play the sound.
6. Exit the **Sound Recorder**.

UNIT 11

LESSON 113

Using the Run Command

In this lesson, you will learn how to run programs using the Run command.

SKILL PRACTICE

NOTE The Run command is similar to the MS-DOS command line. Windows 98 will search the current directory and other directories (called the *path*) specified at startup for the filename you key. If the file cannot be found, you must key the entire path and filename or use the browse feature to locate the file. If your entry in the Run dialog box includes a long filename, you must enclose the entire entry in quotation marks ("").

To Use the Run Command

You can use the Run command to start a program that is not on the Start menu, to start an installation program on a floppy disk, or to browse storage devices for a program.

1. Click the **Start** button.
2. Choose **Run** from the **Start** menu. The Run dialog box appears, as shown in Figure 11-6.

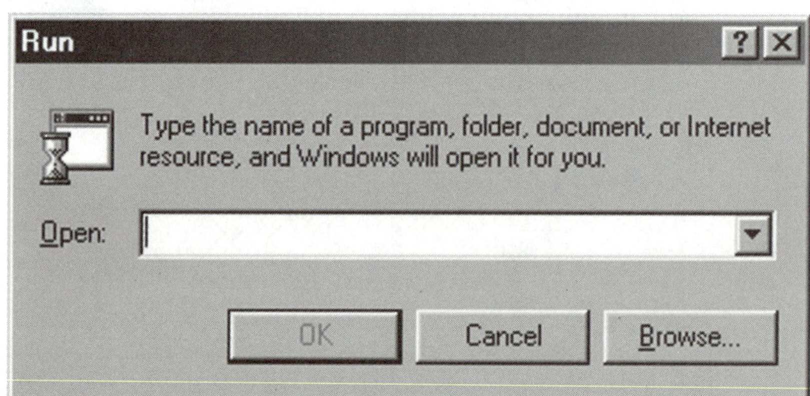

Figure 11-6 The Run Dialog Box

3. Key **Explorer** in the **Open** box and click **OK**. The Explorer starts.
4. Close the **Explorer**.

To Browse for a Program

5. Click the **Start** button.
6. Choose **Run** from the **Start** menu.
7. Click **Browse**. The Browse dialog box appears.
8. Open the **Windows** folder on the **C:** drive.
9. Select **Calc** and click **Open**. The path and filename of the Calculator appear in the Run dialog box.
10. Click **OK**. The Calculator starts.
11. Close the **Calculator**.

(continued on next page)

GLOSSARY TERMS

PATH • the drive letter and directories that lead to a particular file

LESSON
113

ACTIVITY

1. Use the **Run** command to run the **Notepad**.
2. Exit **Notepad**.
3. Access the **Run** dialog box.
4. Click the arrow at the end of the **Open** box.
5. Run the **Calculator**.
6. Exit the **Calculator**.

Skill Practice *(continued)*

To Run a Recently Run Program

12. Access the **Run** dialog box.
13. Click the arrow at the end of the **Open** box. A list of recently run programs appears.
14. Choose **Explorer** and click **OK**.
15. Close the **Explorer**.

UNIT 11

LESSON

114

Startup Applications

In this lesson, you will learn to make an application run at startup. This feature is useful when you have an application that you want to begin running as soon as your computer starts.

SKILL PRACTICE

To Make a Startup Program

To make a program start automatically when Windows 98 is loaded, put the application or a shortcut to the application in the StartUp folder. You can also put a document or shortcut to a document in the StartUp folder, and the document will be opened on startup.

This lesson assumes the Win98 video clip is still on the desktop.

1. Right-click the **Win98** video clip that appears on the desktop.
2. Choose **Cut** from the shortcut menu.
3. Right-click the **Start** button and choose **Open** from the shortcut menu. The Start Menu folder opens.
4. Open the **Programs** folder.
5. Open the **StartUp** folder.
6. Choose **Paste** from the **Edit** menu in the StartUp folder menu bar. The Win98 video clip is copied into the StartUp folder.
7. Close all open windows.
8. Choose **Shut Down** from the **Start** menu.
9. Choose **Restart** and click **OK**. The computer restarts. When Windows reloads, the video clip automatically begins playing.
10. If necessary, close the video clip.

LESSON

114

ACTIVITY

1. Open the **Startup** folder.
2. Delete the **Win98** video clip from the **StartUp** folder.
3. Leave the **StartUp** folder open and open the **Windows** folder.
4. Create a shortcut to the **Calculator**.
5. Move the **Calculator** shortcut to the **StartUp** folder.
6. Restart the computer. The **Calculator** starts automatically after Windows 98 reloads.
7. Delete the **Calculator** shortcut from the **StartUp** folder.
8. Restart the computer.

Using the Disk Defragmenter

In this lesson, you will learn how to use the disk defragmenter. The disk defragmenter reorganizes the data on a disk and puts together any files that are stored on the disk in fragments rather than in one piece.

SKILL PRACTICE

For this lesson, you will need the floppy disk used in the previous two lessons.

To Defragment a Disk

1. Use the Copy Disk command to copy your work disk to a blank floppy disk.
2. Safely store your original work disk and use the copy for the steps which follow.
3. Open the floppy disk window.
4. Delete the **More Documents** folder and the **Reports** folder from the floppy disk.
5. Click the **Start** button. Click **Programs**, then **Accessories** and then **System Tools**.
6. Choose **Disk Defragmenter** from the **System Tools** menu. The Defragmenter starts. The first window prompts you for the storage device you want to defragment.
7. Choose the drive that holds your floppy disk and click **OK**. You may get a message indicating that the disk does not need to be defragmented. If you get that message, click **Start** to start the defragmenter anyway. The defragmenter begins working.
8. Click **Show Details**. The screen expands to show a map of the contents of your drive. Your screen should appear similar to Figure 13-4.
9. While the defragmenter works, click the **Legend** button to display a window that explains the map on your screen.
10. Click **Close** to close the Legend.
11. When the defragmenter is complete, you will be asked if you wish to quit. Click **Yes**. The Disk Defragmenter quits.

NOTE The deletion of these folders leaves blank areas in the data on the floppy disk. The Disk Defragmenter will consolidate the free space on the disk.

LESSON

115

►ACTIVITY

1. Start the **Disk Defragmenter**.
2. Use the Disk Defragmenter to defragment and optimize the free space on your work disk.
3. Quit the **Disk Defragmenter**.

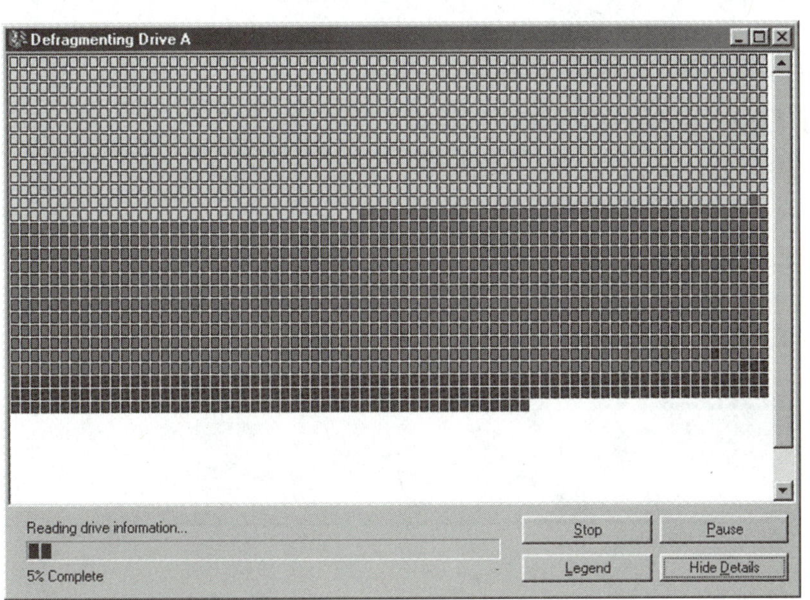

Figure 11-7 Defragmenting

UNIT 11

LESSON 116

Using ScanDisk

In this lesson, you will learn how to use ScanDisk to check disks for problems.

SKILL PRACTICE

For this lesson, you will need the floppy disk used in the Skill Practice of the previous lesson.

To Use ScanDisk

1. Insert the disk you used in the Skill Practice of the previous lesson.
2. Click the **Start** button. Click **Programs**, then **Accessories**, and then **System Tools**.
3. Choose **ScanDisk** from the **System Tools** menu. ScanDisk starts, as shown in Figure 11-8.

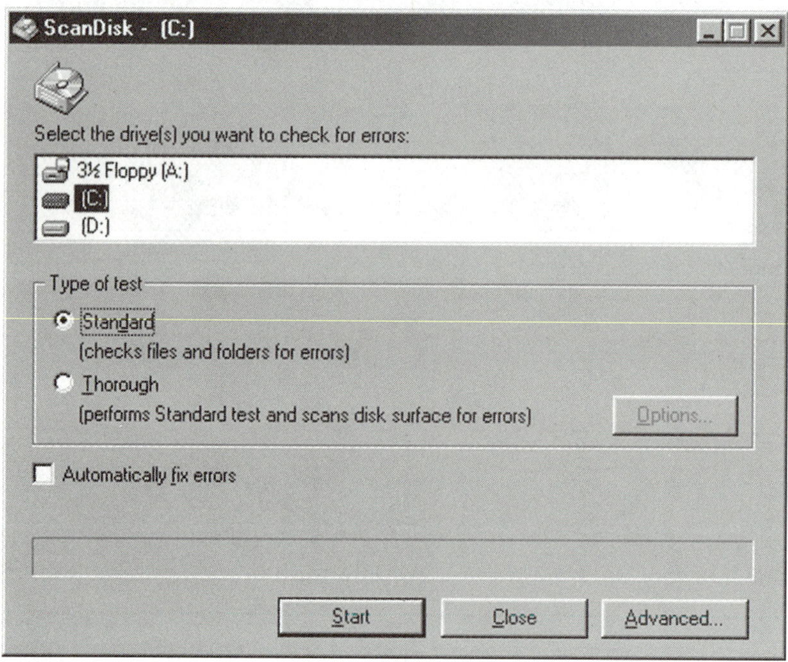

Figure 11-8 ScanDisk

NOTE If errors are found during a scan, you will be asked if you want to repair the problems. If you select the Automatically fix errors check box, errors will be fixed without prompting you for instructions.

4. From the list of storage devices at the top of the ScanDisk window, select the floppy drive that holds the disk you used in the previous lesson. You may have to scroll the list up to see the appropriate drive.

(continued on next page)

LESSON

116

▶ACTIVITY

1. Start **ScanDisk**.
2. Perform a standard scan on the **C:** drive. If problems are reported, consult your instructor.
3. Use **Alt** + **Print Screen** to capture the window that provides the results of the scan.
4. Close **ScanDisk**.
5. Start **Paint**.
6. Paste the captured window into Paint and print it.
7. Exit **Paint**.

***Skill Practice** (continued)*

5. If necessary, click the **Standard** scan option.
6. Click **Start**. ScanDisk begins analyzing the floppy disk. After a few moments, a window will appear summarizing the findings of the scan.
7. Click **Close**.
8. Click **Close** to close ScanDisk.

UNIT 11

LESSON 117

Checking the Properties of a Storage Device

In this lesson, you will learn how to check the properties of a storage device.

SKILL PRACTICE

To Check the Properties of a Storage Device

1. Open the **My Computer** window.
2. Right-click the icon that represents your **C:** drive. A shortcut menu appears.
3. Choose **Properties** from the shortcut menu. The properties for the C: drive appear, as shown in Figure 11-9. The pie graph shows the amount of space used and free on the disk.

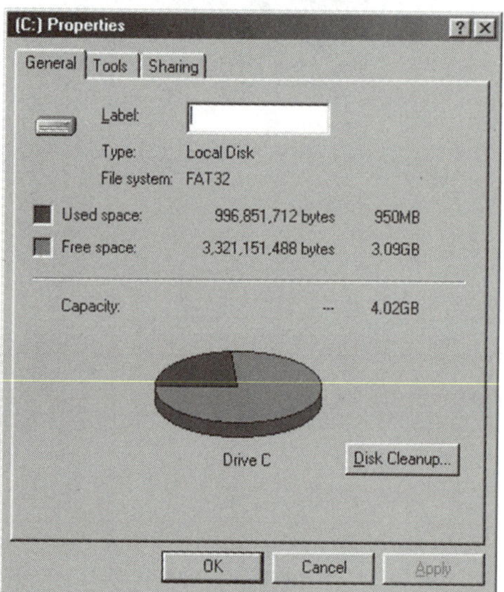

Figure 11-9 Disk Properties

4. Click the **Tools** tab at the top of the dialog box. The Tools section reminds you of how long it has been since you ran ScanDisk, backed up, or defragmented the disk. You can launch each of these system maintenance tools from this dialog box.
5. Click **Cancel** to close the dialog box.

LESSON

117

ACTIVITY

1. Look at the properties of other devices available on your system.
2. If necessary, insert a floppy disk and check its properties.
3. Close all open windows.

UNIT 11

LESSON 118

Running MS-DOS Programs

In this lesson, you will learn how to run MS-DOS programs from Windows 98.

►SKILL PRACTICE

To Run an MS-DOS Program from My Computer or the Explorer

1. Open the **My Computer** window.
2. If necessary, insert your work disk into the floppy disk drive.
3. Display the contents of your work disk.
4. Double-click the MS-DOS program on your work disk called **Mileage**. A window appears, and the program begins to run, as shown in Figure 11-10.

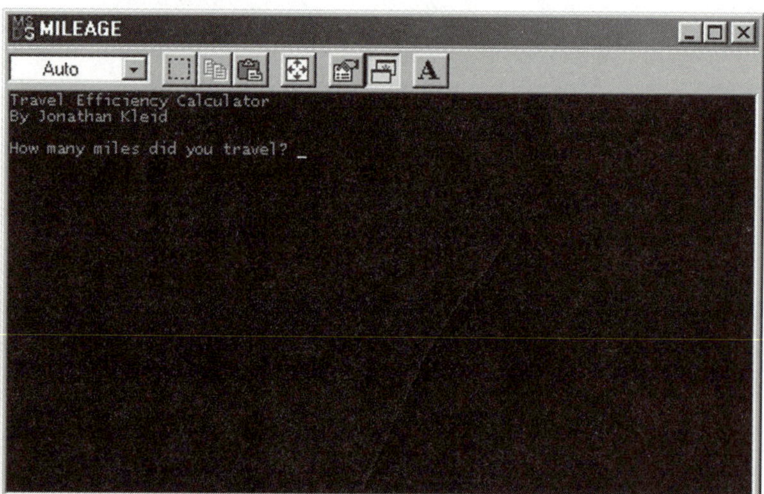

Figure 11-10 An MS-DOS Window

5. Key **100** when prompted for miles and then press **Enter**.
6. Key **4.34** when prompted for the number of gallons used. Press **Enter**.
7. Enter the most recent gas price you have seen. The results of the analysis will appear. Notice the title bar now indicates that the program is finished.
8. Click the close button to close the window.

(continued on next page)

LESSON
118

ACTIVITY

1. Run the MS-DOS program on your work disk called **Temperature Converter** by double-clicking its icon.
2. Enter a temperature in Celsius, and the program returns the temperature in Fahrenheit degrees.
3. Close the program window.

Skill Practice *(continued)*

To Run a Program from the MS-DOS Prompt

9. Click the **Start** button.
10. Choose **MS-DOS Prompt** from the **Programs** menu. A DOS prompt appears.
11. Key either **A:\mileage** or **B:\mileage** (depending on the drive that holds your work disk) and press **Enter**. The Mileage program runs.
12. Enter realistic values when prompted. When the program finishes, you will again see a DOS prompt.
13. Key **exit** and press **Enter**. The window closes.
14. Close all open windows.

UNIT 11

LESSON 119

Copying Between MS-DOS and Windows Programs

In this lesson, you will learn how to run copy text from an MS-DOS program to a Windows 98 program.

SKILL PRACTICE

To Copy Between MS-DOS and Windows

1. Open the **My Computer** window.
2. If necessary, insert your work disk into the floppy disk drive.
3. Display the contents of your work disk.
4. Double-click the MS-DOS program on your work disk called **Mileage**. A window appears, and the program begins to run.
5. Enter realistic values in response to the questions asked by the program. When the program finishes, do not close the window.
6. Click the **Mark** button (see Figure 11-11). A blinking block cursor appears in the upper-left corner of the window.

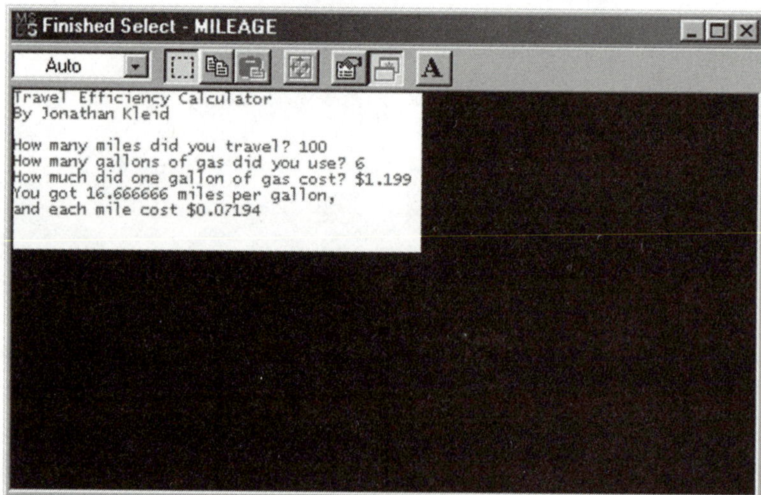

Figure 11-11 The Mark button allows you to copy text from a DOS window.

7. Drag the mouse from the blinking cursor to highlight the entire text in the window.
8. Click the **Copy** button.
9. Close the **Mileage** program window.
10. Start **WordPad**.
11. When WordPad's blank document appears, paste the text into the document.
12. Save the document on your work disk as **DOS Text**, print, and close.

LESSON
119

ACTIVITY

1. Choose **MS-DOS Prompt** from the **Programs** menu.
2. Key **DIR** at the MS-DOS prompt and press **Enter**.
3. Click the **Mark** button and copy the entire window of text.
4. Key **exit** and press **Enter**.
5. Start **Notepad**.
6. Paste the text into Notepad.
7. Save the document on your work disk as **DOS Directory**.
8. Print and close the **Notepad**.

UNIT 12

LESSON 120

Introduction to the Control Panel

In this lesson, you will learn how to access the Control Panel. You will also learn about the kinds of things the Control Panel controls.

►SKILL PRACTICE

TIP The Control Panel can also be accessed from the Explorer. It is found on the same level as your storage devices.

About the Control Panel

The Control Panel is a window that contains tools that allow you to control many features of Windows. Items in the Control Panel allow you to connect to hardware added to your system, add and remove Windows components, set display options, and more. The contents of the Control Panel will vary, depending on the kind of system you have and what programs you have installed.

To Access the Control Panel

You can access the Control Panel from the Settings menu on the Start menu or from the My Computer window.

1. Click the **Start** button.
2. Access the **Settings** menu.
3. Choose **Control Panel** from the **Settings** menu. The Control Panel appears similar to Figure 12-1.

TIP The Control Panel can also be accessed by keying the words "Control Panel" in the address bar of the My Computer window.

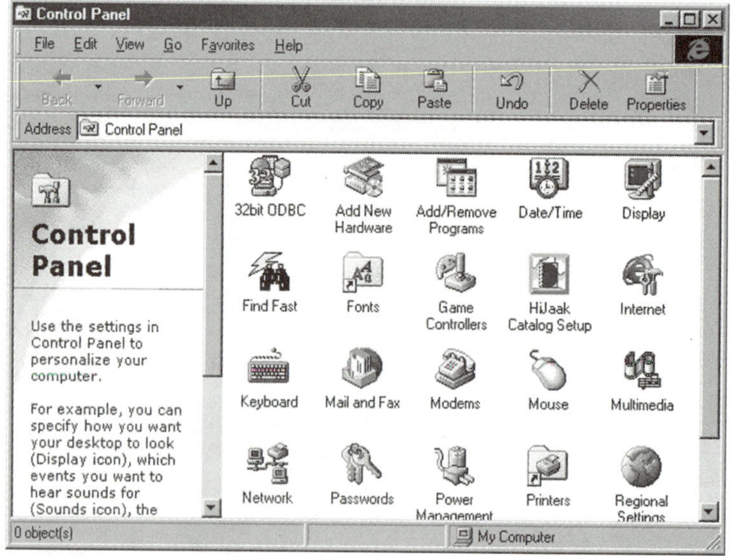

Figure 12-1 The Control Panel

4. Close the **Control Panel**.

(continued on next page)

LESSON

120

ACTIVITY

1. Open the **Control Panel** from the **Start** menu.
2. Close the **Control Panel**.
3. Start the **Explorer** from the **Start** menu.
4. Scroll the left pane to find the **Control Panel** folder. If the My Computer icon is collapsed, you must expand it to make the Control Panel visible.
5. Click the **Control Panel** folder in the left pane. The Control Panel tools appear in the right pane.
6. Close the **Explorer**.

Skill Practice *(continued)*

5. Open the **My Computer** window. The Control Panel is accessible alongside your storage devices, as shown in Figure 12-2.

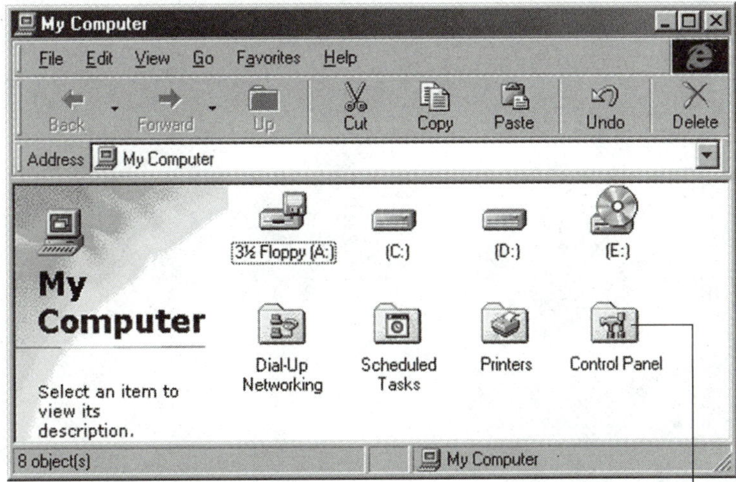

Figure 12-2 The Control Panel can be accessed from the My Computer window.

6. Double-click the **Control Panel** folder. The Control Panel appears.
7. Close the **Control Panel**.
8. Close the **My Computer** window.

UNIT 12

LESSON

121

Using the Hardware Wizard

In this lesson, you will learn about the Hardware Wizard.

►SKILL PRACTICE

TIP You can use the Hardware Wizard to help you properly install devices. You can choose to manually select the new device even if the device is not yet installed. The Hardware Wizard will present you with recommended settings for the new device. You can use the recommended settings to configure the hardware you are installing and then run the Hardware Wizard again after the new hardware is installed.

Figure 12-3 The Add New Hardware Tool

About the Hardware Wizard

The Hardware Wizard is a tool that communicates with your system's hardware to identify any hardware that has been added since Windows was installed. Use the Hardware Wizard after you add new devices to ensure that Windows has properly recognized the changes.

To Run the Hardware Wizard

1. Click the **Start** button.
2. Access the **Settings** menu.
3. Choose **Control Panel** from the **Settings** menu. The Control Panel appears.
4. Double-click the **Add New Hardware** icon (see Figure 12-3). The Hardware Wizard appears, as shown in Figure 12-4.

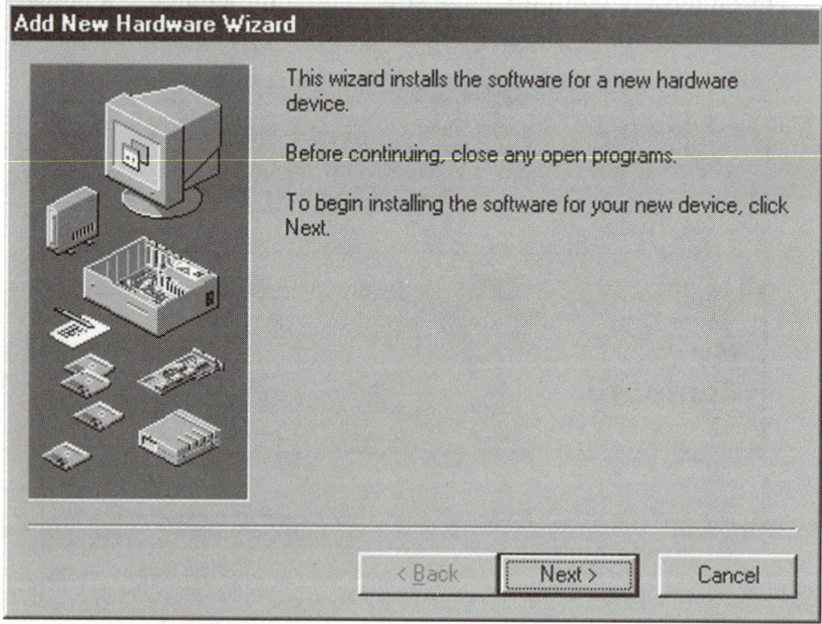

Figure 12-4 The Hardware Wizard

(continued on next page)

LESSON
121

▶ACTIVITY

Prepare a report outlining the hardware installed on your system. Include any specifications that you can determine. End the report with possibilities for upgrade of your system.

***Skill Practice** (continued)*

The Hardware Wizard leads you through a series of screens that detect your hardware and asks you for any necessary information. The detection process is lengthy and can occasionally cause the computer to become unresponsive. For these reasons, we will not continue with the Hardware Wizard in this lesson.

5. Click **Cancel**.
6. Close the **Control Panel**.

UNIT 12

LESSON 122

Adding and Removing Programs and Windows Components

In this lesson, you will learn how to add and remove programs and windows components using the Add/Remove Programs tool in the Control Panel.

SKILL PRACTICE

TIP If you need to remove a program from your system, use the Add/Remove Programs tool when possible to remove all the files installed with the program. Deleting the folder that holds a program often does not properly uninstall the software. Some programs do not have an uninstall option. For those programs, you must delete the files manually.

To Add or Remove Programs

1. Open the **Control Panel**.
2. Double-click **Add/Remove Programs**. The Add/Remove Programs Properties dialog box appears, as shown in Figure 12-5.

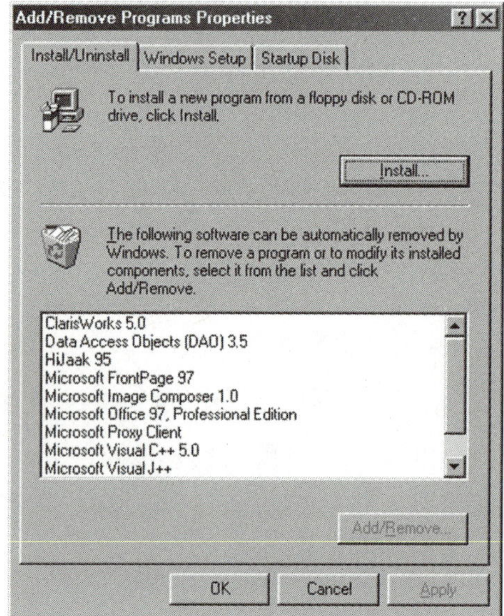

Figure 12-5 Install/Uninstall Programs

The Install button near the top right corner of the dialog box allows you to install new software from a floppy disk or CD-ROM. It will search the available floppy drives and CD-ROM drive for software to be installed. If none is found, a command prompt will appear to allow you to specify the path to the software or browse for it. The bottom portion of the dialog box lists software that can be uninstalled from the Control Panel.

To Add or Remove Windows Components

3. Click the **Windows Setup** tab of the dialog box. The dialog box appears similar to Figure 12-6.

(continued on next page)

LESSON

122

1. Open the **Control Panel**.
2. Double-click **Add/Remove Programs**.
3. If it is not already selected, click the **Windows Setup** tab of the dialog box.
4. Click the **Accessories** component to select it.
5. Click the **Details** button. Make a list of the **Accessories** components that are not currently installed on your system.
6. Click **Cancel** twice and close the **Control Panel**.

Skill Practice *(continued)*

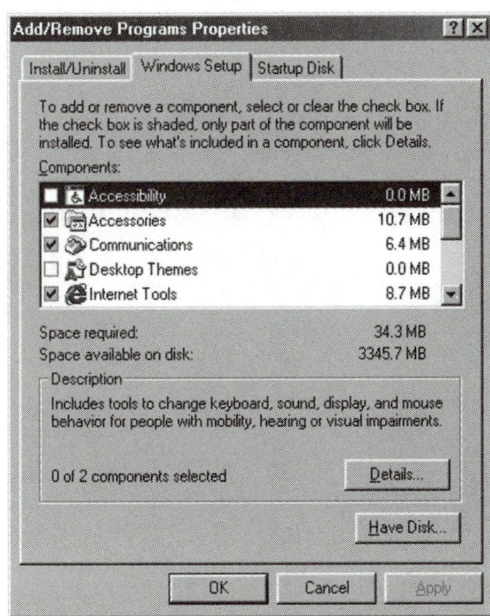

Figure 12-6 Windows Setup

The Components list shows the components of Windows 98 that are currently installed. The scrolling list displays categories of components. A check mark in a white box indicates that all components in that category are installed. No check mark indicates that none of the components in that category are installed. A check mark in a gray box indicates that some of the components in that category are installed.

To see the components in the highlighted category, click the Details button. Remove the check mark from any component you wish to remove and check the components you wish to add. Click OK to remove and/or add the components.

4. Click **Cancel**. The window closes.
5. Close the **Control Panel**.

UNIT 12

LESSON 123

Display Settings and Appearance

In this lesson, you will learn how to change display settings and appearance.

SKILL PRACTICE

To Change Display Settings

You can set the number of colors your screen will display and the size of the desktop area. Many programs will require that your display be set to a minimum of 256 colors. Desktop area is measured by the number of *pixels* (called the *resolution*) that will be used to create the screen. Higher resolutions cause the windows and text to appear smaller and more sharply defined.

1. Open the **Control Panel**.
2. Double-click **Display**. The Display Properties dialog box appears.
3. Click the **Settings** tab. The dialog box appears as shown in Figure 12-7.

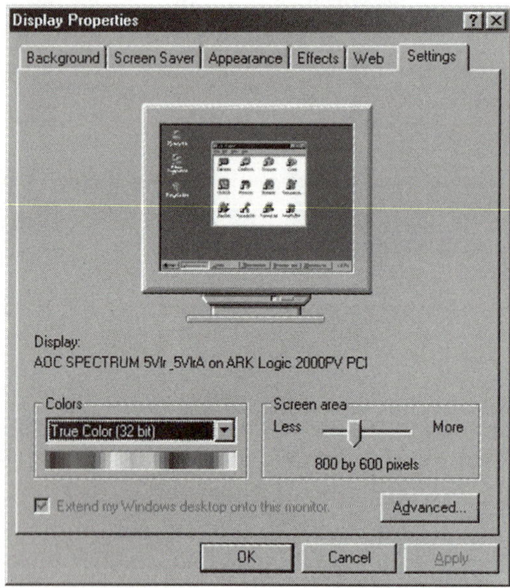

Figure 12-7 Display Properties Dialog Box

The number of colors displayed can be chosen in the Color palette. The display resolution can be selected by sliding the control under Screen Area.

(continued on next page)

NOTE The number of colors and the desktop area available will vary, depending on your monitor and video adapter.

LESSON

123

GLOSSARY TERMS

PIXELS • the dots that make up the picture on a computer screen

RESOLUTION • a measurement of the number of dots that make up the screen

ACTIVITY

1. Experiment with the available color schemes.
2. Set the color scheme back to the **Windows Standard** color scheme.
3. Close the **Control Panel**.

***Skill Practice** (continued)*

To Change Color Scheme

4. Click the **Appearance** tab of the dialog box. The dialog box appears similar to Figure 12-8.

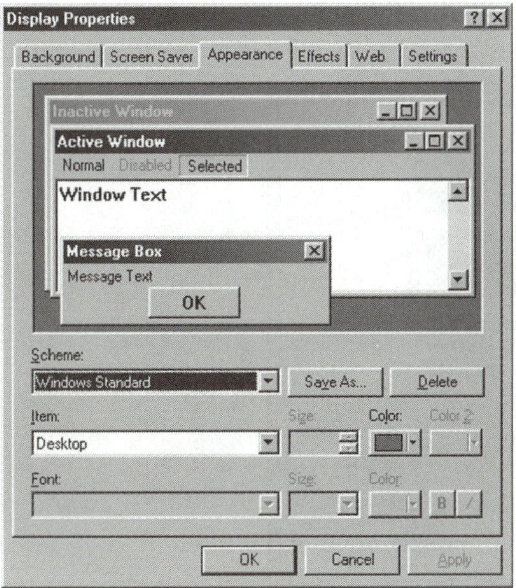

Figure 12-8 Display Appearance

The controls at the bottom of the dialog box allow you to select a color scheme or even select colors individually for each item on the display. The top of the dialog box shows a sample of the selected color scheme.

5. Choose **Wheat** from the **Scheme** box. The sample in the dialog box changes to the selected color scheme.
6. Click **OK**. The Display Properties dialog box closes, and the color scheme is applied.
7. Double-click **Display** in the Control Panel.
8. Click the **Appearance** tab.
9. Choose **Windows Standard** from the Scheme box. The sample in the dialog box shows the standard color selection.
10. Click **OK**. The standard color scheme is applied.
11. Leave the **Control Panel** open for the Activity that follows.

UNIT 12

LESSON 124

Adding Desktop Wallpaper

In this lesson, you will learn how to add desktop wallpaper. Wallpaper is a way to personalize your computer or make the desktop more attractive.

SKILL PRACTICE

NOTE *Wallpaper* can be a graphic as large as the screen or smaller than the screen. The Display option allows wallpaper to be centered on the screen or made to repeat like a pattern.

To Apply Wallpaper

1. Open the **Control Panel**.
2. Double-click **Display**. The Display Properties dialog box appears.
3. If necessary, click the **Background** tab. The dialog box appears as shown in Figure 12-9.

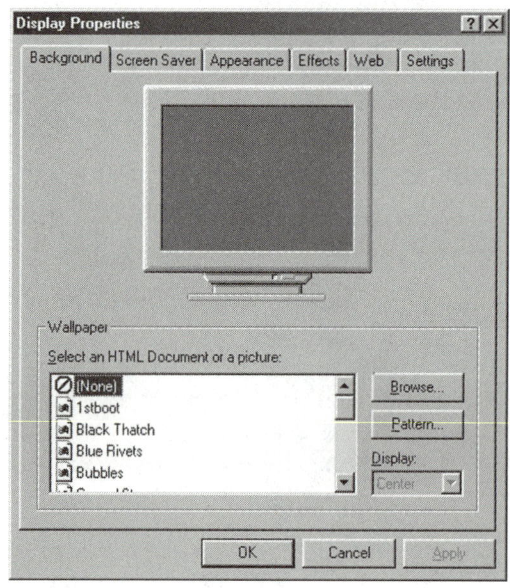

Figure 12-9 Display Backgrounds

4. If necessary, choose **[None]** from the **Wallpaper** list.
5. Choose **Circles** from the **Wallpaper** list. A sample of the wallpaper appears in the graphic of the monitor that appears in the dialog box.
6. Click **Apply**. The wallpaper appears on the desktop.
7. Choose **Setup** from the **Wallpaper** list and click **OK**. The desktop wallpaper changes, and the dialog box closes.

TIP Because wallpaper is just a standard bitmap graphic, it can be created or modified in Paint. Wallpaper files are saved in the Windows folder.

GLOSSARY TERMS

WALLPAPER • a graphic element that can be as large as or smaller than the screen.

LESSON 124

ACTIVITY

1. Experiment with the wallpapers available on your system.
2. Select a favorite wallpaper and leave it selected as you complete this unit.
3. Close all open windows.

UNIT 12

LESSON 125

Using a Screen Saver

In this lesson, you will learn how to use a screen saver. After your computer has set idle for a period of time, screen savers replace the contents of your screen with interesting pictures.

SKILL PRACTICE

To Choose a Screen Saver

1. Open the **Control Panel**.
2. Double-click **Display**. The Display dialog box appears.
3. Click the **Screen Saver** tab.
4. Choose **Flying Windows** from the **Screen Saver** list box. The dialog box appears as shown in Figure 12-10.

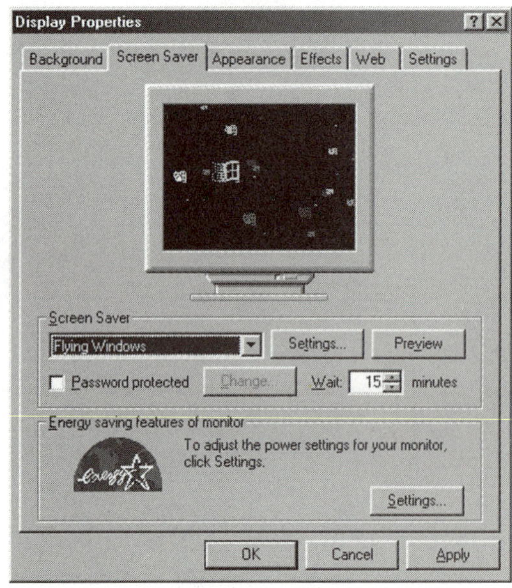

Figure 12-10 Choosing a Screen Saver

5. Click the **Settings** button. A dialog box of options for the Flying Windows screen saver appears. The options will vary, depending on the screen saver selected.
6. Click **Cancel**.
7. Click **Preview** and do not move the mouse for a second or two. The screen saver appears as it will when activated.
8. Move the mouse to end the preview.
9. Double-click in the **Wait** text box and key **20**.
10. Preview some other screen savers available on your system.
11. Select your favorite screen saver and click **OK**.

NOTE Today's computers are not subject to monitor burn-in under normal operating conditions. Set the wait time for your screen saver on the basis of your own personal preference. It is not necessary to set the wait time low in order to save your monitor.

LESSON

125

ACTIVITY

1. Make the **3D Text** your screen saver.
2. Use the screen saver's settings to change the message to **Windows 98**.
3. Preview the screen saver.
4. Click **OK**.
5. Close all open windows.

UNIT 12

LESSON 126

Changing Mouse Settings

In this lesson, you will learn how to change mouse settings.

SKILL PRACTICE

To Change Button Configuration

1. Open the **Control Panel**.
2. Double-click **Mouse**. The Mouse Properties dialog box appears, as shown in Figure 12-11.
3. Choose either the right-handed or left-handed configuration. Choosing the left-handed configuration reverses the functions of the mouse buttons.

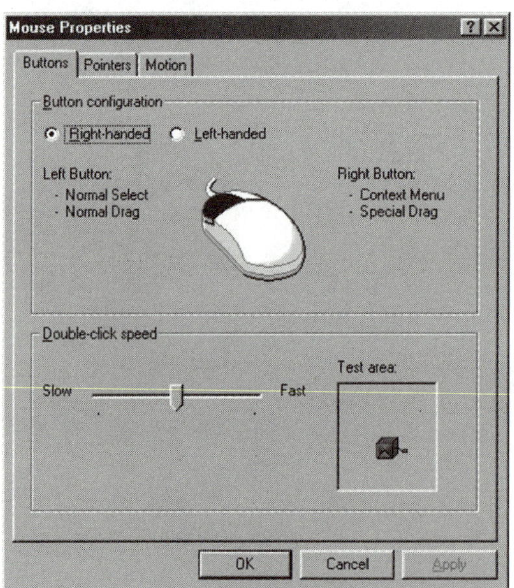

Figure 12-11 Mouse Properties

To Change the Double-Click Speed

You can change the speed at which you must double click for Windows to recognize the two clicks as a double click.

4. Double-click in the **Test area**. The jack-in-the-box pops up.
5. Double-click in the **Test area** again. The jack-in-the-box goes back in the box.
6. Drag the double-click speed slider to its slowest setting.

(continued on next page)

NOTE If the double-click speed is too fast, it may be difficult to double click fast enough for the computer to recognize it. If the double-click speed is too slow, two clicks that were not intended to be a double-click may be interpreted as a double-click.

LESSON
126

▶SKILL PRACTICE (continued)

7. Click twice in the **Test area**. Repeatedly double-click, each time clicking slower, until you find the speed of the current setting.
8. Drag the double-click speed slider near the fastest setting.
9. Double-click in the **Test area**. See if you can double-click fast enough for the fast setting.
10. Drag the double-click speed slider back to its original position or near the center of the range.

To View the Mouse Pointers

The Pointers section of the dialog box allows you to change the appearance of the pointer.

11. Click the **Pointers** tab. The Pointers section of the dialog box appears, as shown in Figure 12-12. The pointer takes on a variety of shapes, depending on the current function.

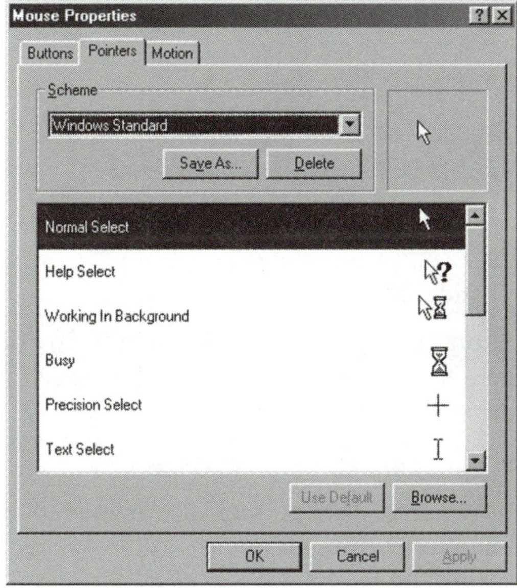

Figure 12-12 Customizing Pointers

12. Scroll through the list of pointer shapes.

(continued on next page)

UNIT 12

LESSON 126

Changing Mouse Settings

►SKILL PRACTICE (continued)

To Change Pointer Speed

13. Click the **Motion** tab. The Motion section of the dialog box appears, as shown in Figure 12-13.

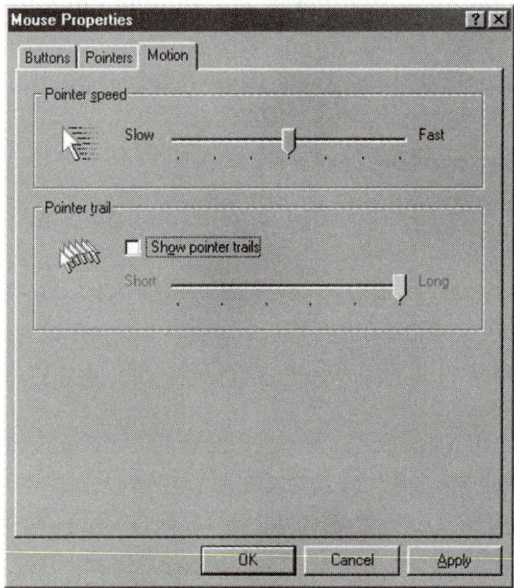

Figure 12-13 Customizing Mouse Motion

14. Drag the pointer speed slider to the slowest setting.
15. Click **Apply**. After a short pause, the new speed will be in effect. Move the pointer. Notice how far the mouse must be moved to move the pointer all the way across the screen.
16. Drag the pointer speed slider to the fastest setting.
17. Click **Apply**. Notice how quickly the pointer moves in response to even a slight movement of the mouse.
18. Return the pointer speed slider to its original position, or about the center of the range.
19. Click **Apply**.

(continued on next page)

LESSON

126

ACTIVITY

1. Change the double-click speed on your computer to the speed you feel most comfortable with.
2. Change the pointer speed to the fastest setting.
3. Turn on pointer trails.
4. Apply the changes by clicking **OK**.
5. Close all windows.
6. Open the **My Computer** window.
7. Open the **Control Panel**.
8. Return the mouse properties to their normal settings.
9. Close all windows.

Skill Practice *(continued)*

To Turn on Pointer Trails

20. Click the **Show pointer trails** check box. If pointer trails are already on, leave them on for the steps that follow.
21. Move the pointer around the dialog box. Notice the trail of pointers that follows your pointer.
22. Click the **Show pointer trails** check box. The pointer trails are turned off.
23. Click **Cancel** to close the Mouse Properties dialog box.

TIP
Pointer trails sometimes make the pointer easier to see on portable computers with liquid-crystal displays.

UNIT 12

LESSON

127

Changing Date and Time

In this lesson, you will learn how to change the system date and time.

SKILL PRACTICE

To Set the Date and Time

1. Open the **Control Panel**.
2. Double-click **Date/Time**. The Date/Time Properties dialog box appears, as shown in Figure 12-14.

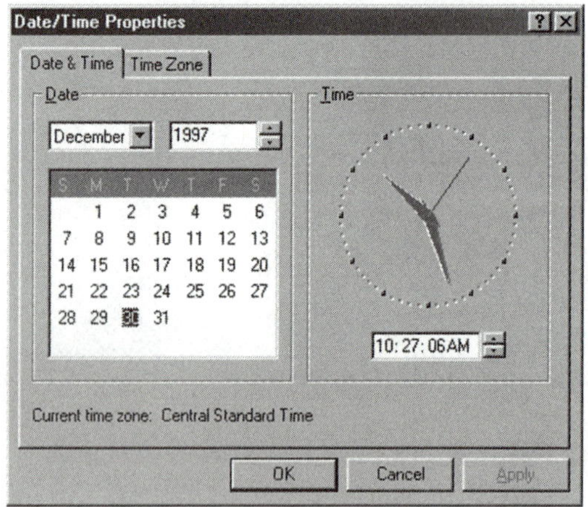

Figure 12-14 Date/Time Properties

3. Click the arrow at the end of the month text box. The month text box has a month selected but is not labeled.
4. Choose **June** from the month text box.
5. Click the **11** on the displayed calendar.
6. Double-click the hour on the digital time display.
7. Click the up arrow at the end of the digital time display to advance the hour.
8. Click **Cancel** to exit the dialog box without changing the date or time.

NOTE The Time Zone tab of the Date/Time Properties dialog box allows you to set your time zone. You can also set an option that causes Windows to automatically adjust for daylight savings time.

LESSON

127

▶ACTIVITY

1. Use the **Date/Time Properties** dialog box to find out what day your birthday falls on in the year 2010.
2. Look at the calendar for February of 2012.
3. Cancel the **Date/Time Properties** dialog box and close the **Control Panel**.

LESSON 128

Viewing Fonts

In this lesson, you will learn how to view the fonts available on your system.

SKILL PRACTICE

To View the Installed Fonts

1. Open the **Control Panel**.
2. Double-click **Fonts**. The Fonts folder opens.
3. Choose **List Fonts By Similarity** from the **View** menu. A font box appears at the top of the window. Windows will compare the fonts in your system with the font selected in the font box.
4. Choose **Times New Roman** from the **List fonts By similarity to:** font box. The fonts in the window are ordered on the basis of their similarity to Times New Roman.
5. Choose **Hide Variations** from the **View** menu. The fonts that are simply style variations (such as bold, italic, and underline) of another font are hidden from view.
6. Scroll down, if necessary, to find the font named **Courier New**.
7. Double-click **Courier New**. A description and sample of the font appears, as shown in Figure 12-15.

NOTE: Deleting a font from the Font window deletes the font from the system. To install a new font, choose Install New Font from the File menu.

Figure 12-15 Font Description and Sample

8. Click **Print**. The Print dialog box appears.

(continued on next page)

LESSON
128

ACTIVITY

1. Open the **Fonts** window.
2. List fonts by their similarity to **Arial**.
3. Print the description for **Times New Roman**.
4. Return the background wallpaper to the original setting.
5. Close all windows.

Skill Practice *(continued)*

9. Click **OK**. The description and sample print.
10. Click **Done**. The font description closes.
11. Close the **Fonts** window.
12. Close the **Control Panel**.

Appendix A

INTRODUCTION TO NETWORKING

For many years, microcomputers existed primarily as stand-alone computers, meaning they had no interaction with other computers. By the mid 1980s, the hardware and software necessary to interconnect microcomputers was available. Interconnecting computers made it possible to share data, storage space, and printers. It also provided new ways for computer users to share information and interact with each other.

WHAT IS A NETWORK?

Strictly speaking, a *network* is two or more computers connected together. Two computers in a small office sharing a printer is a form of network. The worldwide interconnection of computers called the Internet is also a network. And there are many networks that are somewhere between these two extremes.

In this lesson, we will primarily be concerned with networks that serve users within a confined area such as a building or an office. This type of network is called a *local area network* or LAN. Computers on a LAN share data, software, and hardware. Typically, computers on a LAN work more closely with each other and share more resources than larger networks. This is because the close proximity of the computers and devices such as printers make sharing easier.

A network that spans a large geographic region such as a state or county is called a *wide area network* or WAN. The Internet is an example of a WAN. Wide area networks are more likely to share data or messages between users and are less likely to share resources such as printers.

Another type of network is a *dial-in network* such as an *online service*, an *Internet Service Provider*, or a *bulletin board service (BBS)*. These services provide some of the features of a network. However, rather than being constantly interconnected, you connect your computer to the network by *modem*.

NETWORK CONFIGURATIONS

There are three basic network configurations. One configuration requires a computer to be devoted to serving the other computers on the network. The other configuration allows any and all computers on the network to serve each other. The third configuration is a combination of the first two.

Networking with a Dedicated Server

When networking with a *dedicated server*, a computer is on the network solely to provide data, programs, and possibly other resources to the other computers on the network. A dedicated server is usually a high speed computer with one or more high-capacity disks. On these disks, data and programs used by many or all users on the network are stored. For example, a company that sells clothing from a mail-order catalog might use a dedicated server to hold a database of customers and inventory. Each user on the network has access to the same database for entering orders and checking the current inventory.

The server might also include a tape backup system which regularly makes backups of the data on the server. Dedicated servers often have printers attached which can be used by any user on the network. Figure A-1 shows and example of a network with a dedicated server. A network with a dedicated server may have more than one dedicated server on the network.

Appendix A

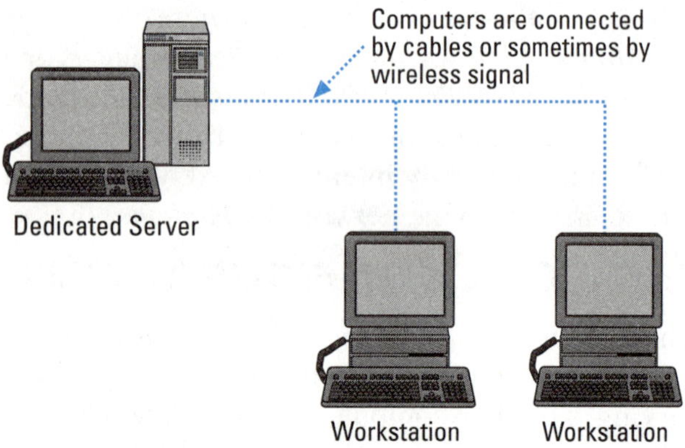

Figure A-1 Network with a dedicated server.

There is an important distinction between a network of microcomputers with a dedicated server and a network of terminals connected to a mainframe or minicomputer. In the case of a microcomputer network with a dedicated server, each microcomputer on the network, called a *workstation*, does its own processing. A workstation may load a program from a server, but the program runs on the workstation.

A computer running Windows 98 can serve as a workstation on a network with a dedicated server. Windows 98 can be used to connect to most popular dedicated servers, such as Windows NT and Novell.

Peer-to-Peer Networks

A *peer-to-peer network* is a network in which any computer on the network has the capability of sharing data or other resources and still functions as a workstation. In effect, any computer on the network can be a server and a workstation at the same time. Figure A-2 illustrates a peer-to-peer network.

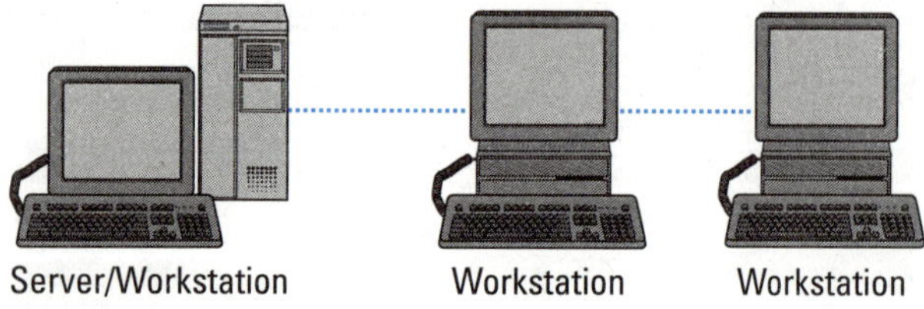

Figure A-2 A peer-to-peer network

Peer-to-peer networks are easier to set up and less expensive because there is no dedicated server. An office with as few as two computers can create a peer-to-peer network and share printers, disks, tape backup, and more. One drawback of a peer-to-peer network is decreased availability of shared resources. For example, if a user on the network must reboot his or her computer for some reason, the resources provided by that computer are temporarily unavailable to others on the network. Because a dedicated server is not serving as a workstation, it is less likely to be taken "offline" with no warning.

Windows 98 provides excellent support for peer-to-peer networking. No additional software is necessary to set up a peer-to-peer network of Windows 98 machines.

Client/Server Networks

A network configuration referred to as *client/server architecture* is becoming increasingly popular. In a client/server network, the processing is split between the server and the workstation (the *client*). In a client/server network, the server may process a request for certain data or do some other processing that is best done on the server. The results are then sent to the client to be processed further (see Figure A-3).

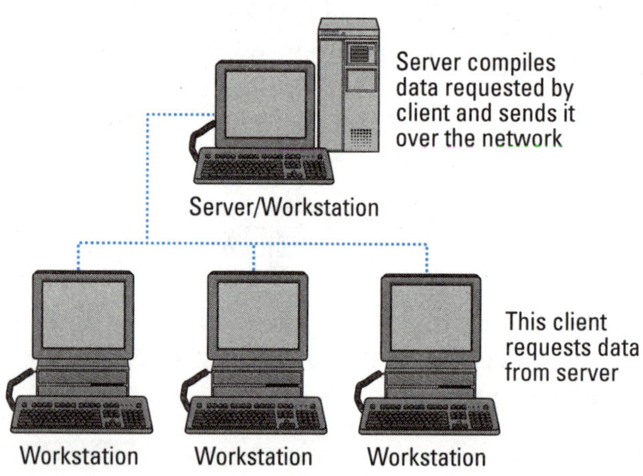

Figure A-3 A client/server network

Appendix A

For example, suppose you work for a company with thousands of employees. You are running an application which uses a client/server architecture to maintain the employee database. The application running on your machine needs to generate a letter for each employee with vacation days which must be used within the next month. Your workstation (the client) makes a request to the server for the records of any employee that fits the given criteria. Those records are located by a program on the server and delivered to the client. The client then retrieves the necessary information from those records and prints the letters to the employees.

Although the client/server architecture requires that the server spend more time processing, the overall speed of the system is improved by reducing the traffic on the network. In the client/server architecture, only the data needed by the client is sent over the network. In a standard dedicated server configuration, each of the thousands of employee records would have to travel over the network to be searched on the workstation.

Some client/server applications can operate in conjunction with Windows 98. Much of the way the Internet works is a client/server model. For example, when you query a Web search engine, the search is taking place on the server and the results are being sent to your Web browser.

SHARING PRINTERS OVER A NETWORK

A resource commonly shared over a network is a printer. Printers can be shared over peer-to-peer networks and networks with dedicated servers. Often a printer available to users on a network is referred to as a *network printer*.

An obvious advantage to sharing printers over a network is that a company or school can purchase fewer and possibly better printers. If several network printers are available, users can select the most appropriate printer for the job. For example, there may be an older laser printer on the network which prints at 300 dots per inch and a newer one which prints at a higher resolution. Some documents may be suited for the 300 dpi printer, while others may take advantage of the higher resolution available on the newer printer.

When a printer is used over a network, documents are stored in a waiting area called a *print queue*. The documents are sent to the printer as quickly as the printer can handle them. The first document to enter the queue is the first to print.

Windows 98 users can share printers. Many office networks have shared printers running on Windows 98 workstations.

USING A NETWORK

Users of a network must learn how to access the shared resources on the server. The first step is to log in to the network. Users must also understand how printers, data, and programs are shared, and how to access these resources.

Logging In

Network resources are not available until the user logs in to the network. Most networks require a *user ID* and a *password* to be entered before access to the network is granted. The combination of a correct user ID and password allows the use of network resources (see Figure A-4).

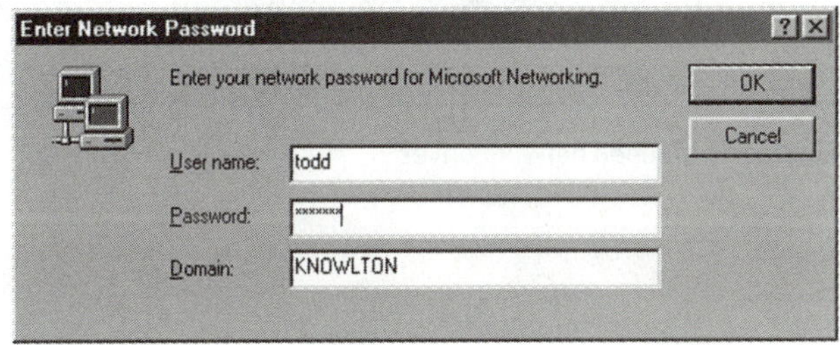

Figure A-4 Logging in to a network

Appendix A

Network administrators can assign different *privileges* to different users. For example, some users may only have access to certain directories or programs. These users will be denied access by the operating system to other files. Figure A-5 shows an example of a message denying access to a file.

Figure A-5 A message denying access privileges

Accessing Network Disks

Most network operating systems allow network disk drives to be seen from a workstation as if the disk were installed in the workstation. In operating systems such as Windows, this process is called *drive mapping* (see Figure A-6).

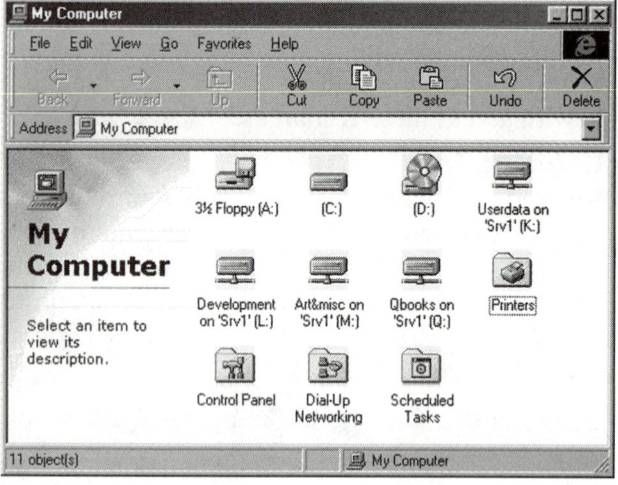

Figure A-6 Mapped network drives

Drive mapping involves giving a hard drive on the server a drive letter on a workstation. Once a network drive has been mapped, the workstation can access programs and data files just as it would on a local drive. Depending upon the network, it can have any number of network hard drives each one would be assigned a different drive letter on the workstation.

Appendix B

THE INTERNET

The Internet was developed by a Department of Defense (DOD) research project in 1969 to connect a number of networks which already existed into a single network, or a network of networks. This project was named ARPANET (Advanced Research Projects Agency Network). ARPANET was primarily used to link DOD research centers with their researchers in universities.

Originally, only computers of the U.S. government, some research institutions, and universities were connected. Eventually, the network was opened up to commercial organizations. As the network of networks grew, it became known as the Internet. Now, of course, even individuals are connected to the Internet.

Individuals and businesses can connect to the Internet through an online service or through a service called an Internet service provider (ISP). An ISP is a company that sells connection time and services to users who dial in to a computer with direct Internet access.

The Internet has exploded with growth, and now connects governments, schools, companies, and individuals around the world. There are tens of millions of people connected to the Internet in more than 100 countries.

Because the Internet is a network of networks, no one individual or organization governs the Internet, although there has been some interest in taking measures to control the Internet—especially to control what kind of information and files can be shared over a system which is so accessible.

THE LANGUAGE OF THE INTERNET

Because the Internet is made up of many networks and every kind of computer in existence, some standard must exist in order for all of these varied computers and networks to successfully communicate with each other. This language of communications is called a *protocol*.

The protocol used by the Internet is called *TCP/IP*. TCP is an acronym for *transmission control protocol* and IP is an acronym for *Internet protocol*. Together these form the protocol of the Internet. TCP handles breaks data into groups, called *packets*, which can be transmitted over the Internet. TCP also recombines these packets on the receiving end of the transmission. IP handles the routing of the data from the individual computers through the connections necessary to reach the global Internet.

WHAT CAN BE DONE ON THE INTERNET?

The Internet provides many different services, such as file transfer, electronic mail, and the World Wide Web. There are also databases which can be searched, and a variety of ways in which information and messages can be shared.

File Transfer Protocol

File transfer protocol (FTP) allows a user on any computer to get files from another computer, or to send files to another computer. FTP is designed to handle file transfer between machines with different character sets and different ways of formatting files. FTP is used any time a user wants to access a file on another system. For example, a company may make information about there products available through FTP to any user on the Internet. Or, a software developer may distribute copies of software through FTP.

Appendix B

Telnet

The network terminal protocol (TELNET) allows a user to log in to other computers on the network. The user can work on the remote terminal as if he or she were connected to the computer via a local network.

A session is started by specifying a computer to connect to. From that time until the session is finished, anything typed is sent directly to the other computer. After making a connection with the remote computer, generally, the remote system will ask the user to log in and give a password.

Electronic Mail

Because millions of people are connected to the Internet, *electronic mail* (or *e-mail*) has become a popular way to communicate. Electronic mail allows you to send a message to any other user of the Internet, providing you know the e-mail address of the user.

To send an e-mail message, a user creates the message with e-mail software such as Outlook Express (see Figure B-1). The message is then transmitted to the local area network or Internet service provider. The message is routed to the Internet and eventually to the server to which the recipient is connected.

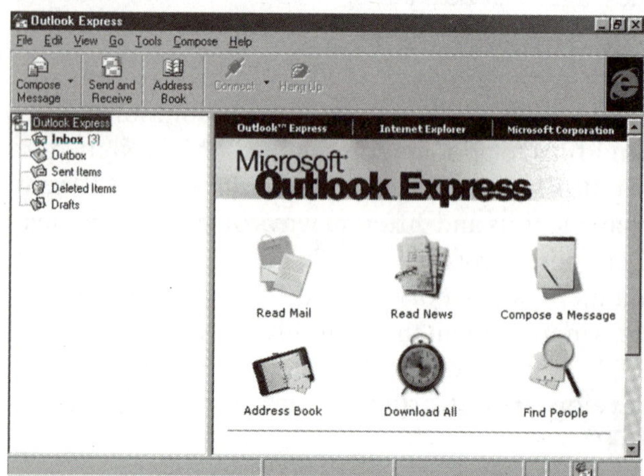

Figure B-1 Outlook Express is one of the many programs for sending and reading e-mail.

Users of the Internet who receive e-mail must have a unique name to serve as their e-mail address. For example, tknowlton@aol.com is an e-mail address used by the author of this book. The aol.com indicates that the computer where the user has an e-mail account is at America Online. The user is tknowlton. The @ character means "at." So taken together, the address tells the system to send the message to tknowlton at aol.com.

The com extension on the name gives an indication of the type of system the computer is. The extension divides the computers on the Internet into domains. Table B-1 shows some of the common extensions used in the United States.

Table B-1

Domain Extension	Meaning
com	A commercial service of business
net	Companies and groups involved with the Internet network
gov	Government servers
mil	Military servers
org	Organizations

Outside the U.S., domains are typically organized by country and are two characters in length. For example, uk for the United Kingdom. The .us extension is used in the United States. It is mostly used by schools.

Mailing Lists

A mailing list is an Internet service which sends electronic mail to a list of subscribers. Mailing lists might be formed among people with a similar interest. Members of the list can send messages to a server called a *list server*. The messages are then distributed to the members of the mailing list by the list server. For example, a mailing list of teachers of a particular subject might be formed to allow a discussion forum through e-mail.

Appendix B

Other mailing lists are intended to release information from a company or organization to a list of e-mail addresses. For example, a company might use a mailing list to distribute press releases or other information to an interested audience.

To join a mailing list, users send a message to the list server. The message must contain commands the list server understands. Often the message must contain the word SUBSCRIBE in order to subscribe to the list. If you wish to remove yourself from the mailing list, you can send an UNSUBSCRIBE message to the list server.

Newsgroups

Newsgroups are like bulletin boards on the Internet. Thousands of topics are open for discussion by sending messages to a newsgroup and reading the messages left by others. Topics range from the serious to the silly. You can probably find a newsgroup for people discussing your favorite television show. There are also newsgroups where individuals discuss computer programming, and others where people buy and sell goods.

The World Wide Web

The World Wide Web (WWW) is the fastest growing and probably the most exciting service of the Internet. The WWW is a form of client/server networking. Servers on the Internet run a *Web server* that communicates with client software (called a *Web browser*) on the user's computer. Information sent to the client is in a special format called *hypertext markup language (HTML).*

The information on the WWW is in a multimedia format. Each document is called a page. Web pages can present text, graphics, and even animation and sound. Individuals and businesses can have their own *home page* with information they wish to share with the world. Pages are linked using *hypertext links* which allow you jump from one page to another by clicking objects and text on the screen. For example, a Web page on a server in Kansas City may have a hypertext link to a Web page in Australia. The user merely clicks the link to access the computer in Australia. Figure B-2 shows a typical Web page being viewed by a Web browser.

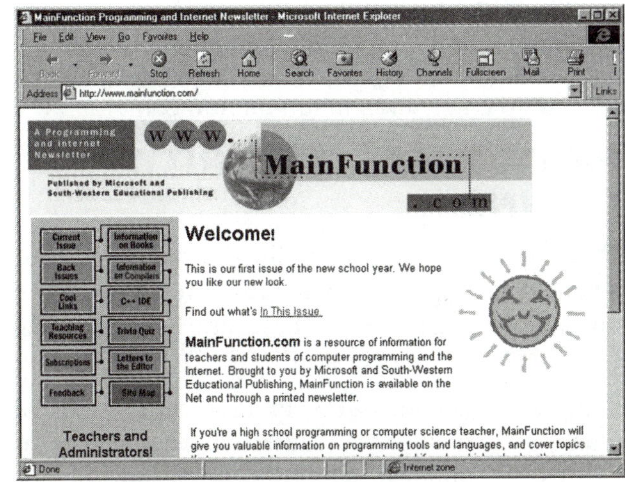

Figure B-2 The World Wide Web

Like e-mail addresses, Web pages also have unique addresses that allow users to access the page. WWW addresses are somewhat similar in appearance to e-mail addresses. An address on the WWW is called a *uniform resource locator (URL)*. An example of a URL is *http://www.thomson.com*. Just like with an e-mail address, each part means something. First, *http://* means that the document being retrieved is to use a special protocol called *hypertext transfer protocol (HTTP)*. The *www* means that this is a WWW page. The name *thomson.com* is the *domain name*. The domain name follows the *Domain Name System (DNS)*. This system allows each particular page to have its own individual name, and gives it the ability to be accessed by users throughout the world.

The Domain Name System is important because it allows resources on the Internet to have easy-to-remember addresses. However, the names in the Domain Name System actually equate to a numbering system. Every computer on the Internet is identified by a group of numbers, called an IP address. For example 205.231.180.104 is the IP address of the computer where the Web site www.mainfunction.com resides. The numerical address is difficult to remember, so the address is referenced by names that are easier to understand. In your Web browser, you could enter 205.231.180.104 to visit MainFunction, or you could enter www.mainfunction.com.

PRIVACY AND SECURITY ONLINE

Users of the Internet and online services should be aware of security and privacy issues related to going online. While going online has many benefits, some caution should be exercised.

Electronic mail is a useful communications tool for many individuals and businesses. The privacy of electronic mail, however, is not guaranteed. Although most e-mail is not regularly monitored, some employers do reserve the right to read e-mail messages coming or going from their servers. System administrators may also see your messages in the course of maintaining the system, and e-mail can be accidentally misdirected to the wrong recipient. Sending confidential information via e-mail is not recommended.

Most systems allow files and programs to be attached to e-mail messages. If you receive an e-mail message with a file attached and you do not know what the file is or do not recognize the sender of the message, do not download the file. It could be a virus or other program designed to cause harm.

When browsing the WWW, be aware that the Web servers know what system you are connecting from and sometimes other information about your account. Do not assume that you are completely anonymous as you surf the Net.

Also be cautious when downloading files from WWW sites, especially executable files. Anytime you download a program and run it, you are putting your computer and your data at risk. Online services carefully verify the files they make available for download. There is no guarantee of control on WWW sites. Download only from sources you know and trust.

Finally, when using the Internet, you will likely meet other Internet users from your area and from around the world. Keep in mind that people can misrepresent themselves when online. It is difficult to know much more about a person you meet online except what they tell you. When participating in discussions online, you should be very careful about giving out your full name, phone number, or address. This information could be misused.

The online world is not a dark world with danger around every corner. But like any large community, the online community has some less than exemplary citizens. However, being aware of the dangers that exist, and taking a few steps to prevent problems can protect you from most problems.

Appendix C

INTRODUCTION TO THE ACCESSIBILITY OPTIONS

Having an impairment of vision, sound, or dexterity can sometimes make it difficult to operate a computer effectively. Microsoft kept this in mind when creating Windows 98 by including special features called accessibility options. For example, there are options to make the keyboard easier to use and to allow you to use the keyboard in place of the mouse. Other options allow you to change the colors to high contrast colors, and increase the font size of the Windows' environment.

The Accessibility Options are accessed from the Control Panel. The Accessibility Properties dialog box appears as shown in Figure C-1. The five sections of the dialog box (Keyboard, Sound, Display, Mouse, and General) each contain options to make using the computer easier.

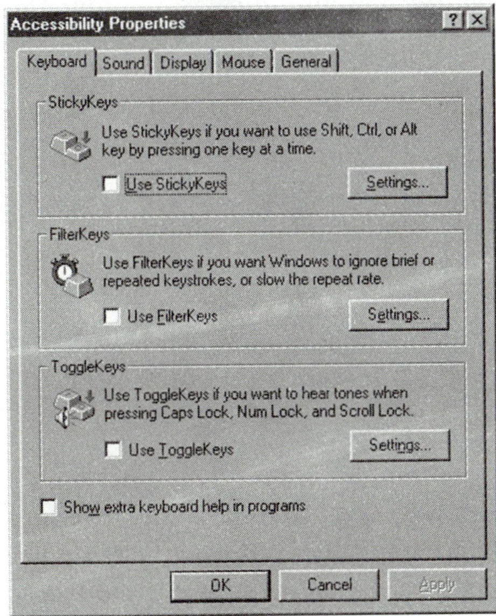

Figure C-1 Keyboard options of the Accessibility Properties dialog box

KEYBOARD OPTIONS

The Keyboard section of the Accessibility Properties dialog box contains three options that will help people with dexterity impairments issue commands more easily.

StickyKeys

The StickyKeys option makes entering key combinations such as Ctrl+C easier. When the Use StickyKeys option is checked, Windows begins treating the function keys (Shift, Ctrl, and Alt) as "sticky." This means that to issue a command, the user simply has to press one of the function keys and then release it. Windows keeps this key active until another key is pressed, making it possible to issue a command without pressing two keys simultaneously. The Settings button in this section give you more options for controlling the way StickyKeys are used.

FilterKeys

By clicking the Use FilterKeys option, you can make Windows ignore repeated keystrokes, or make Windows slow down the repeat rate of letters. This makes it possible for Windows to recognize when the user is wanting to repeat a character, or is accidentally holding a key down too long. The Settings button on the right side of this section allows you to adjust the sensitivity of FilterKeys.

ToggleKeys

The ToggleKeys option makes Windows produce a sound when the Caps Lock, Num Lock, or Scroll Lock keys are pressed. A high-pitched sound indicates that the lock is being turned on. A low-pitched sound indicates that the lock is being turned off. This is useful for those who have difficulty seeing the small lights on the keyboard.

SOUND OPTIONS

Users who are hearing impaired can be assisted by the options in the Sound section of the Accessibility Properties dialog box (see Figure C-2).

Appendix C

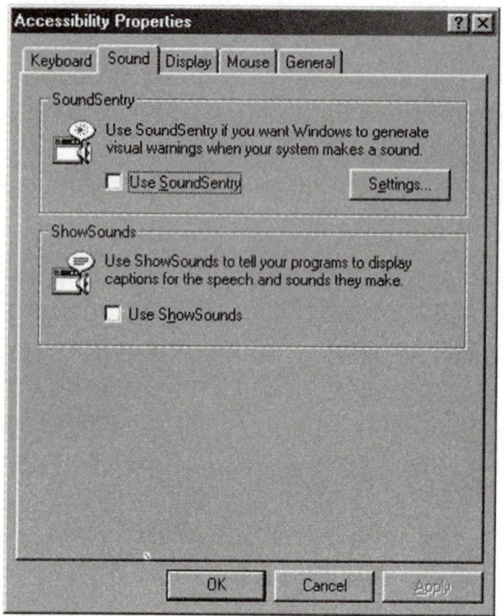

Figure C-2 Sound Options

SoundSentry

The SoundSentry replaces the usual beep that the computer's speaker produces with a flash of a selected screen element. The Settings button allows you to choose the part of the screen which you want to flash.

ShowSounds

Programs which are written to support the ShowSounds option will display text or icons in the place of sounds when the ShowSounds option is on.

DISPLAY OPTIONS

For people with a vision disability, seeing the text on the screen can be very difficult. The Display section of Accessibility Options helps with this problem by allowing the user to make the text larger and the colors high contrast. By checking the Use High Contrast option, Windows will change its settings to make almost everything easier to read. The Settings button on the right opens a dialog box which allows the user to adjust the color scheme which Windows displays. It also lets you activate the shortcut to toggle this option on and off.

MOUSE OPTIONS

Windows 98 was designed to be used with a mouse or other pointing device. Those who have difficulty manipulating a mouse may use the mouse options to cause the numeric keypad to move the mouse pointer and to perform clicks and dragging. The Use MouseKeys option (see Figure C-3) causes the arrows on the numeric keypad to move the mouse pointer. The 5 key performs a click, and the plus key (+) on the numeric keypad performs a double-click. The Ins key begins dragging and the Del key ends a drag operation.

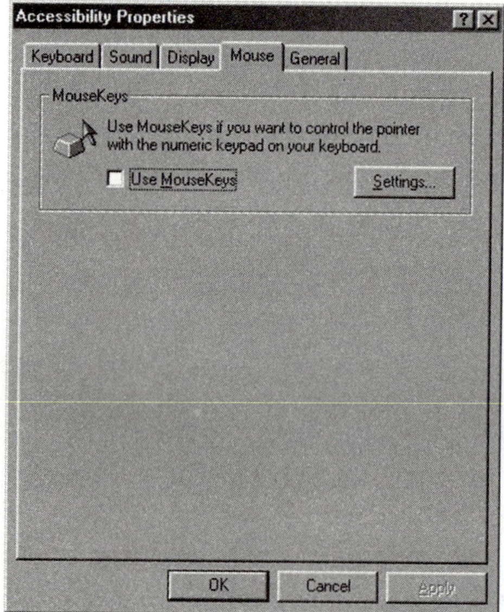

Figure C-3 Mouse options

The Settings button gives the user the ability to change the speed at which the cursor moves when an arrow key is pushed, along with the ability to use a shortcut to switch between the mouse and the keyboard.

GENERAL OPTIONS

The General options apply to the administration of the Accessibility Options (see Figure C-4). The Automatic reset option causes the accessibility options to turn off after the computer has been idle for a specified length of time. The Notification option provides a message if any accessibility option is turned on or off using a shortcut key. The Notification option may prevent accessibility options from being turned on or off accidentally. The SerialKey devices option allows alternative input devices to have access to the computer if they are unable to use a standard keyboard or mouse. With the Settings button you can choose the port, and the speed at which this input device will operate. The device must be a SerialKey compatible device.

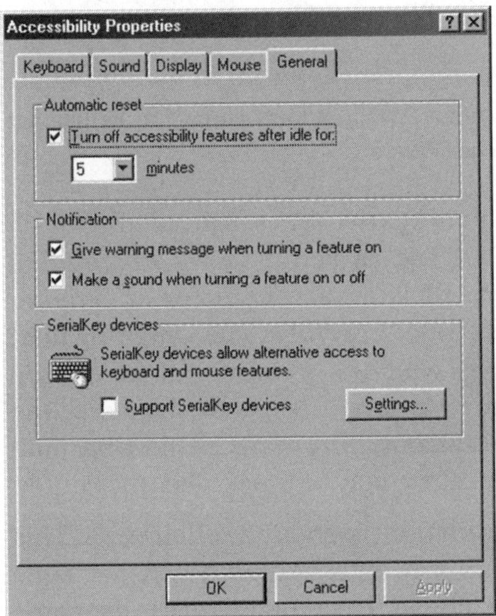

Figure C-4 General Options

Appendix D

OUTLOOK EXPRESS

Outlook Express is a mail client that is packaged with Windows 98. A *mail client* is software that can send and receive e-mail. Outlook Express also contains an address book that stores information on your family, friends, and business contacts. The search feature easily locates people who are either in your address book or located on the Internet. In addition to sending and receiving e-mail, Outlook Express also can subscribe to newsgroups. Outlook Express can be customized to download the newsgroup messages every 15 minutes.

Starting Outlook Express

To open Outlook Express, click the Start button. Open the Internet Explorer menu from the Programs menu. Click Outlook Express. You can also click the Outlook Express button on the Quick Launch Toolbar.

Adding an Internet Account

Before you can start using the e-mail features of Outlook Express, you must have an e-mail account on an e-mail server somewhere on the Internet. To configure Outlook to access your mail account, click Accounts from the Tools menu. Click the Mail tab to view the already-created accounts. Click the Add button and select mail from the three options that appear. The Internet Connection wizard appears.

The Internet Connection wizard asks you a series of questions to set up your e-mail account. The first question it will ask you is your display name. The display in most cases will be your full name. Click next. A screen appears asking for your e-mail address as shown in Figure D-1. Type your e-mail address in the blank. Click next. The next screen that appears asks for the type of e-mail server you are using. The e-mail servers send, receive, and store e-mail messages.

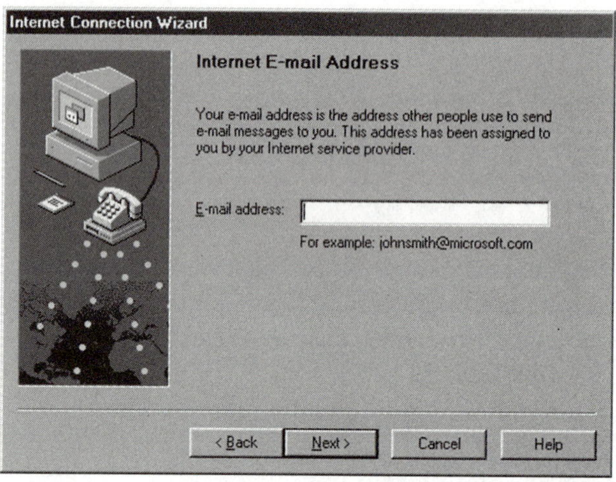

Figure D-1 The Internet E-mail Address portion of the Internet Connection Wizard

The incoming mail has two types of protocols: POP3 and MAPI. POP3 is an acronym for *Post Office Protocol 3*. MAPI is an acronym for *Messaging Application Protocol Interface*. The Outgoing mail server is SMTP, which is an acronym for *Simple Mail Transport Protocol*. Most of the time, the incoming mail and outgoing mail use the same mail server; however, there may be times when they differ.

Once the information is entered, click next. This screen requires you to enter your POP account name and password. The POP account name is the name by which the server identifies you as. Key your POP account and password. If your server requires you to log on using a Secure Password Authentication, click that option. Click next. Type a name that identifies your account. This name will be displayed when selecting different e-mail accounts. Click next. Choose the kind of Internet connection you are using and click next. Click finish. The Internet Connection wizard closes and your e-mail account is added to Outlook Express.

Appendix D

WRITING E-MAIL

To begin writing an e-mail message, click the Compose Message button on the upper left corner of the screen. A blank e-mail message appears as shown in Figure D-2. An e-mail message is comprised of three sections: the address fields, subject field, and message field.

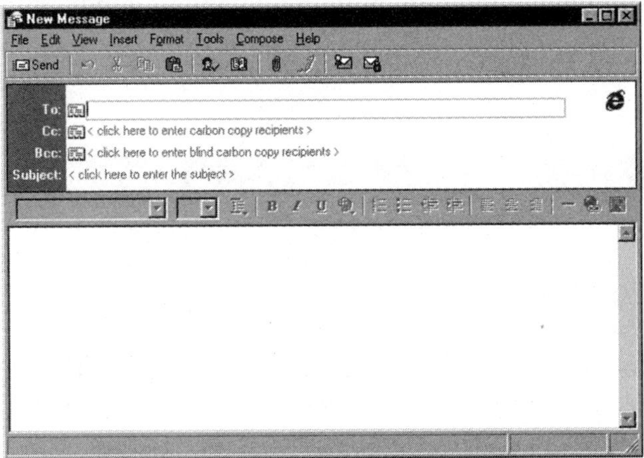

Figure D-2 A blank e-mail message

There are three different kinds of address fields. The primary e-mail addresses are typed in the To address field. This field is required to send a message. The second type of address field is the Cc field. Cc is an acronym for Carbon Copy. To send a copy of the message, use this field. The Bcc is an acronym for Blind Carbon Copy and is similar to the Cc field. It is different in that the e-mail address is not included in the primary recipient's message.

The subject field gives the e-mail recipient an idea of what the message is about. The subject is not necessary, but it is usually helpful to include it in the message.

The message field contains the actual message. Typing in the message field is similar to typing in a word processor such as WordPad. It has all the same formatting options. The message can include text, attached files, and even a background. The background, however, will not appear if the recipients mail client is not compatible with this option.

SENDING AND RECEIVING E-MAIL

Once the e-mail message is finished, you are ready to send it. Click the send button in the tool bar. The e-mail window closes and the message is sent to the Outbox. All the mail that is in the Outbox is stored on the hard drive until the message is actually sent. Connect to the Internet and click the Send and Receive button on the toolbar. Outlook Express checks your server and downloads all your spooled e-mail, and all of the messages in your outbox are sent. The messages that were in the Outbox are moved to the Sent Items box, and all your new e-mail is imported to the Inbox.

Appendix E

WINDOWS TUNE-UP WIZARD

The Windows Tune-Up wizard is a combination of system tools that optimize and speed up your computer. There are different programs that are scheduled to run depending on what configurations you choose.

Starting the Windows Tune-Up Wizard

To begin the Windows Tune-Up wizard, click the Start button. Open the Systems Tools menu from the Accessories menu in the Programs menu. Click Windows Tune-Up. The Windows Tune-Up wizard appears.

Tuning Your Computer

Start the Windows Tune-Up wizard. If the program has been configured before, a dialog box will appear. Select Change my tune-up settings or schedule, so you can reconfigure the Windows Tune-Up wizard. Click OK. The next dialog box that appears asks if you want to customize the Windows Tune-Up wizard or have an express tune-up. The customized tune-up gives you many options, while the express tune-up offers only the most common options. If selecting the Express option, you will specify when you want the Windows Tune-up to occur. The Express Tune-Up is complete.

TASK SCHEDULER

Once the Windows Tune-Up wizard is complete, the options that were chosen are saved in the Scheduled Tasks folder. The Scheduled Tasks folder lists all the regularly run programs and the date of when they where last run. The Task Scheduler allows you to automatically run programs that include programs that are not found in the Windows Tune-Up such as an anti-virus. To open the Scheduled Tasks folder, click the Start button. Open the Systems Tools menu from the Accessories menu in the Programs menu. Click the Scheduled Tasks folder icon. The Scheduled Tasks folder opens and looks similar to Figure E-1. You can also open the Scheduled Task folder by double clicking the Task Scheduler icon located next to the clock in the toolbar; however, the icon will not appear if no tasks are scheduled.

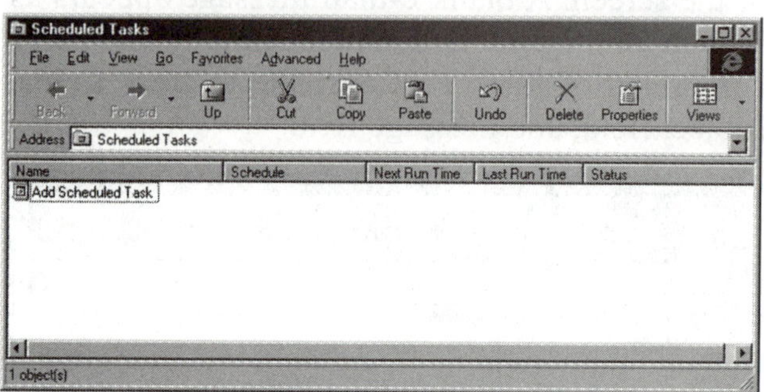

Figure E-1 The Scheduled Task folder

To Schedule an Additional Task

With the Scheduled Task folder open, double click the Add Scheduled Task icon. The Scheduled Task wizard appears. Click Next. A list of programs appears in the next dialog box. Choose one of the programs listed. A dialog box that asks when to run the program appears. Select an option. Click next. A dialog box appears and verifies the options that you chose. Click Finish. The programs icon is added to the Scheduled Tasks folder.

To Edit and Delete a Program from the Scheduled Tasks folder

Double click the icon you added. A dialog box appears as shown in Figure E-2. The dialog box has three different tabs: Task, Schedule, and Settings. The Task tab allows you to change the path of the program. The Schedule tab allows you to change the time of the day that the program will automatically run. The Settings tab contains many options to further customize the program. Click OK.

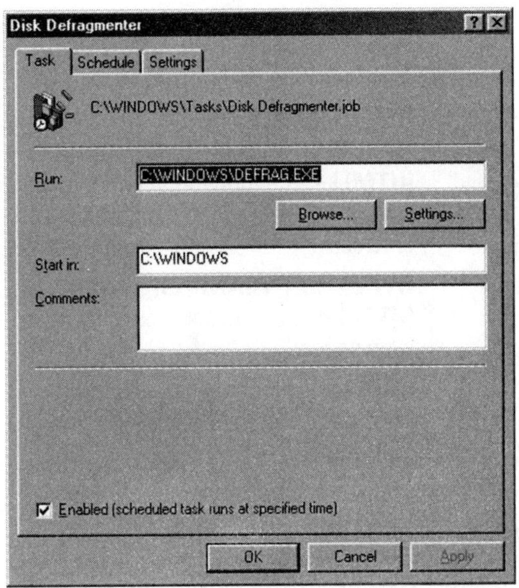

Figure E-2 The dialog box allows you to modify the setting of the program.

Click the icon of the program you added. From the file menu, choose Delete. The program is removed from the Scheduled Task folder.

Glossary

APPLICATION SOFTWARE • The programs that perform useful tasks for the user.

BOOK • A category of Help topics.

BULLETIN BOARD SERVICE (BBS) • A private telecommunication service generally set up by an individual to earn money or as a hobby.

CASCADE • To arrange and resize windows in such a way as to stack them neatly on top of each other with the title bars showing.

CD-ROM DRIVE • A device that allows computers to access data stored on compact disc.

CENTRAL PROCESSING UNIT (CPU) • The device that is the brain of the computer.

CHECK BOX • A dialog box control which allows you to choose one or more of a group of options.

CLICK • To quickly press and release the left mouse button.

CLIENT • A workstation in a local area network based on the client/server architecture.

CLIENT/SERVER ARCHITECTURE • A design model for a local area network where processing is divided between the server and the workstations (clients).

CLIPBOARD • The area in the computer's memory where text that has been cut or copied is held.

COMMAND BUTTONS • Buttons which carry out commands.

CURSOR • The blinking vertical line that indicates the position at which the next character keyed will appear.

DEDICATED SERVER • A computer on a network that's sole purpose is to provide data to other computers on the network.

DESKTOP • The background against which the windows and icons appear.

DIALOG BOX • A window which provides information to the user or asks the user to supply more information.

DIAL-IN NETWORK • A server to which users connect by modem.

DOMAIN NAME SYSTEM (DNS) • The system that allows each WWW site to have its own individual name, and gives it the ability to be accessed by users throughout the world.

DOUBLE-CLICK • To quickly press and release the mouse button twice in rapid succession.

DRAG • To press and hold the mouse button while moving the mouse pointer.

DRAG AND DROP • Dragging an item from one location to another to perform an operation.

DRIVE MAPPING • Assigning a drive letter to another computer on a networks physical drive.

ELECTRONIC MAIL • (also called e-mail) Allows users to transmit messages to other computer users.

FAX MODEM • A device that allows computers to communicate and send and receive faxes via telephone lines.

FILE • A program or document stored on a computer's storage device.

FILE TRANSFER PROTOCOL (FTP) • Allows a user on any computer to get files from another computer or send files to another computer.

FOLDER • An item used to organize files into groups.

GRAPHICAL USER INTERFACE (GUI) • A way of interacting with a computer through graphic images and controls.

HARDWARE • The devices that make up a computer system.

HIDDEN FILES AND FOLDERS • Files and folders that are usually hidden from view.

HYPERLINKS • The way pages are linked allowing a user to jump from one page to another by clicking objects and text on the screen.

HYPERTEXT MARKUP LANGUAGE (HTML) • The format that information is sent from a web server to a client's web browser.

HYPERTEXT TRANSFER PROTOCOL (HTTP) • The protocol used to retrieve Web pages.

ICONS • Tiny pictures used to represent files and to identify controls.

INTERNET • A world-wide network of computer systems that allows for the exchange of electronic mail, public messages, data, and files.

INTERNET PROTOCOL (IP) • The protocol that handles the routing of packets on the Internet.

KEYBOARD • The device used to input text and numbers into the computer.

LANDSCAPE ORIENTATION • Printing text sideways on the page.

LIST BOX • A dialog box control which allows you to choose an item from a scrolling list.

LOCAL AREA NETWORK • A group of computers connected together in order to share resources and data.

MAIL CLIENT • Software that can send and receive e-mail.

MAINFRAME COMPUTERS • A multi-user computer designed to be used in large organizations, generally used with dumb terminals.

MARGIN • The space between the edge of the page and the printed text.

MAXIMIZE BUTTON • Expands a window to fill the screen.

MENU BAR • The bar below the title bar from which menus pull down.

Glossary

MESSAGING APPLICATION PROTOCOL INTERFACE • A protocol used to interface with other Internet servers.

MODEM • A device used to send and receive data over telephone lines to other computers.

MONITOR • The computer's video display.

MOUSE • A hand-held input device that allows you to point and select items on the screen.

MULTIMEDIA APPLICATIONS • Programs that combine text, graphics, and sound.

NETWORK • Two or more computers that are connected in order to share files and resources.

NETWORK INTERFACE CARD • A circuit board that connects a computer to a local area network.

NETWORK PRINTER • A printer available to users on a network.

ONLINE SERVICE • A commercial service which provides online information, files, and messaging to its subscribers.

OPERATING SYSTEM • Coordinates the application software's interaction with the computer.

OPTION BUTTONS • A dialog box control which allows you to choose only one of a group of options.

PASSWORD • A tool used to increase security on a network by requiring a user to type a specific word in order to log in.

PATH • The drive letter and directories that lead to a particular file.

PEER-TO-PEER • A network in which any computer on the network has the capability of sharing data or other resources and still functions as a workstation.

PICA • A unit of measurement that equals 1/72 of an inch.

PIXELS • The dots that make up the picture on a computer screen.

POINT • A unit of measurement that equals 1/6 of an inch.

POINT • To position the mouse pointer on an icon or control on the screen.

PORTRAIT ORIENTATION • Printing text upright on the page, in the normal reading position.

POST OFFICE PROTOCOL 3 • A protocol used to receive files over the Internet.

PRINTER • An output device that puts text and images on paper.

PRIVILEGES • The rights given to a user regarding files and printing on a network.

PROTOCOL • The language of communication between computers.

RANDOM ACCESS MEMORY (RAM) • A computer's temporary storage.

RESOLUTION • A measurement of the number of dots that make up the screen.

RESTORE BUTTON • Returns a maximized window to the size it was before being maximized.

RIGHT-CLICK • To quickly press and release the right mouse button.

SCROLL • To move the contents of a window within the bounds of the window's size.

SCROLL BARS • Graphic elements which allow you to scroll the contents of a window.

SELECT • To highlight text in order to perform operations on it.

SIMPLE MAIL TRANSPORT PROTOCOL • A protocol used to send files over the Internet.

SOFTWARE • The instructions a computer follows.

SYSTEM SOFTWARE • The software needed to control the hardware and load application software.

SYSTEM UNIT • The case that holds the processing unit and storage devices of the computer.

TASKBAR • The bar that displays the Start button, as well as buttons for each open program and window.

TEXT BOX • A dialog box control which allows you to key text in response to a question.

TILE • To arrange and resize windows in such a way as to make all of the windows fully visible at the same time.

TRANSMISSION CONTROL PROTOCOL (TCP) • The protocol that breaks down information into packets to be transmitted .

UNIFORM RESOURCE LOCATOR (URL) • An address on the World Wide Web.

USER ID • When logging onto a computer system, the name that the computer recognizes as the users.

WALLPAPER • a graphic element that can be as large as or smaller than the screen.

WEB BROWSER • Client software that communicates with a web server to view a Web page.

WEB SERVER • A program that communicates with a web browser.

WIDE AREA NETWORK (WAN) • A network that spans a large geographic region.

WINDOWS • An environment created by Microsoft that gave IBM type machines a graphical user interface.

WINDOWS NT • The network version of Windows.

WORK STATION • Each microcomputer on a network with a dedicated server.

WRITE-PROTECT • To protect the contents of a disk by preventing the computer from making changes to the disk.

Index

A

accessibility options 289
Active Desktop 78, 164-166
Add New Hardware icon 262
Address toolbar 26, 80-81, 106, 162
Advanced Research Projects Agency Network (ARPANET) 102, 285
applications software 4
ARPANET *See* Advanced Research Projects Agency Network
Arrange Icons 84
arranging
  desktop 148-149
  icons in Windows Explorer 176
  items in My Computer 84
Auto Arrange 149

B

book
  how to use iv-v
browsing
  disks 174
  in Internet Explorer 106
  in Run 246
  using hyperlinks 106
  with Address toolbar 162
buttons, help with 132

C

calculator 236
capturing screens and windows 232-233
cascading windows 40
CD Player 240
CD-ROM drive 2, 72
central processing unit (CPU) 2
check boxes 48
checklist, start-up 1
classic style clicking 77, 79
clearing Documents menu 146
clicking, with mouse 10
client/server architecture 282
clipboard 67
close button 26
closing
  documents in WordPad 56
  menus 18-19
  minimized programs or windows 156
  programs 20
  windows 28
color scheme 267
colors, in Paint 222
command buttons 48
Contents, in Help 128
control menu button 26
Control Panel
  accessing 260-261
  adding programs and Windows components 264
  changing display settings and appearance 266-267
  date and time 176
  fonts 278-279
  Hardware Wizard 262-263
  mouse settings 272-275
  removing programs and Windows components 264
  screen savers 270
  wallpaper 268
copying
  between Windows and MS-DOS 258
  disks 188-189
  documents to desktop 144
  folder items in My Computer 88
  in Windows Explorer 183
  paintings 230
  text in WordPad 66
  to another disk 90
CPU *See* central processing unit
cursor 12

D

date and time 276
date modified 202
dedicated server 281
Delete key 140
deleting
  Active Desktop items 166
  files or folders 140, 184
  Recycle Bin 142
  restoring items 142
Department of Defense (DOD) 102, 285
desktop
  arranging 148-149
  copying documents to 144
  defined 9
  moving Active Desktop item to 165
  saving documents to 144-145
  starting Internet Explorer from 104
  wallpaper 268
Details view 82
dial-in network 281
dialog boxes 8, 48
  help with 136
Disk Defragmenter 250
disks, browsing 174
display settings and appearance 266-267
DNS *See* Domain Name System
documents
  closing in WordPad 56
  copying to desktop 144
  creating in WordPad 58
  menu 146
  opening from Windows Explorer 174
  opening in WordPad 50
  printing in Internet Explorer 111
  printing in WordPad 54
  renaming 92
  saving in Internet Explorer 110
  saving in WordPad 64-65
  saving to desktop 144-145
DOD *See* Department of Defense
Domain Name System (DNS) 102, 287
double-clicking
  speed 272
  with mouse 10
drag and drop 153
dragging
  in My Computer 88
  to delete files or folders 140
  with mouse 10
drawing, with Paint
  lines 216-217
  shapes 220
drive mapping 284

Index

E

electronic mail (e-mail) 286, 293
emptying Recycle Bin 143
Esc key 12, 18
exiting
  programs 20
  WordPad 56
Explorer, Windows
  adding and removing background to folders 194-195
  arranging icons 176
  browsing a disk 174
  copying a disk 188
  copying files and folders 183
  creating folders 180
  deleting items 184
  displaying toolbar 174
  expanding and collapsing folders 172
  formatting disks 186
  moving files and folders 182
  opening documents 174
  running MS-DOS programs 256
  selecting objects 178
  sorting files 176
  starting Find 198
  starting programs 174
  starting 170-171
  viewing extensions and paths 190
  viewing hidden files and folders 192-193
extensions, viewing 190

F

Favorites 114
fax modem 2
features, new xi
file transfer protocol (FTP) 285
filenames, viewing 190
files
  copying 183
  deleting 140, 184
  finding 200-206
  hidden 192-193
  moving 182
  opening 201
FilterKeys 289
Find
  by contents 206
  by date modified 202
  by file type and size 204
  by name and location 200-201
  saving search criteria 208
  saving search results 209
  starting 198
floppy disks
  copying 188-189
  drives 72
  formatting 186
  sending to 91
Flying Windows 270
Folder Options 76-78
folders
  adding and removing background of 194-195
  copying items among 88-89
  creating new 96, 180
  deleting 140
  expanding and collapsing in Windows Explorer 172
  finding 200-206
  hidden 192-193
  in My Computer 74
  moving items among 88
  opening 74, 201
  renaming 92
fonts 278-279
formatting disks 186
FTP *See* file transfer protocol

G

graphical user interface (GUI) 6

H

hard disk, space necessary 1
hard drive 72
Hardware Wizard 262-263
hardware
  defined 2-3
  needed to run Windows 98 1
Help
  accessing topics by Index 124
  buttons 128
  hiding Contents 128
  identifying button names 132
  opening books 122
  opening topics 123
  printing topics 130-131
  searching 126
  viewing previously opened topics 128-129
  with dialog boxes 136
  with menu commands 134
hidden files and folders 192-193
History function of Internet Explorer 116
home page 287
HTML *See* hypertext markup language
HTTP *See* hypertext transfer protocol
hyperlinks 106, 287
hypertext links *See* hyperlinks
hypertext markup language (HTML) 102, 287
hypertext transfer protocol (HTTP) 102, 287

I

icons
  arranging 84, 176
  defined 6
  dragging 88
  opening document from 98
  printing from 98
  views 82
Index 124
Internet Connection wizard 292
Internet Explorer Channel Bar option 164
Internet Explorer
  entering addresses 106
  Favorites 114
  History function 116
  moving between Web pages 108
  opening 104
  printing documents 111
  saving HTML documents 110

Index

searching 112
starting from desktop or taskbar 104
viewing previously opened pages 107
Internet protocol *See* TCP/IP
Internet Service Provider (ISP) 281, 285
Internet
browsing with My Computer 118
history 102
parts of 102
searching 112
inverting selection 178
IP address 287
ISP *See* Internet Service Provider

K

keyboard
defined 3
using 12-13
keys
hold 12
important 12
using combinations 12

L

LAN *See* local area network
Large Icon view 82
list box 48
List Form view 82
list server 286
local area network (LAN) 281
logging in 283

M

MacOS 4
mail client 292
mailing lists 286
MAPI *See* Messaging Application Protocol Interface
margins 52
maximize button 26
maximizing a window 30
Media Player 242
memory needed to run Windows 98 1
menu bar 18, 26
menus
choosing a command 19
closing without choosing a command 18
Documents 146
help with commands 134
pulling down 18
Messaging Application Protocol Interface (MAPI) 292
minimize button 26
minimizing a window 32
monitor 2
mouse
defined 3
pointer speed 274
pointer trails 275
pointers 273
settings 272-275
using 10-11
moving
Active Desktop items to desktop 165
between Web pages 108
in My Computer 88
in Windows Explorer 182
taskbar 158
text in WordPad 68
to another disk 90
to another folder in Windows Explorer 174
window 34
MS-DOS 4
copying to Windows 258
prompt 257
running programs 256-257
multimedia applications 6, 242
music CDs 240
My Computer
arranging items 84
backing up one level 80
browsing Internet from 118
browsing using classic style clicking 77, 79
browsing using Web style clicking 76, 78
copying items among folders 88-89
copying to another disk 90
creating new folders 96
displaying toolbars 80
dragging icons 88
hiding toolbars 81
icon 72
moving items among folders 88
moving to another disk 90
opening documents from icons 98
opening drives from 74
opening folders 74
printing documents from 98
renaming documents and folders 92
running MS-DOS programs 256
selecting items 86
sending to a floppy disk 91
sorting items 85
starting Find from 199
switching views 83
undoing operations 94
using address bar 81
using Cut, Copy, and Paste 88
view options 82

N

network 2, 281
network configurations 281-283
networking 281
new features xi
newsgroups 287
Notepad 238

O

online service 281
opening
documents from icons 98
documents in WordPad 50
drawings in Paint 214
drives 74
folders 74, 201
Help books 122
Help topics 123
Recycle Bin 142
text files 238
windows 28
operating systems 4

Index

option buttons 48
OS/2 4
Outlook Express 286, 292-293

P

packets 285
Page Setup, in WordPad 52-53
Paint
  adding text 228
  capturing screens and windows 232-233
  colors 222
  copying to another application 230
  drawing lines 216-217
  drawing shapes 220
  erasing 224
  opening a drawing 214
  pasting to another application 230
  printing 218
  reversed colors 223
  saving 218
  selection tools 226-227
  starting 212-213
  Undo 224
password 283
pasting
  in My Computer 88
  paintings 230
pathnames, viewing 190
peer-to-peer networks 282
pixels 266
pointing, with mouse 10
pointer trails 275
POP3 *See* Post Office Protocol 3
portrait orientation 52
Post Office Protocol 3 (POP3) 292
print queue 283
Print Screen key 232, 233
printer 2
  sharing over a network 283
printing
  from My Computer 98
  from shortcut 152
  Help topics 130-131
  in Internet Explorer 111
  in Paint 218
  in WordPad 54
privacy 288
privileges 284
processor 2
programs
  adding 264
  closing 20, 156
  exiting 20
  removing 264
  starting 14-15, 174
  switching between 16-17
protocol 102, 285

Q

Quick Launch button 106

R

random access memory (RAM) 2
recording sounds 244
Recycle Bin 142, 184
redisplaying windows 32
refreshing Web pages 108
renaming 92
resizing
  Active Desktop items 165
  taskbar 158
  toolbars 160
  windows 36
resolution 266
restoring
  deleted items 142
  windows 30
ruler 46
Run command 246-247

S

Save As 64
saving
  documents to desktop 144-145
  drawings in Paint 218
  in Internet Explorer 110
  in WordPad 64-65
  search criteria in Find 208
  search results in Find 209
  text files 238
ScanDisk 252-253
screen savers 270
screens, capturing 232
scrolling 42
search criteria 208
search engine 112
Search, in Help 126
security 288
Select All 60
selecting
  all text in WordPad 60
  items in My Computer 86-87
  objects in Windows Explorer 178
  paragraph(s) in WordPad 60
  text in WordPad 60
selection tools, in Paint 226-227
Send To 91
SerialKey 291
servers
  dedicated 281
  Web 287
shortcuts
  creating 150
  for printers 152
  properties 154
ShowSounds 290
shutting down Windows 98 22-23
Simple Mail Transport Protocol (SMTP) 292
sizing handle 26
Small Icon view 82
SMTP *See* Simple Mail Transport Protocol
software 4
sorting
  files in Windows Explorer 176
  items in My Computer 85
Sound Recorder 244
sounds
  playing 242, 244
  recording 244
SoundSentry 290
standard button bar 26, 80
start button 14

Index

start-up checklist 1
starting
  Active Desktop item 164-165
  CDs 240
  Find 198
  Internet Explorer 104
  Media Player 242
  Paint 212-213
  programs 14-15, 174
  Windows 98 8-9
  Windows Explorer 170-171
  WordPad 46-47
startup applications 248
status bar 26
StickyKeys 289
storage devices 72, 254
subscribe 287
switching
  between programs using the taskbar 16-17
  between windows 38
system software 4
System Tools menu 250
system unit 2

T

Task Scheduler 294
taskbar
  adding toolbars to 160
  defined 17
  hiding 158-159
  identifying full name of buttons on 132
  positioning 158
  properties 146
  starting Internet Explorer from 104
  switching between windows with 38
TCP/IP 102, 285
telnet 286
text boxes 48
text
  adding in Paint 228
  copying in WordPad 66
  editing in WordPad 62
  finding file by 206
  inserting in WordPad 62
  moving in WordPad 68
  selecting in WordPad 60
tiling windows 40
time 276
title bars 26
ToggleKeys 289
toolbars
  adding to taskbar 160
  Address 162
  displaying in My Computer 80
  hiding 81
  in Windows Explorer 174
  in WordPad 46
  making new 160
  removing 161
  resizing 160
transmission control protocol *See* TCP/IP
tree 173
Tune-Up wizard 294

U

Undo 94, 224
uniform resource locator (URL) 102, 287
user ID 283

V

video clips 242-243

W

wallpaper 268
WAN *See* wide area network
Web browsers 287
Web pages
  moving between 108
  printing 111
  refreshing 108
  saving 110
  stopping 108
  viewing 104, 106
Web servers 287
Web style clicking 76, 78
wide area network (WAN) 281
windows
  arranging 40
  capturing 233
  cascading 40
  closing when minimized 156
  elements of 26
  making taller 36
  maximizing 30
  minimizing 32
  moving 34
  opening and closing 28
  redisplaying 32
  resizing 36
  restoring 30
  scrolling contents of 42
  switching between 38
  tiling 40
  widening 36
Windows 98
  adding components 264-265
  removing components 264-265
  shutting down 22-23
  starting 8-9
WordPad
  closing a document 56
  copying text 66
  creating new document 58
  dialog boxes 48
  editing text 62
  exiting 56
  inserting text 62
  moving text 68
  opening a document 50
  Page Setup 52
  printing 54
  saving a document 64-65
  selecting text 60
  starting 46-47
workstation 282
World Wide Web (WWW) 102, 287
write-protect 188
WWW *See* World Wide Web

Name

Progress Record

UNIT 1 Windows Basics

		Score	Date	Instructor
Lesson 1	Your Computer's Hardware			
Lesson 2	Software and Operating Systems			
Lesson 3	Introducing Windows 98			
Lesson 4	Starting Windows			
Lesson 5	Using the Mouse			
Lesson 6	Using the Keyboard			
Lesson 7	The Start Button			
Lesson 8	Switching Between Programs Using the Task Bar			
Lesson 9	Using Menus			
Lesson 10	Exiting a Program			
Lesson 11	Shutting Down Windows			
	Reinforcement Exercise 1			
	Challenge Exercise 1			

UNIT 2 Working with Windows

		Score	Date	Instructor
Lesson 12	The Elements of a Window			
Lesson 13	Opening and Closing Windows			
Lesson 14	Maximizing and Restoring a Window			
Lesson 15	Minimizing a Window			
Lesson 16	Moving a Window			
Lesson 17	Resizing a Window			
Lesson 18	Switching Between Windows			
Lesson 19	Arranging Windows			
Lesson 20	Scrolling			
	Reinforcement Exercise 2			
	Challenge Exercise 2			

UNIT 3 Introduction to WordPad

		Score	Date	Instructor
Lesson 21	Starting WordPad			
Lesson 22	Dialog Boxes			
Lesson 23	Opening a Document			
Lesson 24	Using Page Setup			
Lesson 25	Printing a Document			
Lesson 26	Closing a Document and Exiting WordPad			
Lesson 27	Creating a New Document			
Lesson 28	Selecting Text			
Lesson 29	Editing Text			
Lesson 30	Saving a Document			
Lesson 31	Copying Text			
Lesson 32	Moving Text			
	Reinforcement Exercise 3			
	Challenge Exercise 3			

UNIT 4 My Computer

		Score	Date	Instructor
Lesson 33	Storage Devices and Organization			
Lesson 34	Opening Drives and Folders			
Lesson 35	Web and Classic Clicking			
Lesson 36	Customizing Clicking			
Lesson 37	Navigating with the Toolbars			
Lesson 38	View Options			
Lesson 39	Arranging and Sorting Items			
Lesson 40	Selecting Items			
Lesson 41	Copying and Moving Items Among Folders			
Lesson 42	Copying and Moving Items to Another Disk			
Lesson 43	Renaming Documents and Folders			
Lesson 44	Undoing File and Folder Operations			
Lesson 45	Creating a New Folder			
Lesson 46	Opening and Printing a Document from Its Icon			
	Reinforcement Exercise 4			
	Challenge Exercise 4			

Name

Progress Record

UNIT 5 The Internet

		Score	Date	Instructor
Lesson 47	The Internet			
Lesson 48	Opening Internet Explorer			
Lesson 49	Entering an Address and Clicking Links			
Lesson 50	Moving Between a Web Page Using Back and Forward			
Lesson 51	Saving and Printing a Web Page			
Lesson 52	Searching the Internet			
Lesson 53	Favorites on the Internet			
Lesson 54	History			
Lesson 55	Browsing the Internet with My Computer			
	Reinforcement Exercise 5			
	Challenge Exercise 5			

UNIT 6 Working with Windows

		Score	Date	Instructor
Lesson 56	Using Help Topics by Content			
Lesson 57	Using Help Topics by Index			
Lesson 58	Using Search			
Lesson 59	Help Buttons			
Lesson 60	Printing Help Topics			
Lesson 61	Help with Button Names			
Lesson 62	Help with Menu Commands			
Lesson 63	Dialog Box			
	Reinforcement Exercise 6			
	Challenge Exercise 6			

UNIT 7 More Desktop Features

		Score	Date	Instructor
Lesson 64	Deleting a File or Folder			
Lesson 65	Restoring Deleted Items and Emptying the Recycle Bin			
Lesson 66	Copying and Saving to the Desktop			
Lesson 67	The Documents Menu			
Lesson 68	Arranging the Desktop			
Lesson 69	Creating a Shortcut			
Lesson 70	Creating a Printer Shortcut			
Lesson 71	Shortcut Properties			
Lesson 72	Closing a Minimized Program or Window			
Lesson 73	Positioning the Taskbar			
Lesson 74	Adding Toolbars to the Taskbar			
Lesson 75	Address Toolbar			
Lesson 76	Active Desktop			
Lesson 77	Customizing Active Desktop			
	Reinforcement Exercise 7			
	Challenge Exercise 7			

UNIT 8 Using the Explorer

		Score	Date	Instructor
Lesson 78	Starting the Windows Explorer			
Lesson 79	Expanding and Collapsing Folders			
Lesson 80	Browsing a Disk			
Lesson 81	Arranging Icons and Sorting Files			
Lesson 82	Selecting Objects			
Lesson 83	Creating Folders			
Lesson 84	Moving and Copying Files and Folders			
Lesson 85	Deleting a File or Folder			
Lesson 86	Formatting a Floppy Disk			
Lesson 87	Copying a Floppy Disk			
Lesson 88	Viewing MS-DOS Filename Extensions and Paths			
Lesson 89	Viewing Hidden Files and Folders			
Lesson 90	Customizing Folders			
	Reinforcement Exercise 8			
	Challenge Exercise 8			

Name

Progress Record

UNIT 9 Using Find

		Score	Date	Instructor
Lesson 91	Starting Find			
Lesson 92	Finding Files and Folders by Name and Location			
Lesson 93	Finding Files and Folders by Date Modified			
Lesson 94	Finding Files by File Type and Size			
Lesson 95	Finding Files by the Text Contained in the Files			
Lesson 96	Saving Search Criteria and Results			
	Reinforcement Exercise 9			
	Challenge Exercise 9			

UNIT 10 Painting

		Score	Date	Instructor
Lesson 97	Introducing Paint			
Lesson 98	Opening a Drawing			
Lesson 99	Drawing Lines			
Lesson 100	Saving and Printing a Painting			
Lesson 101	Drawing Shapes			
Lesson 102	Using Colors			
Lesson 103	Erasing and Using Undo			
Lesson 104	Using the Selection Tools			
Lesson 105	Adding Text			
Lesson 106	Using Paintings in Other Applications			
Lesson 107	Capturing Screens and Windows			
	Reinforcement Exercise 10			
	Challenge Exercise 10			

UNIT 11 Other Applications and Multimedia Features

		Score	Date	Instructor
Lesson 108	Using the Calculator			
Lesson 109	Using the Notepad			
Lesson 110	Playing a Music CD			
Lesson 111	Using the Media Player			
Lesson 112	Recording Sounds			
Lesson 113	Using the Run Command			
Lesson 114	Startup Applications			
Lesson 115	Using the Disk Fragmenter			
Lesson 116	Using ScanDisk			
Lesson 117	Checking the Properties of a Storage Device			
Lesson 118	Running MS-DOS Programs			
Lesson 119	Copying Between MS-DOS and Windows Programs			
	Reinforcement Exercise 11			
	Challenge Exercise 11			

UNIT 12 Working with Windows

		Score	Date	Instructor
Lesson 120	Introduction to the Control Panel			
Lesson 121	Using the Hardware Wizard			
Lesson 122	Adding and Removing Programs and Window Components			
Lesson 123	Display Settings and Appearance			
Lesson 124	Adding Desktop Wallpaper			
Lesson 125	Using a Screen Saver			
Lesson 126	Changing Mouse Settings			
Lesson 127	Changing Date and Time			
Lesson 128	Viewing Fonts			
	Reinforcement Exercise 12			
	Challenge Exercise 12			